The Unknown Soldiers

The Unknown Soldiers

African-American Troops in World War I

Arthur E. Barbeau and Florette Henri

New Introduction by Bernard C. Nalty
Foreword by Burghardt Turner

DA CAPO PRESS

This book is dedicated to the black Americans who served their country in World War I

Library of Congress Cataloging in Publication Data

Barbeau, Arthur E.
   The unknown soldiers: African-American troops in World War I / Arthur E. Barbeau and Florette Henri; new introduction by Bernard C. Nalty; foreword by Burghardt Turner.—1st Da Capo Press ed.
      p.   cm.
   Originally published: Philadelphia: Temple University Press, 1974.
   Includes bibliographical references and index.
   ISBN 0-306-80694-0
   1. World War, 1914–1918—Participation, Afro-American. 2. United States. Army—Afro-American troops. I. Henri, Florette. II. Title.
D639.N4B37   1996   95-45862
940.54'03—dc20   CIP

First Da Capo Press edition 1996

This Da Capo Press paperback edition of *The Unknown Soldiers* is an unabridged republication of the edition first published in Philadelphia in 1974, here supplemented with a new introduction by Bernard C. Nalty. It is reprinted by arrangement with Temple University Press.

Published by Da Capo Press
A Member of the Perseus Books Group
http://www.dacapopress.com

Contents

That shameful record is going to be written up, and published, so that the whole world may read it, and learn how these black men, who went out from these shores to die at their country's call, were treated simply because of the color of their skin. . . .

REV. FRANCIS GRIMKE

Plates

Introduction

The Unknown Soldiers appeared in 1974 and promptly established itself as the most thorough and best written account of its subject, a preeminence that it still enjoys. The diligent research and precise writing of Arthur E. Barbeau and Florette Henri produced an instant classic, invaluable to students of the history of African Americans in the military and fascinating to the casual reader. Da Capo Press deserves our thanks for making this work available once again.

When it first appeared, *The Unknown Soldiers* shed light on an aspect of the African-American contribution to American military history that was largely ignored while scholarly and public attention focused on either earlier black troops or the racial integration of the armed forces, which President Harry S. Truman had directed in July 1948, and its consequences. African Americans had seen limited military service in colonial times, in the American Revolution beginning with the battles at Lexington and Concord, and in the War of 1812, especially with the navy and in the defense of New Orleans. These topics had aroused scholarly and popular interest, as had the Civil War, in which African-American soldiers, serving in separate units, helped destroy slavery and gain the rights of citizenship.

African Americans had little time to enjoy the fruits of victory in the Civil War. The constitutional safeguards protecting their hard-won rights came to be interpreted narrowly or utterly ignored. The repeal of the results of the Civil War became complete in 1896, when the Supreme Court established in *Plessy v Ferguson* the principle of separate but equal and thus provided a legal basis for imposing racial segregation on almost every aspect of American life.

When the United States went to war with Spain in 1898, some African-American leaders saw an opportunity to regain the rights of citizenship through heroism on the battlefield, in effect shaming white America into abandoning racial discrimination. Black troops fought competently, often heroically, in Cuba, Puerto

Rico, and the Philippines, but their contributions to victory brought no lowering of racial barriers. The African-American soldiers found that Jim Crow—the personification of racial discrimination—followed the flag overseas.

The fate of the 1st Battalion, 25th Infantry, transferred from Nebraska to Brownsville, Texas, in 1906, exemplified the status of the black soldier in Jim Crow's America. Gunfire erupted on the streets of Brownsville in the early hours of August 14, killing one civilian and wounding two others. The blame fell upon the recently arrived African-American soldiers, but Army investigators could find no concrete evidence pointing to specific members of the battalion. Convinced that the black troops had to be guilty, President Theodore Roosevelt resorted to mass punishment and, on his own authority as commander in chief, issued dishonorable discharges to all who might possibly have been involved. The Senate Military Affairs Committee looked into the Brownsville incident. A majority endorsed the president's action, but a minority report—put together largely by Senator Joseph B. Foraker of Ohio, a bitter foe of the president—demolished the basis for Roosevelt's decision, invalidating the evidence he found so persuasive and demonstrating that the black soldiers had been framed, presumably by racists among the townspeople. The president remained adamant, however, and the dishonorable discharges were not changed to honorable until 1972, after a revolution in race relations within the nation and the military. Only one victim of the injustice, Dorsie Willis, was still alive.

Although the African-American contribution to the defeat of Spain did not force Jim Crow to relax his grip on the United States, when the nation entered World War I against Germany, a number of influential blacks still believed that sacrifices for victory would ensure progress toward racial equality. At the onset of hostilities W. E. B. DuBois, the scholar and civil rights advocate, used the pages of *The Crisis*, the publication of the National Association for the Advancement of Colored People, to urge his fellow African Americans to put aside their just grievances, close ranks with white citizens, and help win the war. Two years later, with Germany beaten, DuBois denounced whites who "cheat us and mock us, . . . kill us and slay us, . . . [and] deride our misery."

In this volume Barbeau and Henri accurately describe the cruel events that shattered the illusions of those, like DuBois, who believed that black Americans could better their condition by enthusiastically supporting World War I.

The Unknown Soldiers deals with tragedy and triumph. The tragedy that did most to determine the wartime role of African-American soldiers was the mutiny at Houston, Texas in August 1917, when soldiers of the black 24th Infantry rebelled against the city's Jim Crow laws, killing fifteen civilians and one Army officer, who apparently was mistaken for a local policeman. The brutality by the police toward both the soldiers and black civilians that had goaded the troops to violence did not mitigate the swift punishment exacted by the War Department. By the end of September 1918, nineteen of the mutineers had died on the gallows. The uprising at Houston frightened the War Department into reducing the number of black combat units—ultimately retaining just the 92d Division and the understrength 93d Division (Provisional)—and training them in small contingents, easily outnumbered by white troops stationed nearby. Fear—along with racial segregation and a devout belief in white supremacy—caused the Army to divert most African-American draftees into units that loaded and unloaded ships, built roads and encampments, or performed other military labor.

Members of the labor battalions proved to be the least known of the unknown African-American soldiers. The authors, however, have drawn upon the records of the War Department and other sources to show how the Army used the draft to provide black laborers in the United States and in France. At one camp, labor troops, supposedly undergoing military training, devoted just an hour in the evening to basic subjects like close-order drill after working all day on construction or housekeeping projects. At another camp the African Americans gathered firewood in a nearby national forest.

The authors further demonstrate that the treatment of black soldiers by the American Expeditionary Forces in France was itself a tragedy. Although an occasional white officer showed respect for his men, the 92d Division suffered from indifferent, at times contemptuous, leadership. Indeed, the division's chief of staff, though he conceded that the African-American troops had exerted steady pressure on the Germans in the final weeks of the war, would nevertheless dismiss them as being "dangerous to no one but themselves and women." When a battalion of the division's 368th Infantry advanced bravely in an attack that enabled French troops to break contact with a stronger German force, the African-American unit received the *Croix de guerre* from the French, but higher American headquarters rejected every recommendation for awards to individual black soldiers in the battalion.

The notorious reluctance of American commanders to approve decorations for African-American soldiers eventually caused the Department of the Army to look for evidence of racial discrimination in awarding the Medal of Honor, the highest decoration for individual valor, during World War I. This investigation, however, had to await the uprooting of legalized racial segregation and did not begin until 1988. Three years later, it resulted in the posthumous award of the Medal of Honor to Corporal Freddie Stowers, killed while leading an attack on a machine gun nest in September 1918. He had served in the 93d Division (Provisional).

The authors also describe such triumphs as the combat record of the 93d Division (Provisional), which served almost exclusively with French forces that ignored American advice to enforce rigid racial segregation and avoid "spoiling" the black soldiers. The French, who had been fighting more than three years, needed the African-American soldiers and could not risk treatment that would stir up resentment and undermine their military efficiency. Treated as real soldiers, the men of the division responded with the skill and heroism that earned the *Croix de guerre* for three of its four regiments. Another triumph consisted of the appointment of African-American wartime officers—some of them students at black colleges, recent graduates, or former enlisted men in the four black regiments of the Regular Army, and still others mobilized with the National Guard. While these new officers, the vast majority of them lieutenants, were pinning on their insignia, the highest-ranking black officer in the Regular Army, Colonel Charles Young, a graduate of the U. S. Military

Academy, languished on the inactive list, where he remained until the final weeks of the fighting. The War Department shelved this experienced officer rather than run the risk that he might somehow command white troops as a result of his seniority and the frenzied wartime expansion.

After the armistice that ended the struggle, Jim Crow asserted control at the ports where American troops waited to return to the United States. In one instance cited by Barbeau and Henri, black veterans loaded their baggage on a ship, only to unload and resume their wait when the captain flatly refused to allow African Americans to sail on board his vessel. After suffering harassment and humiliation at the ports, the soldiers returned to a nation where wartime prosperity had begun to ebb, pitting blacks against whites in a competition for a dwindling number of industrial jobs and fanning the flames of racism. Violence by whites against blacks, whether riots or the lynching of individuals, erupted throughout the nation, and members of the mobs usually escaped punishment. No wonder that in 1919 a disillusioned and angry DuBois urged African Americans to abandon cooperation and fight for their freedom.

The record of African-American troops in World War I, thoroughly explored by the authors, demonstrates that they performed best when treated fairly, as by the French. The War Department, though it studied the history of the war, refused to learn this basic lesson and tried to fight a second world war adhering to the racial policy of the first. The demands of total mobilization for World War II—and the stirrings of militancy on the part of blacks—compelled the armed forces to accept large numbers of African Americans and assign them tasks that would help win the war. Consequently, although racial segregation prevailed, black tank or artillery battalions supported white infantry, African-American fighter pilots escorted bombers with white crews, and for a brief time, late in the war in Europe, platoons of black soldiers served alongside whites in the same rifle companies.

President Truman, for reasons of politics and simple justice rather than to increase military efficiency, ordered the racial integration of the armed services in July 1948. The manpower demands of the Korean War, which began two years later, at last taught the army the lesson it should have learned from World War I. Efficient use of manpower—limited because a limited war involved only a partial mobilization of American resources—required that military necessity, rather than the accident of race, determine the training, assignment, and treatment of all soldiers.

In brief, *The Unknown Soldiers* remains the best account of African-American troops in World War I. As such, it explains the transition from hope to despair, from a belief that civil rights could be won on the battlefield to a conviction that any strategy dependent on the goodwill of white Americans was bound to fail. The experience of World War I explains why African-American leaders on the eve of World War II demanded assurances of better treatment and opportunity in the armed forces and in defense industries before supporting President Franklin D. Roosevelt and his rearmament program. Charles H. Houston, a civil rights activist and veteran of World War I, told a House committee in 1940 that he had come home in 1919 so angered by the racism encountered in the service that he did not even apply for the campaign medal he had earned. How, he asked, could the nation expect African Americans to fight overseas, as he had, when their friends and families were being oppressed, even lynched, at home?

BERNARD C. NALTY
Hyattsville, Maryland
April 1996

Bernard C. Nalty worked as a historian for the U.S. Air Force for 25 years and later in the History Offices of the Marine Corps and Joint Chiefs of Staff. He is the author of the groundbreaking and definitive Strength for the Fight: A History of Black Americans in the Military.

Foreword

Even though several full-length accounts have been written of the remarkable exploits of Afro-American soldiers in World War I, none of them have revealed the sordid realities of the racist, debasing indignities committed against the black soldier, both as enlisted man and officer. W. E. B. DuBois made an excellent start at revealing this shameful record in "An Essay toward a History of the Black Man in the Great War," published in the *Crisis*, June 1919, but the three-volume work he projected unfortunately was never completed.

Of those accounts that were published within a few years after the end of the war, all left much to be desired. They were without index, footnotes, or bibliography, and none was written by an historian who applied rigid tests to his sources. The titles of these books tell more about the authors' intentions than about their products: Emmett Scott's was titled the *Official History;* J. A. Jamieson edited the *Complete History;* Kelly Miller gave a worthless *Authentic History;* while W. Allison Sweeney issued a plain *History*. These four books were rushed into print in 1919. Charles Williams took a little more time with his *Sidelights on Negro Soldiers*, which appeared in 1923. All of them were mainly catalogues of events, splattered with editorial opinion, detailing the heroic exploits of medal winners and quoting praise from letters, military communications, and press reports, rather than analyses in depth of the more seamy side of the Afro-American experience in training, in labor battalions, and in combat.

Now, fifty years later, Arthur E. Barbeau and Florette Henri have dug through the military records and personal papers of participants and have spelled out in detail the record of racist discrimination, from the prewar handling of the four black Regular army units through the draft to postwar demobilization. It is not a pretty story, full of romantic military heroics. Rather, it reflects, on the one hand, the determined efforts of the government and the army to prevent the Afro-American from realizing his potential, and, on the other, the determination of the Afro-American to realize it despite those efforts.

Professor Barbeau and Mrs. Henri have shown us the absurdity of the established policies, designed to support and maintain racist social patterns rather than to produce an efficient military machine. With the army and navy clamoring for manpower, black volunteers were being rejected or kept waiting
for all-black units to be authorized and activated. DuBois in the
Crisis of June 1919 noted a "persistent campaign. . . . First, was
the effort to get rid of Negro officers; second, the effort to discredit Negro soldiers; third, the effort to keep Negroes out of
the Regular Army." Earlier, in the March issue of the *Crisis*,
DuBois had written that "the American army is going to return
to America determined to disparage the black officer and eliminate him from the army despite his record." DuBois was right.
The smear campaign was so successful that, as the next war
approached, the question was still being asked: "Do Negroes
make good soldiers?" In my own service with the 92d Division
in World War II, I still felt the effects of that unjust disparage-
ment of the Afro-American soldiers who had fought a generation earlier. I recall General Almond, the division commander,
calling all the Afro-American officers to the field house to tell
them that he did not believe they should be promoted above the
rank of captain.

In the face of such humiliating treatment, one may well ask,
"Why has the Afro-American been so persistent in pressing for
military service in his nation's wars?" Frederick Douglass gave
this answer in 1863: "Let the black man get upon his person the
brass letters U.S.; let him get an eagle on his buttons and a
musket on his shoulder, and bullets in his pocket, and there is
no power on the earth which can deny that he has earned the
right to citizenship." * DuBois, who was sharply criticized by
many Afro-Americans in 1918 for urging that, for the duration
of the war, the black man should set aside his special cause and
let the country come first, answered in the September 1918 issue
of the *Crisis* by pointing out the gains that had come from each

* *Addresses of the Honorable W. D. Kelley, Miss Anna E. Dickinson and
Mr. Frederick Douglass at a Mass Meeting Held at National Hall, Philadelphia, July 6, 1863, for the Promotion of Colored Enlistment* (Philadelphia,
1863), p. 5.

of the wars in which the Afro-American had performed so admirably and selflessly. Richard Dalfiume, in *Desegregation of the United States Armed Forces* (Columbia, Mo., 1969), summarized the attitude of the Afro-American community: "Throughout American history the black American viewed his military service in the nation's conflicts as proof of his loyalty and as a brief for his claim to full citizenship. White Americans appear to have realized this, and they continually sought to restrict or downgrade the black soldiers's military service" (p. 1).

In *The Unknown Soldiers*, Barbeau and Henri have provided an outstandingly well-documented appraisal of the heroic role of the Afro-American combat and service troops; of the obstacles placed in the path of the Afro-American, resulting in a partially hobbled black combat force whose record was excellent in spite of deterrents to still greater achievement; of the willingness of high military officials to sabotage military effectiveness rather than change their racist policies. The authors reveal the persistent demands of the black community for the organization of black combat units and the political pressures operative in the formation of the 92d and 93d divisions.

At last a clear picture is presented of the obstacles and the morale-destroying insults and humiliations directed uniquely against the black soldier. Chiefly, this important book will help us appreciate that the price of valor and service to his country for the Afro-American in World War I was very high.

BURGHARDT TURNER

Preface

The unknown soldier of World War I was the American black man, and it is the purpose of the authors to make his history known.

Some will be indignant at the story. Others will be indignant at the authors. But it has at no point been our purpose to arouse emotion, only to tell the truth as nearly as we can from thorough research. If, at points in this study, it seems to any reader incredible that the black soldier can have been so maligned, misused, and abused, or that the United States government and army can have been so wasteful of manpower in a time of need, we can only refer him to the sources, especially official sources. A good cure for doubt would be a small dose of the appendix, the plan of the Operations Branch of the Army General Staff for the "Disposal of the Colored Drafted Men."

That black soldiers could be good soldiers is amply attested and illustrated. It is also undeniable from the evidence that an entire division of black soldiers was permitted, even encouraged, to do less than its best by everything that was done to it, from its organization through its battles.

It seems quite clear, from all the evidence of both success and failure, that the "Negro problem" in the army was made by the army. Army draft policy, assignment, training, and leadership of black soldiers were all based upon racist presuppositions. All black troops, both labor and combatant, were objects of the ambivalence of racism, the double-barreled desire to use the black man like an inferior yet have him perform like an equal; to deal with him according to a double standard but judge him by a single standard.

Unfortunately for the investigator who seeks enlightenment as to the innate potential of black American soldiers in the Great War, prejudice as usual obstructs the view. In the light of disparities in the treatment of white soldiers and black soldiers, it is impossible to guess how the black men would have performed given equal treatment. Would they, on the average, have done as well as, worse than, or better than white soldiers? If the army had wanted to prove black inferiority, it would have first had to give blacks the same chance as whites to do their best. This it did not do. But it made assertions without proof, which condemned the black man in the army to segregation and discrimination for the next thirty years.

In 1948, at hearings of President Harry S Truman's Committee on Equality of Treatment and Opportunity in the Armed Services, the old story—incomplete, inaccurate, and unproven—of the "failure of the 92d Division" was retold. It is hoped that this study of the unknown soldier and officer of World War I will lay bare the extent of that failure, only fractionally as great as represented, and the reasons for it, greater than anyone could surmise without the information that was made available to the authors.

Many people helped point the way to that information or made suggestions and criticisms. Without their help, the present volume could not have been completed; but any errors of information, fact, or analysis are solely the responsibility of the authors. The contributions of some people were so significant as to require specific mention. First, the authors owe a lasting debt to those black Americans who bore the burdens of racism in the army and in America in order to make the history that we are only retelling. This book is dedicated to their behavior.

Special mention must be made of the generous assistance of the staff of the Army and Air Force Branch of the National Archives under the direction of Victor Gondos, Jr. John E. Taylor, of that branch, was helpful in finding desired information and in recommending materials that the authors were unaware of; Mrs. Sarah Jackson, who remembered the whereabouts and field of interest of every researcher, provided invaluable leads and clues. The entire staff of the 135th-Street branch of the New York City Public Library were most helpful in assisting us in the use of the Schomburg Collection. Among the many others to whose willing assistance we are indebted are: Beulah Davis and her staff at the Emmett J. Scott Collection, Morgan State College; the staff of the Amistad Research Institute at Fisk University; Alfred S. Kramer, staff consultant with the National Council of the Churches of Christ; Stetson Conn, director of the Office of the Chief of Military History, the United States Army; and professors Samuel P. Hays, Peter Karsten, Norman Dixon, and Robert G. Colodny, of the University of Pittsburgh, who nursed along the original investigation of this subject as an academic project. In addition, both authors take particular pleasure in thanking librarians close to home, who, by cheerful and informed use of library facilities and services saved us an incalculable amount of time and energy: Donald Strong and his staff at West Liberty State College, and Melvon L. Ankeny, Robert J. Trudell, and the entire staff of Harborfields Public Library, Greenlawn, New York.

Always, deepest thanks must be saved for the spouses who saw us through manic and depressed periods, our delightfully biased and least severe critics, Patricia Ann Barbeau and Raymond Henri.

A.E.B.
F.H.

The Unknown Soldiers

1. Who Was the Black American of World War I?

Cheapness characterizes almost all the donations of the American people to the Negro:—Cheapness, in all the past, has been the regimen provided for the Negro in every line of his intellectual, as well as his lower life . . . cheap wages and cheap food, cheap and rotten huts; cheap and dilapidated schools; cheap and stinted weeks of schooling; cheap meeting houses for worship; cheap and ignorant ministers; cheap theological training; and now, cheap learning, culture, and civilization!

Alexander Crummell, *The Attitude of the American Mind toward the Negro Intellect* (1898).

SINCE the arrival of the first Negroes at Jamestown, Virginia, in 1619, black people in all areas of American life had received less than their share of the joy, the goods, and the freedom promised by the New World. From the first, black Americans had suffered from white society's conviction that they were inferior and therefore that giving them inferior treatment was justified. Then the cultural lag produced by cheap everything was cited by white society as proof of the racial inferiority which had served as justification for the cheapness that produced the cultural lag. This is the seminal argument in American racism.

For example, figures for 1911 and 1912 indicate that the South spent an average of $10.32 in educating each white child, but only $2.89 for each black child. In 1916, 87.2 percent of all funds expended in the South on agricultural and vocational education benefited whites only. In the light of such additional disparities, it can scarcely be laid to racial inferiority that black people in the South had a much larger proportion of illiteracy than whites—in 1900, black illiteracy was 44.5 percent; that of native-born whites, 4.6 percent—yet illiteracy was commonly cited as evidence of racial inferiority. Despite many obstacles, black illiteracy was dramatically reduced in the next two decades; in 1910, it was 30.4 percent (native white, 3.0 percent); by 1920, it had dropped to 22.9 percent (native white, 2.0 percent).[1] The cultural leap was possible because of vastly increased educational opportunity in those twenty years as Southern blacks moved to Northern cities and served in the armed forces. It was certainly due to increased educational and occupational opportunities that by 1910 there were 75,000 black professionals, including about 3,400 physicians, 500 dentists, and 30,000 teachers;[2] and that by 1920 the number of professional-level black people had increased by more than another 5,000.[3]

One reason often given for the small expenditures on black education in the South was that tax contributions of blacks amounted to so little—in fact, some Southerners held, less than was spent on educating them. In one Georgia county for which figures are available, the per capita valuation of white property was $118,440, and of black, $656.[4] (The significance of these figures as an indication of economic exploitation of blacks was ignored.) But inequities in educational expenditures existed even in Southern cities where blacks paid substantial taxes, as in Norfolk, Virginia, where 25 percent of tax collections came from black citizens. Yet only half the eligible children were accommodated in the black schools—which in any case were inferior and stopped at the seventh grade.[5]

Northerners and liberals, even politically radical Socialists, to a large extent shared the Southern belief—well propagandized—that black people had such undesirable characteristics as low intelligence and criminality.[6] A considerable portion of the Northern press assumed that lynchings occurred in almost all cases as a result of rape or other sexual crimes against white women—"Lynched for the Usual," as Southern newspapers would head their articles.[7] However, unassailable figures disprove that assumption. Of the fifty-four blacks lynched in 1916, fewer than one-quarter were even charged with sexual crime. Listed among the many causes of mob murder were such offenses as "slapping boy" and "speaking against mob in act of putting a man to death."[8] One of the black people lynched that year was a woman.

The black American was no better off politically than socially. Sold out by the Republican party in the Hayes administration, and gradually disfranchised all through the South, Negroes had cause to be disillusioned with the party of Lincoln. A good many of those who could vote helped elect the Democratic candidate Woodrow Wilson in 1912. But he too disappointed them deeply. The Southern migrant who said he moved north to Washington to be "as near the flag as I can" [9] must have been a saddened man to find that Wilson and his Progressive administration did not reappoint black officeholders; deliberately and systematically segregated blacks in civil service jobs; permitted the introduction of discriminatory bills into Congress; and for six years did nothing to discourage lynching. All too many of the influential Southern Progressives in Congress were outspoken racists—such men as James K. Vardaman and John Sharp Williams of Mississippi, Coleman Blease of South Carolina, and Hoke Smith of Georgia.

There is little doubt that the public position of black Americans deteriorated during the Wilson years, and that this was part of the reason for the increasing radicalism of blacks during the decade. [10] Black leaders and press protested Wilson's acquiescence in racist measures, but to no effect. Those most often and most vehemently castigated by black protesters were, in addition to Wilson himself, two of the five Southerners in his ten-man Cabinet: William Gibbs McAdoo of Georgia, secretary of the treasury, who became Wilson's son-in-law; and Albert Sidney Burleson of Texas, postmaster general, in whose department, long a haven for black workers, the strict segregation of blacks began. [11] Shortly after America's entry into the war, Chicago's militant black newspaper, the *Defender*, said of the government: "We are loathe to believe that it is the sentiment of the majority to belittle and discredit one-eighth of the entire population. The South being in the saddle, we can expect anything from that source, however." [12] And Oswald Garrison Villard, grandson of the abolitionist William Lloyd Garrison, wrote: ". . . we hear solemnly that the only way out is to govern the inferior race by violence, by defiance of law and order, by the negro's exclusion from a share in government as from its benefits." [13]

Black grievances were well founded. A black job seeker in government might be hired sight unseen, ordered by telegraph to report for work, and then, when his black face appeared, be informed that the appointment was an error and the job not available. The Philadelphia shipyard and other government facilities had been segregated and remained so. In Louisville and Memphis black women were employed by military authorities at tasks considered too hard or disgusting for white women to perform. Black messenger girls in the Munitions Building in Washington had to stand around in the halls all day awaiting assignments, because their desk space had been taken from them; they had no place to eat, either. And they were told that "if they didn't like it, to take their coats and hats and BEAT IT any time of day." [14]

Although it is not certain that Wilson shared the racism of many of his political allies, it is incontestable that he was too dependent on their political aid in his reform program to interfere with or discourage their unconstitutional practices. From time to time some protest would be read into the *Congressional Record* by a Northern congressman like Frederick H. Gillet of Massachusetts, but without effect. Vardaman was perhaps the leading racist in Washington; yet apparently Wilson never attempted to stifle Vardaman's views until he opposed the President's international policies. [15] As Kelly Miller, a Howard University professor, said of Wilson: "He believed in democracy for humanity but not for Mississippi." [16]

When war broke out in Europe in the summer of 1914, not many black or white citizens felt personally involved. Perhaps the black population had a slight edge in indifference because they were less informed; more likely to live poor and isolated lives in the rural South; and, unlike white immigrants, had no ties with any of the combatant nations. In New York's Harlem, Negroes generally favored the cause of France, but only because they felt France had been liberal in its attitude toward colored peoples. Still, as one black is quoted as saying, "The Germans ain't done nothin' to me, and if they have, I forgive 'em." [17] That's a lesson the "good nigger" had been taught by Southerners—to forgive any trespasses by white people.

But, as with most other Americans, black interest in the conflict grew slowly from the neutral stance of 1914 to one of keen sympathy with the Allies by 1917. H. H. Proctor, a Southern Negro minister and a follower of Booker T. Washington, thought the worldwide struggle to extend the limits of liberty would eventually create a new meaning for democracy in the American South.[18] Adam Clayton Powell, a Harlem minister and the father of the future congressman Adam Clayton Powell, Jr., told his flock that the war would bring a new world which the "little, narrow, two-by-four people" who had oppressed Negroes would find uncomfortable.[19] The more militant Northern blacks found a well-informed spokesman in William Edward Burghardt DuBois, who had the same point of view as Powell about the war. DuBois, editor of the influential *Crisis* magazine of the National Association for the Advancement of Colored People (NAACP) said: "This war is an End, and, also, a Beginning. Never again will darker people of the world occupy just the place they have before." [20] A Southern Negro teacher told a black audience that they were "soldiers of freedom"; and that "when we have proved ourselves men, worthy to work and fight and die for our country, a grateful nation may gladly give us the recognition of real men, and the rights and privileges of true and loyal citizens of these United States." [21] Many black Americans gave voice to these delirious hopes.

Whatever the President had done to them and not done for them, black Americans were as stirred as any other people in the world by his pledge to make the world "safe for democracy." In March 1917, Robert R. Moton, Booker T. Washington's close friend and successor as head of Tuskegee Institute, wrote to Wilson pledging Tuskegee's aid in the event of America's participation in the war. After the *Lusitania* was sunk by a German U-boat, Napoleon Marshall, a black lawyer who was a captain in New York's 15th National Guard Regiment, offered to raise a regiment of Negro troops for whatever service Wilson desired.[22]

The war fever seemed to lift certain Jim Crow restrictions, but the pattern was not consistent. Walter White, who became assistant secretary of the NAACP in 1918, reported that the pro-war meeting held by blacks in Atlanta was the first time blacks had been permitted to use the city auditorium.[23] In Jacksonville, Florida, blacks were permitted to attend a Liberty Bond drive in the city auditorium, with black speakers on the program and black bond subscribers welcome. However, in an armory in the same city, when some "colored" citizens wished to attend a rally at which the music of a black English composer was to be played, the militia officer in charge of the armory refused to admit them.[24] Examples like these say plainly that the rules were stretched when something was wanted from blacks—support or money—but not otherwise.

Although the outbreak of war in Europe brought the black man of America no social or political change, it did revolutionize how and where he lived. In 1914, about two-thirds of the cultivated land in the South was rented, sharecropped, worked, and (some of it) owned by blacks.[25] After a brief drop in the price of cotton, some black farmers seem to have shared in the countrywide increase of prosperity. A study of Clarke County, Georgia, made at that time by a Southern teacher, Francis Long, shows that the earnings of blacks there rose between 67 percent and 150 percent over prewar levels.[26] Whites complained that newly rich blacks lavished their money on gaudy clothes and other items of display.[27] Statistics in the Clarke County study seem to bear out the stereotype of the flashy, extravagant, showy, improvident black—but statistics can be used to "prove" almost anything. It is instructive to examine Long's study to see how figures, chosen because they flesh out an existing stereotype, are presented as the irrefutable and complete facts on which the stereotype is based. Long, for instance, found that in Clarke County blacks enormously increased their property in automobiles, while adding slightly less than 500 acres to their property in land. The total value of all black-owned cars, he says, rose from $400 in 1913 to $14,875 in 1918—a thirty-six-fold increase—while the value of all white-owned cars increased only threefold, from $80,885 to $257,450. What Long does not point out, however, is that calculations based on these figures in relation to black and white population in the county will show the per capita increase for blacks to be only $127, against a per capita increase for whites of $1,535. Such omissions lead one to wonder about Long's information on land sales. He does not say, for instance, how much land was offered for sale, the price of such land, and if it was offered to blacks at a higher price than to whites, which was common practice. He does not tell how much land changed hands within each color group.

In any case, those Clarke County farmers, black and white, were lucky to have money to buy anything in a period that brought most Southern farmers disaster. A boll-weevil cycle, persistent drought, and then floods that eroded the naked fields caused terrible suffering to many in the rural South. But other jobs beckoned from a distance. Northern employers were scouring the country for replacements for the cheap immigrant labor stopped by the war just as war production skyrocketed. Black migration from the South, fairly significant since 1900, after 1914 turned into a mass exodus. The most reliable estimates of the number that went North are in the neighborhood of 400,000.[28] The black population in key Northern industrial centers jumped dramatically. Chicago was the goal of many blacks, because the *Chicago Defender* had inspired and abetted migration: Chicago blacks increased from 44,000 in 1910 to 109,000 in 1920. It was estimated that 20 percent of all workers in Northern meatpacking plants were black, and that 25,000 blacks were employed in shipbuilding. In 1910, there were 552,815 black workers in Northern industry, or about 10 percent of all working blacks. By 1920 the number had increased to 960,039.[29]

Probably most black Southerners went North for better jobs and pay, but there were many other motives. Adam Clayton Powell cited the most important: "They are tired of being kept out of public parks and libraries, of being deprived of equal educational opportunities for their children, for which they are taxed, or reading signs 'negroes and dogs not admitted': the men are tired of disfranchisement, the women are tired of the insults of white hoodlums, and the whole race is sick of seeing mobs mutilate and burn unconvicted negro men." [30]

Southern states became truly alarmed as the pace of emigration quickened, and tried by legal and extralegal methods to prevent the disappearance of the black labor force that supported the Southern economy. The magazine *World's Work* felt that the exodus would create grave problems for both South and

North, the South because it was losing badly needed agricultural laborers and the North because it would be saddled with large numbers of ignorant and undisciplined men who were unskilled at any trade and impossible to assimilate.[31] But according to other publications, employers were finding Negroes from the South as efficient laborers as any group of European immigrants.[32]

The *New York Times* expressed the opinion that a change was about to sweep the South which would make it a better place for blacks: "If this change does come, and comes quickly, it will do much to keep the negro where by nature and endowment he is most at home, where he is best understood, and in reality where he is best liked, and where his best service and highest happiness lie." [33] That's what Southerners said, and probably in many cases believed. But such changes as occurred after America entered the war were for the worse, not the better; "work or fight" laws gave the Southern black laborer the alternative of working at what the white man wanted him to, for what the white man was willing to pay, or being summarily inducted into military service. Such vagrancy laws, plus tighter Jim Crow restrictions and a great increase in mob violence against blacks, cannot exactly be said to illustrate the proposition that the black man was best liked and happiest in the South. In any case, the black American of 1900–1920 was not so interested in popularity as in success; and happiness seems to have been not so much a matter of munching on a slab of watermelon in the shade of the cottonwood as casting his vote, choosing his job, ending the month with a little spare cash, and sending his children to school. Although life in a Northern ghetto was far from idyllic for the black man, it is undeniable that he had more freedom and less fear there than in the South. Also, a man or woman with outstanding talents could make good, as many of the black Southern migrants did.[34]

Although the "work or fight" laws were deeply resented, the expression of opinion by a broad range of black society indicates strong patriotism and a desire to serve in the armed forces. Most black leaders backed American entry into the war, when that finally came; and the fact that they remained leaders indicates that they mirrored the views of the black masses. James W. Johnson, secretary of the NAACP, said that, with the American declaration of war, patriotism was "fanned into a flame" in Harlem.[35] In a speech in Harlem, Captain Marshall of the 15th National Guard declared that "any man who was not willing to fight for his country was not worthy to be one of its citizens." [36]

There is solid evidence that the submerged black tenth of America's population was stirred by the ringing words of President Wilson. Again and again in the writings and remarks of black leaders can be found Wilson's magic phrase about making the world safe for democracy. Roscoe Conkling Simmons, nephew of Booker T. Washington, gave total allegiance to Wilson: "Where he commands one to go I shall go." [37] DuBois, in the *Crisis*, joined other black journalists in urging support of the war effort, using a rhetoric as ringing as Wilson's. In his famous editorial "Close Ranks" DuBois said: "This is the crisis of the world. . . . We of the colored race have no ordinary interest in the outcome. That which the German power represents today spells death to the aspirations of Negroes and all darker races for equality, freedom and democracy. Let us not hesitate." [38] And earlier he had asked blacks to join the army and work in the fields and factories so that the goal of world liberty might be realized: "We urge this despite our deep sympathy with the reasonable and deep-seated feeling of revolt among Negroes at the persistent insult and discrimination to which they are subject and will be subject even when they do their patriotic duty." [39] What patriotism could be purer than that which expects no fair recompense? And DuBois clearly expected none.

Not all black leaders could so totally swallow their bitterness. Said Henry Hewlett: "What the Chief Executive said to the world the Negro says to America. . . . I am a full-blooded American; every time I hear a band play a national air my blood steams up to the boiling point and I feel as much buoyed up as anyone else, but when it is all over and I begin to meditate and reflect, cold chills sweep over me." [40] Francis Grimke, a prominent and outspoken Washington, D.C., clergyman, said: "Men of darker hue have no rights which white men are bound to respect. And it is this narrow, contracted, contemptible undemocratic idea of democracy that we have been fighting to make the world safe for, if we have been fighting to make it safe for democracy at all." [41]

Most of the black press supported Wilson and his prosecution of the war, even when government actions ran counter to the interests of the black community. In such situations, most of the black leaders and press urged patience until the end of the struggle with Germany. But there were some publications that took a more radical and immediate stand. The *Washington Bee* argued that "self-styled spokesmen" of the black people had no right to offer the services of Negroes to the government; such "bootlickers," as the *Bee* called them, who slavishly accepted disfranchisement and segregation, could volunteer their own services for any fighting that was to be done. [42] The *Messenger*, a labor publication edited by A. Philip Randolph and Chandler Owen and considered by the U.S. Department of Justice "the most able and the most dangerous" of black publications, [43] suggested that these flag-waving leaders should "volunteer to go to France, if they are so eager to make the world safe for democracy. We would rather fight to make Georgia safe for the Negro." [44] Randolph and Owen later spent some time in jail for allegedly pro-German writings.

But most black people went along with DuBois's "Close Ranks" position; and it was important that they affirm their unquestionable loyalty because even before the United States entered the war the government suspected that German agents were propagandizing blacks, which in fact they were trying to do. The *Washington Post* found it not surprising that whites feared a lack of loyalty among the black people, whom they had disfranchised, mistreated, and lynched. [45] In the general xenophobia of wartime, blacks were sometimes accused of being simply transplanted Africans, not Americans. Black leaders protested that Negroes were loyal only to their native land. [46] Carter Woodson, director of the Association for the Study of Negro Life and History, said that only a very few of the Negroes who were approached by German agents felt sympathy for Germany's position, although a great many blacks thought that making America a decent home for their race took priority over fighting to free Europe from the German yoke.

Most white people, including Southerners, accepted without

question the loyalty of the black American. Rep. Edward W. Pou of North Carolina said he had never doubted colored support for the war effort and voiced the dubious compliment that "if these German agents ever went among the negroes they would be taken care of in a very proper and effective manner without any assistance whatever from the Department of Justice or any Government officials." [47] Even a virulent racist, while attacking the blacks for almost everything else, asserted that "no question as to his patriotism is ever raised." [48]

One of the very best ways to demonstrate patriotism, the administration firmly conveyed to all citizens, was to buy Liberty Bonds. Black citizens subscribed heavily in proportion to their wealth, eager to show loyalty and love of country. A bond rally among New York blacks raised about $60,000. Robert Abbott, publisher of the militant *Chicago Defender*, advised his employees to buy bonds, and he himself bought $12,000 worth "to substantiate my sincere feelings for the great cause of Democracy." Black members of the Regular army and newly raised black troops at bases subscribed almost $800,000 in the 1917 drives.[49] Although the Southern states feared they could not meet a $20 per capita Liberty Loan quota because of their many poor blacks, it appears that all Southern states except South Carolina managed to reach their quotas by virtue of generous contributions from Negroes; and, as the publicity chairman of the North Carolina drive remarked, blacks suffered more to give their allotted share than whites did. A black citizen of Louisiana made the largest individual contribution from that state.[50]

Not all bonds were bought out of pure selflessness by either blacks or whites. According to an editorial in the *Negro World*, quoted in a Justice Department document, a black minister urged his congregation to buy bonds not because of patriotism but "in a spirit of hypocritical public service." [51] Black businessmen like white businessmen bought bonds because it was good for business to demonstrate patriotism. And there were stronger pressures. The NAACP protested that a physician in Vicksburg, Mississippi, was tarred and feathered and run out of town for not buying $1,000 worth of bonds, which he claimed he could not afford, although the local drive chairman assured Secretary of the Treasury McAdoo that no such incident had occurred. It was alleged that some draft boards changed the classifications of black businessmen to Class I if they refused to buy the required amount of bonds.[52] In all, the black population, for whatever motives, contributed a quarter of a million dollars in the various loan drives. A very few blacks, like the Reverend Mr. Grimke, publicly refused to subscribe because of the mistreatment of their people.[53] But, black or white, a man had to be in an unassailable position or recklessly courageous to take such a stand. On the whole, blacks willingly bought what Liberty Bonds they could because "Liberty" was a beautiful word to men only a generation removed from slavery.

Despite all efforts blacks made to show themselves loyal citizens, they won no respite from discrimination and injustice, in small matters or great. A Columbia, South Carolina, judge sentenced a black man to three years in jail for stealing a bicycle, although a white man drew only a three-month term for stealing an automobile. A Texas judge fined a white man $25 for selling alcohol to soldiers; four black men were fined $225 each for the same offense.[54] White sailors threw black passengers off a Philadelphia streetcar. White draftees beat a black train porter to death when he called them down for damaging the interior of a railway coach.[55] Reported offenses and miscarriages of justice like these number by hundreds, and certainly there must have been as many or more that no one ever heard about. And this at the very time the black American was being asked to give his labor, his wealth, and his life for his country.

For his labor he got tangible rewards. He gave his wealth, in most cases, for pure belief in the principles for which the war was being fought. He was willing to risk his life, in the form of military service, for several reasons: being in the armed forces was not only a steady job, but a status job among blacks, and although the pay was small it came regularly; also, like so many white Americans in World War I, black Americans wanted to be soldiers to defend their country.

There had always been blacks in American fighting forces, from colonial times. An unspecified number served in the Revolutionary War, and a battalion fought with Andrew Jackson at New Orleans in the War of 1812. But it was not until the Civil

War that many blacks were used in service. By the end of that war about 150 regiments of segregated black troops, more than 180,000 men, had been mustered into the Union army. There are no accurate reports on black officers, although some served in the Massachusetts regiments and with the Louisiana Guards, and at least eight surgeons and seven chaplains held commissions from the United States Army. Black troops fought in forty-six or more engagements and suffered 2,894 battle deaths. There were also, of course, black soldiers in noncombatant positions, such as guard and garrison duty and railroad construction. Reports on their performance were generally favorable.[56] Blacks were used by the Confederate army also, as military laborers. The Confederate command discussed enlisting blacks into the military service, but the war ended before any such plan was put into action.

During the Reconstruction period, Congress retained some of the black Union troops in the Regular army. Four regiments of infantry were created, which were later consolidated into two, the 24th and the 25th; and two regiments of cavalry, the 9th and 10th. All of these units were kept busy fighting Indians and Mexicans, and they won the reputation of being tough, brave, efficient, though often brawling troopers. Of the ninety-three medals and certificates issued to Regular army troops from 1865 to 1892, twelve went to blacks. One great convenience to the government in having these four regiments was that they provided officer billets for the very few black West Point graduates—only three up to the time of World War I. The only complaint military officials seemed to have about the black regiments was that the high rate of illiteracy among black noncommissioned officers resulted in incomplete paper work.[57]

During the Spanish-American War, all four regiments were sent to Cuba, where they served creditably. Some took part in the siege of Santiago and others assisted Theodore Roosevelt's Rough Riders in their charge up San Juan Hill.[58] Then the four black regiments and the 48th and 49th Volunteer Infantry (Colored) were sent to the Philippines to help put down the native insurrection against American colonial rule. In the kind of guerrilla warfare that was waged in the Philippines, a good deal of responsibility fell to the junior officers, many of whom were black. One battalion of the 24th Infantry was credited with a successful march across 200 miles of difficult and unknown country.[59]

After that, the black regulars were assigned to garrison posts in the American Southwest, Hawaii, and the Philippines. The 10th Cavalry and the 24th Infantry were called on for a punitive expedition against the Mexican leader Pancho Villa after his raids on American territory, and it was then that black troops ran into trouble for the first time. At Carrizal, Mexico, part of the 10th Cavalry broke under fire. Apologists argued that the unit was surrounded and under heavy fire, and that the cavalry mounts had been stampeded. Many of the officers were killed in the early stages of the action, and the noncoms proved unable to rally and regroup their men.[60] Whatever justification there may have been, the performance of the black troops was officially considered unsatisfactory.

For forty years the record of the black troops had been unmarred by any large-scale racial conflict. Then a very serious incident occurred at Brownsville, Texas, in 1906. Members of the 25th Infantry, on service there, were irritated by what seemed to the self-confident troopers intolerable discrimination on the part of townspeople and police. On the night of 13 August, it was alleged, parts of three companies of the regiment left their posts without permission, marched into the town, and fired into business places where they had been offended. A bartender was killed, and a police officer and one other white man were wounded. When the three accused companies involved refused to cooperate in turning over the culprits, President Theodore Roosevelt ordered all members of all three companies—167 men and officers—dismissed "without honor." [61] This excessively severe and unjust punishment for an unproved offense shocked the black community.

Fear of black soldiers became so firmly implanted in white minds that ten years after Brownsville a bill was introduced in Congress that would have prohibited the enlistment or reenlistment of blacks in the military service of the United States. Time and exaggerated press stories added lurid details to the Brownsville incident, so that as late as 1942 a high-ranking military officer wrote of it: ". . . who could imagine that American soldiers in a body would try to murder unoffending women and innocent children?" [62] Nothing of the sort had happened at Brownsville, but an unshakable myth had grown up around it in the military. As for black Americans, Brownsville remains such a tender spot in memory that as late as 1971 a black congressman introduced a bill to clear the name of the 25th, and the Department of the Army shortly thereafter declared it cleared. [63]

Tales of black military service remained one of the glories of black history, becoming more glorious in the retelling. El Caney, San Juan Hill, and Carrizal were rallying cries to black Americans as much as the halls of Montezuma and the shores of Tripoli are to United States Marines. The battles black troops had fought were symbols of equal citizenship that could not be erased by Jim Crow or disfranchisement. With America's entrance into World War I, the black community hoped and pleaded that their own soldiers would have a chance to serve.

There were nonwhite soldiers in the Great War from the very beginning, because all the major powers used troops from their colonies in Africa and Asia. The *Literary Digest* pointed out that the French army included 340,000 natives of North Africa, mostly Berbers; at least a quarter of a million black men from the Soudan and Senegal; and 30,000 from the French West Indies. A number of black men held high command in the French army, and at least two were generals. [64]

Reports varied as to the efficiency of these troops in battle. Early in the war, a white American reporter wrote that such troops could not possibly be of any value in modern European warfare, and that only in desperation could France delude itself into using them. [65] It does indeed appear that the first black troops in France performed unevenly. Two battalions of Senegalese, under modern artillery fire for the first time, held their lines and managed to advance under heavy fire, but a French regiment from West Africa broke in its first experience of combat. There was good reason for these troops to have difficulties. Men from different parts of Africa, speaking different languages, were put into the same units; in some cases, their officers could not communicate with them. They were assembled in haste, and their equipment and training were below the general standards of the French army. In addition, those from a tropical climate suffered severely during the extraordinarily bitter winter of 1915–16.[66]

Yet, in its desperate need, France continued to make use of all available human resources. In 1917, 73,000 West Africans were recruited for service on all fronts. Every account of France's fighting in the Great War carried favorable mention of the achievements and gallantry of the black Africans. One regiment of Senegalese was reported to be the most highly decorated unit in the entire French army. Of the thousand Senegalese used in the Gallipoli campaign, three-quarters were killed or wounded in just ten days.[67] The commander of a black battalion said that his men, "full of a sacred frenzy, carried away in ecstasy, rushed forward, striking and killing, tearing eyes and flesh with steel, nails, and teeth"; then the machine guns found their target, and soon only one captain and ten men were left alive of all those black fighters.[68] American whites, especially in the South with its huge black population, cannot have read such stories of blood-crazed blacks without a prick of terror.

England was more reluctant than France to use nonwhite troops against white Europeans, although in extreme need this was sometimes done. Apparently, however, no African or West Indian black was ever knowingly commissioned in the British army, and with a very few exceptions no nonwhite British troops fought in Europe. West Indians were used in the Dardanelles campaign, were complimented for bravery in the Palestine campaign of 1917, and served in the Jordan Valley campaign the following year. Other black colonials of Britain fought the Germans in Cameroon and had to bear the racism of South African whites who directed the campaign. They were barred from YMCA facilities, denied supplies by white quartermaster personnel, and had to ship their sick and wounded to India for treatment.[69] Their low status and poor treatment, said one of their white officers, were explained by the low opinion held by the War Office of West Indians as fighters. "Hence the employment of West Indians as Shell Carriers and finally as laborers," said this lieutenant colonel.[70] Or, at least, it was easy for the War Office when shell carriers and laborers were needed to assign these jobs to the West Indians, who were organized only into battalions and therefore had no high-ranking officer to intercede for them; such labor assignments could always be justified by the claim that the West Indians did not have the qualities necessary for fighting men, whether or not that was true. The masses of Englishmen would not care what happened to the West Indian blacks; their own hostility to the colored colonials resulted in race violence in several cities of England and Wales in 1917, the most serious incident being eleven days of rioting in Liverpool.[71]

Americans read about black colonial troops in Europe, interpreting reports according to their own biases. Black Americans regarded all reports as favorable to black troops, and whites were equally convinced that they had failed. Black writers featured stories of French Negro troops who were such fierce fighters that they were being used exclusively as shock troops; of German troops so terrified of combat with black soldiers that the German High Command had to offer a reward of 400 marks for each one captured; and of African soldiers who were expert with knife and bayonet—men who took no prisoners—who doted on cold steel.[72]

Reports on black troops of the Allies convinced American officers of what they already believed, that Negroes were virtually useless in combat. The War Plans Division of the General Staff informed the chief of staff that England had been forced to remove its Indian troops from France because they had cracked under the strains of modern warfare—which appears not to have been generally true—and added that the British Indians undoubtedly were of higher intellectual development than American blacks.[73] Gen. Charles C. Ballou declared that the French had no faith in black officers—also untrue according to the evidence—and never used black men in positions of command.[74]

Nevertheless, black Americans were needed in the war effort, and the army planned to draft them along with white Americans. Immediately after the severance of diplomatic relations with Germany, more than a month before the United States declared war, the First Separate Battalion (Colored) of the Washington, D.C., National Guard was mustered into federal service. The black unit was mobilized to guard the White House, the Capitol, and other federal buildings, and facilities such as bridges and water supply, against possible enemy sabotage.[75]

It appears that the First Separate Battalion (Colored) was chosen for this sensitive mission because of army confidence that a German agent could not possibly conceal himself in a black unit; and besides, blacks' loyalty might be presumed to belong undividedly to the United States, unlike that of "hyphenated Americans." But black Americans preferred to regard the selection of the black Washington battalion as a due reward for their total, nonhyphenated Americanism. And so the black war story, which was to add a new chapter in the humiliation and degradation of black Americans, began on a note of high hope.

2. Violence in the Summer, 1917

They are saying a great deal about democracy in Washington now, but
while they are talking about fighting for freedom and the Stars and
Stripes, here at home the whites apply the torch to the black man's
homes, and bullets, clubs, and stones to their bodies.

> Hubert H. Harrison, president of the Liberty League
> of Negro Americans, quoted in the
> *New York Times*, 5 July 1917.

AT THE very time when patriotism and sacrifice were
being demanded of black Americans, a nationwide surge of
violence was directed against them. In 1916 there had been fifty-
four lynchings. In 1917 there were seventy, and as in earlier
years the offenses were often trivial or not at all outside the law.
A black man was lynched in Elgard, Louisiana, for the "crime"
of vagrancy; in Kissimee, Florida, for not surrendering his farm
when ordered to; in Letchatchie, Alabama, for insolence; in Sale
City, Georgia, for questioning a white man's word. At Quit-
man, Georgia, absurdity and obscenity combined in the lynching of an illiterate Negro on the charge of writing an insolent letter to a white woman.[1]

But if excuses for lynching followed the traditional pattern,
methods sometimes showed a shocking new tendency toward
hysterical hatred and sadism. On the flimsiest circumstantial evidence and a confession extracted by force, a man named Ell (or
El) Persons was arrested for the murder of a white girl in Memphis, Tennessee. A mob snatched him from the jail. First they
hacked his ears off, and then, to the cheers of a crowd of thousands of men, women, and children, they soaked him with gaso-
line and set him afire. The crowd's only complaint was: "They

21

burned him too quick!" [2] Later in the year another lynch mob of Tennessee, this time in Dyersburg, did a more leisurely job. Lation (or Ligon) Scott, accused of assault on a white woman, was snatched by a torchlight gang even though the woman had been unable to identify him in a police lineup. Red-hot pokers were thrust into Scott's eyes and down his throat; more hot irons were pressed against his feet, torso, and genitals. Only then was the pyre lighted and his body thrown on it. [3]

Why was there this increase in murder and sadism? No doubt the war in Europe was having the usual coarsening effect of wars, with pictures and stories of atrocities making brutality a familiar daily matter. But certainly part of the reason was white resentment of the advances being made by blacks. Black people were leaving the South in great numbers, disrupting the Southern economy as servants and laborers vanished. In the North they were getting white men's jobs and making unheard-of money, and like white men they were to be drafted into military service. There was even to be a training camp for black officers. Such a situation must have been intolerable and terrifying to many whites, especially in the South, and the mutilation and bestial murder of black individuals would have provided a fearsome lesson to black people as a whole to stay "in their place."

Here and there, a white man raised his voice against lynchings. Sen. Charles S. Thomas of Colorado said the nation should not expect black men to fight for democracy in France while their relatives were being butchered at home. Gov. A. O. Stanley of Kentucky personally prevented a lynching, and there was an instance where Baltimore police rescued a black from a mob. [4] But local authorities seldom tried to protect lynch victims or punish lynch mobs, and in fact they sometimes played more than a passive role in these murders.

President Wilson was urgently asked to speak out against lynching and violence, but he replied that he had no authority in such matters, which by the Constitution were left to state control. The Military Intelligence Bureau, aware of black unrest because of the increase in lynchings, suggested a way of getting around the constitutional restriction by passing an antilynching bill as a war measure, and thus within federal jurisdiction. The bill was to make it a federal offense to kill or threaten to kill any person in the service of the nation or subject to such service, or any relative of such a person through the degree of first cousin. With blacks being drafted into the army, almost every black person would have come under the broad umbrella of this law. But the bill never had a chance to become law, because it was never reported out of committee for a vote.[5]

Kelly Miller said: "If the Negro is allowed to be lynched in the South with impunity, he will soon be lynched in the North. . . ."[6] Events proved him right. Resentment of the advance of black people was not limited to the South, and there were incidents of mob violence in the North more dreadful than any individual Southern lynching. That summer of 1917 a rash of racial clashes spread through major cities, North and South: Chicago, New York, Newark, Danville (Va.), Lexington (Ky.), Waco (Tex.), and Chester (Pa.). But the worst of all took place in Illinois, in the tough industrial town of East St. Louis.

Railroading, metalworking, meat packing, and other such heavy industries in East St. Louis were enjoying a wartime boom. Several thousand—perhaps up to 10,000—black migrants from the South added their numbers to an existing black population of about 6,000.[7] Many migrants were showing up at the plant gates looking for work. This situation coincided with labor troubles in the city. In 1916, race relations became tense when the Aluminum Ore Company and some meat packers took on migrant blacks as strikebreakers. Black workers, whom the unions would not admit to membership, could in any case be had for less pay than white workers. The *New York Times*, not particularly sympathetic to blacks at that time, did not think job competition a major cause of racial conflict; it pointed out that, generally, black workers got only jobs that white workers didn't want.[8] In any case, there is little doubt that employers exploited the situation, and many whites were jobless. The labor unions berated the employers for the consequent deterioration in race relations, and the employers blamed the unions for taking their members out on strike.[9] A congressional committee that later investigated the riot of East St. Louis reported that racial clashes were products of a corrupt city government which worked hand in hand with local industrialists, protected vice and crime in the Negro districts, and then blamed the black criminal element for the city's troubles.[10] Still others believed that German agents were instigating these disruptions in war production. Possibly all these charges were in some degree valid and contributory to numerous racial incidents which culminated, in the summer of 1917, in an unprecedented disaster of mob violence.[11]

It began on 28 May with a meeting of the Central Trades Union of East St. Louis, at which angry demands were made that black criminals in the city jail be turned over to the committee and that the city government halt the influx of blacks. As the meeting ended, a rumor spread that some Negroes had just killed a white man. A mob formed to hunt down and beat blacks. Three thousand people took part in this Negro-hunt for two days, unchecked by the police or the National Guardsmen who were called in.[12] After a relative lull through June, much worse rioting broke out on the night of 1 July, triggered by events still unclear. It seems that a carful of white joyriders drove through the red-light district called Black Valley, the riders shooting at random into Negro homes. A number of blacks armed themselves and swarmed angrily into the streets. When another car with white riders drove through the black district the blacks fired at it and killed two of the whites. Afterward it was claimed that the second car was an unmarked police car and that the two men killed were policemen. According to one story they were not recognized because they were not in uniform; according to another, they flashed their badges before the blacks fired. Sen. Lawrence Y. Sherman of Illinois later described this incident as "lawless and savage" blacks murdering policemen on their way to disperse an unlawful meeting. But the blacks continued to insist that the car they had shot at was not a police car carrying policemen.[13]

Nevertheless, next day the bullet-riddled car was parked in front of the police station, and indignant white civilians thronged to see it. Enraged by the display, bands of whites began to rampage through the city, indiscriminately clubbing, stabbing, shooting, and hanging all blacks they met, including women and children. The National Guard was called in again but did nothing to protect the blacks or restore order. According to considerable testimony, they helped the mobbists or at least did not interfere with them. "A number of soldiers openly stated that 'they didn't like niggers' and would not disturb a white man for killing them," the investigating committee reported. The guard commander took no disciplinary action and in fact was not even in uniform.[14]

For days the newspapers were filled with tales of the horrors perpetrated by the mobs. Women were among the pursuers and the pursued. One black woman had her throat slashed by a white woman; gangs of white girls beat every black woman they could find. One mob immolated a cripple. A two-year-old black boy was shot and his body thrown into a burning building.[15]

By the end of four days of rioting eight whites had been killed and "over 100 negroes were shot or mangled and beaten to various degrees of helplessness," Senator Sherman told the investigating committee. Senator Tillman of Georgia explained that "white blood becoming once aroused grows savage and very, very cruel." [16] At least four of the eight murdered whites appear to have been killed by bullets intended for blacks, and among the injured whites two had been hurt by the mobbists for trying to aid blacks. The black casualty figure probably omits a number whose burned or drowned remains were never found, or who dragged themselves away from the city to die elsewhere. The *Times* said that half of the city's black population had fled by the fourth day of the rioting. In addition to bodily harm the blacks had suffered an estimated $3-million property damage as the mobs looted and burned.[17]

For days after the riots it was openly boasted in East St. Louis that "the niggers would be finished shortly, together with anyone who interferes with the rioters." [18] There was little reason to doubt this, considering the actions of the city police as reported by the House investigation:

The police shot into a crowd of negroes who were huddled together, making no resistance. It was a particularly cowardly exhibition of savagery.

When the newspaper reporters were taking pictures of the mob, policemen charged them with their billies, broke their machines, destroyed the negatives, and threatened them with arrest if any further attempt was made to photograph the rioters. . . .[19]

Any lingering hope that black people could get a fair shake in that city was dispelled by figures on arrests and sentences. Eleven blacks drew long prison terms for the deaths of four white men; eight whites drew similar sentences for the deaths of thirty-nine blacks, including women and children.[20]

The horrors of East St. Louis got wide coverage in the nation's press. Responsible Southern papers generally took the line of the *Atlanta Constitution* that such riots were deplorable but could be avoided if blacks stayed in the South where "every man is safeguarded in the right to work—and to live in peace and security if he works and leads the life of a decent, self-respecting citizen." [21] When Senator Sherman called for an investigation by a congressional committee, not all his colleagues agreed that this was necessary to get at the reasons for the riots. Senator Vardaman said they demonstrated that the Anglo-Saxon race would not give up any of its privileges to an inferior group, and that showering benefits on blacks would lead to mongrelism and national decay. Sen. Ben Tillman of South Carolina, one-time Populist who had courted the black vote with promises of equality, said that "the more the Northern people know of the negro the less they like him. I have epitomized it by saying 'they love him according to the square of the distance.' The further off he is the better they like him." [22]

The black community responded to the riot with shock and anger. In New York, 5,000 blacks marched in a silent parade on 28 July, with 20,000 more standing in silence along the route, to protest the injustice of East St. Louis. One poster showed kneeling women pleading with President Wilson to make America safe for democracy before trying to do that job for the world—but police confiscated it. President Wilson declined to see a black delegation about East St. Louis, claiming the press of urgent business. Kelly Miller, referring to Wilson's snub in an open letter to the President, wrote: "The Negro, Mr. President, in this emergency, will stand by you and the nation. Will you and the nation stand by the Negro?" [23] There was no answer.

A month after the East St. Louis riots, violence of a different sort burst out in Houston, Texas, where a battalion of the 24th Infantry Regiment, black Regular soldiers, was stationed. This clash cannot be considered in a vacuum but must be related to the increased lynchings and to what had happened at East St. Louis. The black soldiers involved knew what blacks had suffered in that riot, and they must have been primed with anger, quick to resent any slur or insult by whites. Also, these troops came from all over the country and, as the *New York Times* commented, were not docile like Southern Negroes and might irritate Southern whites by their lack of respect for the Southern code.[24] It was probably an error of judgment for the army to send black Regulars to Houston, but men were needed in connection with the building of Camp Logan near the city, and black troops drew this duty.

Army authorities had, in fact, quickly decided not to use any of the Regular black regiments in France, but instead to depend on black draftees and National Guard units. The 9th Cavalry therefore, was stationed at Stotsenburg Camp in Luzon, Philippines, throughout World War I. The 10th Cavalry was stationed at Fort Huachuca near Tombstone, Arizona, and several of its companies spent the war years patrolling the border and putting down uprisings on the Mexican side. When the war began, the 25th Infantry was at Schofield Barracks in Hawaii, but when native troops were activated in the summer of 1918 the 25th was brought stateside for Mexican border patrol, and thus a white regiment was released for service in France.

By such assignments the black Regulars were kept out of the way of trouble. While this policy deprived the country of the services of trained black troops in France, the talents and experience of the four regiments were not entirely wasted. They provided from their staffs many of the officers and specialists who organized the new black draft units. Twenty-five members of the 9th Cavalry went to the black officer training school at Des Moines when that was established, and twenty-one of them won commissions. Of the 10th Cavalry, more than sixty noncoms became officers in the new units, and about 600 experienced troopers were made noncoms. More than 1,000 men of the two infantry regiments were transferred as specialists or noncoms, and many of the best personnel left the regiments for officer training school.[25] So, despite the disappointment of black troopers and many other black people that the four regiments were not sent to France, the country did make use of its experienced black troopers while at the same time keeping them near the border or in the Pacific area where they performed vital functions and were not likely to "cause trouble."

Only the 24th Infantry was an exception. Regimental headquarters was at Camp Furlong, near Columbus, New Mexico, but the battalions were separated: the 1st was sent to Waco, Texas, the 2d to Denning, New Mexico, and the 3d to Houston.

Houston welcomed the black soldiers by tightening up enforcement of its omnipresent Jim Crow laws. The men of the 24th, 3d Battalion, seasoned and self-confident troopers, responded by ignoring those laws. In the city they refused to sit in the Jim Crow sections of streetcars and theaters. They tore down Jim Crow signs and made them objects of ridicule by wearing them at a dance. At camp they refused to drink from water barrels provided for Negro workmen.[26] In short, they insisted on their dignity as members of the United States Army.

To citizens and police of Houston, such behavior on the part of Negroes was not dignity but insolence. City officials knew how to break black insolence. Men of the battalion were insulted and beaten by police. The provost guard was forbidden to carry arms within the city limits, a flagrant breach of courtesy and precedent, and members of the guard were harassed by the city police.

On 23 August, about a month after the battalion's arrival, one of the soldiers tried to prevent a white policeman from beating up a black woman. He was pistol-whipped and arrested for drunkenness. Later that day a Corporal Baltimore of the battalion's military police went to inquire about him. The police officers found Baltimore's manner offensive and pistol-whipped him too. He fled, was caught, beaten again, and arrested.[27] Although the corporal was released soon and returned to camp that afternoon, somehow a rumor spread among the men that he had been killed, and they determined to avenge his death. They warned their friends not to come to camp that evening. This was known to the (white) battalion commander, and he must have recognized it as a sign of trouble brewing, but he took no security steps beyond forbidding the men to leave camp for any reason.[28]

The official version of the story is that, early in the evening, men of one company stole ammunition from an unguarded supply tent and made a dash for town, reportedly urged on by Corporal Baltimore. As this group approached the city it met some white men and fired on them, thus sounding an alarm for the town. By the time they reached Filipo Street the soldiers were intercepted by police and armed civilians who were waiting for them. For a short time shots were exchanged, and then the group of soldiers dispersed and drifted back to camp.

The clash does not appear to have been a carefully organized attack, even in the official version. These men were experienced soldiers; yet it was said that they gave notice of their approach by casual gunfire and broke up after the brief outburst of shooting on Filipo Street. However, the casualties were serious. Two black soldiers and seventeen white men, including five police officers, had been killed.[29]

Two companies of white coast artillerymen and a battalion of white infantrymen were at once rushed to Houston. The 24th Regiment men were disarmed and immediately sent back under arrest to their headquarters in New Mexico.[30] In the course of the next month, 156 members of the 24th's 3d Battalion were tried by courts-martial for participating in what was officially labeled a mutiny.

At the first group of trials in early December of 1917, sixty-three soldiers were tried. Thirteen were condemned to death, forty-one were sentenced to life imprisonment and four to shorter jail terms, and five were acquitted. For the thirteen, sentence of death was pronounced on 8 December, a Sunday; the following Wednesday, before dawn, the thirteen were hanged.[31] In subsequent courts-martial sixteen more men were sentenced to death, and many more were given life imprisonment.[32]

Despite all the trials and testimony, it is doubtful that the truth of that night in Houston was ever arrived at. The men of the regiment maintained a wall of silence. The white commander of Company L, Capt. Barlett James, scheduled to appear as a witness before the first court martial, committed suicide a week before that court opened. Whatever had happened, there was no doubt of the indecent haste in the hanging of the first thirteen men. They had been dead three months before the records of their trials reached the judge advocate general's office for review as to their legality. Because of this circumstance, the black community emotionally hailed the thirteen who had been executed as martyrs.[33] Still, those thirteen lives bought something valuable. Provost Marshal Gen. Enoch Crowder drafted General Order No. 7, which stated that in the future no death sentence could be carried out until it was reviewed and upheld by the President. Crowder was possibly motivated by fear that a congressional investigation of the hanging of the Houston thirteen might result in the creation of a civilian court of appeals for the decisions of courts-martial.[34]

In 1918 President Wilson, on the recommendation of Secretary of War Newton D. Baker, commuted the sentences of ten of the remaining sixteen who were under sentence of death, but the other six were hanged. The President took no action on those men serving prison terms, one of whom committed suicide. This was indeed retribution with a vengeance, because, in addition to all the man-years spent in prison, nineteen black men were legally killed for the deaths of seventeen whites.[35]

Vengeance seems to have played a large part in the Houston affair. It was in a spirit of vengeance that the State of Texas demanded that the mutineers be tried in state courts on murder charges, and that local authorities be given "a hand in the punishment of the negro soldiers." [36] Also, it seems more like an avenging spirit than a passion for justice that motivated an investigation by a citizens' committee of Houston. Its report was sure to inflame white opinion, and many of its allegations were not substantiated by evidence, only by testimony heard by the committee: that the black attack had been planned for two days before it occurred, and that the soldiers intended to kill every white they could find. The latter directly contradicted a report in the *New York Times* that the mutineers on their way to town had passed some whites by without molesting them; and as for killing all whites, it is certain that no white women or children were molested in any way.[37] Finally, the speedy disposition of the first thirteen does not resemble justice so much as it does a lust to make some black men—guilty or innocent—pay at once with their lives for white lives lost.

It is incontrovertible that white men died in Houston that night, and although accounts of the riot or mutiny are extremely confused there is little reason to doubt that black men killed them. But where did the guilt really lie? An investigating officer of the War Department said:

> The ultimate cause of the riot were [*sic*] racial. Certain men of the 24th Infantry apparently resolved to assert what they believed to be their rights as American citizens and United States soldiers. They failed, and in some cases refused to obey local laws and regulations affecting their race, they resented the use of the word "nigger." Their attitudes and actions undoubtedly gave rise to a spirit of restlessness on the part of certain portions of the colored community, especially the laborers at Camp Logan. On the other hand, the Police Department and many citizens of Houston resented the presence of colored soldiers and resented on the negro the badge of authority of the United States uniform. It is my belief that the tension had reached that point where any unusual occurrence would have brought on trouble.[38]

Secretary Baker told the President the same thing—that the "so-called Jim Crow laws" in Houston were the real source of the trouble.[39]

Through the press, too, the spirit of vengeance cried out. The *Outlook* called for the speedy trial and execution of the mutineers as if their guilt were established fact. The magazine advised black leaders to condemn the mutiny as fervently as white leaders condemned the rioters of East St. Louis; and it declared that if proper apologies were not forthcoming the black men who were training at Des Moines to become officers would not be commissioned. Also, said *Outlook*, white troops would always have to be stationed near blacks to insure that they behaved properly. "A great majority of those Negroes who have taken the enlistment oath have rendered faithful service," the editors continued, "but neither they nor Negroes in civil life can afford to ignore the stain cast upon their racial honor by Brownsville and Houston." [40]

It is important to analyze this last statement to discover just what the country wanted of its black soldiers. Reasonably enough, it wanted them to render faithful service. It also wanted them never to repeat Brownsville and Houston, stains on their racial honor—but what precisely does that mean? It seems to mean that black soldiers were to do just as the white man told them to, to obey his rules without protest; they were not to stand up for their own people, not to use initiative or daring. To break the rules, to act like men, the black man was taught at Brownsville and East St. Louis and Houston and at the noose end of many a lynch rope, was to bring swift and inordinate punishment upon himself. A Memphian put the idea plainly, in referring to the recent lynching of the man named Persons: "Say nigger you have said lots more than a brute should say. Come down; we will *show you* where the El Person tree is. No *fire* there now—just plenty rope. Come nigger, and see. You can *go away easy*. We will see to it." [41]

The lesson was clear. To survive, the black man would have to agree that he was an inferior brute; that he must not defend himself; that he could not lead and must not follow other black men; and that, above all, he could not advance except under the guidance of white men. Not long after, on a French battlefield, members of a black battalion were required to defend themselves, the officers to lead the soldiers, the soldiers to follow the officers, and to advance to an objective without the guidance of white men. But they had learned their lesson too well to do well.

3. Choosing and Using Black Draftees

It would be no use to exempt such men from the draft. Such exempted men would be replaced by others of a similar kind and the draft boards could run through the colored race in the United States and exempt a large part of them. In these days of conservation, when every rag and bone and tin can is saved, human beings cannot be wasted. These colored men have to be inducted into the service by draft in their turn and it is believed that they ought to be put right to work at useful work which will be of real significance to the United States in prosecuting the war, and will release men available for other services.

Report of Col. E. D. Anderson, Operations Branch,
War Plans Division, 16 May 1918.

THERE were three categories of black Americans available to the army for service in France: the four regiments of Regulars, the National Guard units of various states, and ordinary civilians. The Regulars, as we have seen, were to remain stateside. Members of the National Guard were to be organized into units of the National Army. As for the black civilians, it was the army's intention from the very beginning of the war to draft them and set them to the hard manual labor required in vast quantity by modern warfare. Whatever had to be done to accomplish this plan was done, and the desirable end was believed quite enough justification for the often dubious means. The effect on black Americans for many years to come, right up until today, was ignored.

Negro spokesmen, disappointed that the four Regular regiments were not to be sent to France, demanded that black citizens be used in the war effort. DuBois in the *Crisis* said: "I believe that this is our War and not President Wilson's War and that no matter how many blunders the administration makes, or how many obstacles it puts in our way we must work the harder to win the war." If black men were not given a chance to fight, the *Crisis* pointed out, the labor shortage would offer them new job opportunities:

> Will we be ousted when the white soldiers come back?
> THEY WON'T COME BACK
> So there you are gentlemen, and take your choice,—
> We'll fight or work.
> We'll fight and work.
> If we fight we'll learn the fighting game and cease to be so "aisly lynched."
> If we don't fight we'll learn the more lucrative trades and cease to be so easily robbed and exploited.
> Take your choice, gentlemen.
> "We should worry." [1]

The draft law, passed in May 1917, required the registration of all male citizens between the ages of twenty-one and thirty-one. There were both blacks and whites who wondered whether Negroes, bitter from their long history of oppression, might not resist the call to fight for the white America that had oppressed them. The postwar report of Provost Marshal General Crowder laid to rest any lingering question about the response of blacks: "How groundless such fears, how ill considered such doubts, may be seen from the statistical record of the draft with relation to the Negro. His race furnished his quota, and uncomplainingly, yes, even cheerfully." [2] The response was not quite so unanimously enthusiastic as General Crowder stated, but in general he was right. Negro speakers were organized into a "flying squadron" by Howard University and other black institutions, and toured the South fanning Negro patriotism. [3]

Although black opposition to the draft was negligible, a number of white Americans vehemently opposed a black draft. In the South especially it was feared that military service would make black laborers less docile and might lead to dangerous black militancy after the war. Senator Vardaman, in whose view blacks were subhuman, was most vitriolic on the subject of a black draft: "Universal military service means that millions of negroes who come under this measure will be armed. I know of no greater menace to the South than this." Vardaman was not alone in this opinion; similar objections came from Northerners as well as Southerners.[4]

A very perceptive comment was made by the journalist and writer Herbert Seligmann soon after the war: "The penalty for the social and political disabilities imposed upon the Negro has been that he is constantly in the minds of white people. From contempt, with its admixture of self-reproach, to hostility is a short step and an easy one. Hence the apprehension with which the white South looked upon the induction of Negroes into the army; hence in the past, the quick resort to the rope, the pistol, the torch." [5]

But, as Colonel Anderson pointed out, the war effort required every rag, bone, and tin can; and the draft law required blacks as well as whites to register for possible military service, whatever Vardaman and others might think. The registrants would be examined and classified according to their ability and usefulness; those unfit to serve in any capacity would be culled from those acceptable for either full or limited service. But, in accord with Anderson's philosophy, draft boards culled few blacks, the expectation being that they would become only pick-and-shovel troops so it didn't matter what they had wrong with them—they did their day's work with these handicaps as civilians and could just as well do it as soldiers.

Discrimination was the rule throughout the draft processing. The registrant was required by the draft circular to list his race as "Caucasian," "negro" [*sic*], "Mongolian," "Malayan," or "Indian." [6] In Washington, D.C., blacks and whites were lined up separately for physical examination; excess furniture jammed the black side of the room, and blacks were given no pegs to hang their clothes on. Although black inductees were often examined by white physicians, a board in Detroit was formally reprimanded for permitting black doctors to examine whites. The board in Fulton County, Georgia, granted exemptions to 526 of the first 815 white registrants examined but turned down only 6 out of 202 black men; in this case of blatant discrimination, the criticism was so loud that President Wilson had to remove the entire board. In an effort to counter complaints of unequal treatment, the white and black presses were flooded with propaganda supporting the administration policy on race relations.[7]

In 1917 there were two separate draft calls, on 5 June and 12 September. A total of 23,779,997 men were registered, of whom 2,290,527 (9.63 percent) were blacks. As these enrollees were examined, those immediately available for the draft were placed in Class I, with the rest deferred for the time being. Of the 1,078,331 blacks examined under the first call, 556,917 (51.65 percent) were put in Class I. Of the 9,562,515 whites examined at the same time, 3,110,659 (32.53 percent) were put in Class I. Taking 19.12 percent more blacks than whites would seem to indicate that draft boards found black registrants superior material, mentally and physically; but, of course, it meant nothing of the sort.

Furthermore, of blacks put into Class I in the first draft call, 36 percent were inducted into the service; of whites put in Class I, only 24 percent. Of the number called into the service at that time blacks formed about 22 percent. But many more whites than blacks had entered the service of their own volition. The percentage of blacks to the total number of men entering the service, including enlistees and those accepted in the first draft call, comes to a more reasonable 12.6 percent. Still, blacks, who were 10.19 percent of registrants during the entire war, provided 12.6 percent of those actually taken.[8]

In the South, blacks provided grossly more than their share. By the end of the war, figures for Alabama, Florida, and Virginia showed that blacks made up more than 30 percent of their total registrants; for South Carolina, Georgia, and Louisiana, more than 40 percent; for Mississippi, 50.42 percent. Five states, all in the South, inducted more blacks than whites; Florida (+900), Georgia (+1,800), Louisiana (+1,200), Mississippi (+4,700), and South Carolina (+7,500).[9] In Clarke County, Georgia, blacks formed 45 percent of those registered, but 58 percent of those mustered into the service.[10]

Men who failed to register or who, having registered, failed to report for induction, were classified under the draft law as delinquents or deserters. Of the 475,000 so listed throughout the war, 22 percent were black. Of the total of each race registered under the draft law, the white desertion rate was 3.86 percent and the black rate 9.81 percent.[11] However, military authorities were almost unanimous in alleging ignorance, illiteracy, and frequent changes in place of employment as the major causes of black delinquency.[12] General Crowder, who believed blacks so cheerful and uncomplaining in their war service, commented, "With equal unanimity the draft executives report the amount of wilful delinquency or desertion has been almost nil," and offered the information that a major factor in delinquency among blacks was "the withholding of [draft board] mail by the landlord (often himself an aristocratic slacker) in order to retain the man's labor." [13] There is little doubt of Southern reluctance to have black farm labor drafted. In fact, it was a not uncommon policy for draft boards to take blacks who owned their own land while exempting those who worked for whites as sharecroppers or tenants.[14] The encouragement of desertion for profit was another reprehensible tactic more common in the South than in the North. The draft law provided that an apprehended deserter be fined, usually $50, this amount to be deducted from his pay and given to the person who apprehended him. Some Southern officials, in collusion with postal authorities, would deliberately prevent delivery of a registrant's notice of induction and later turn him in and collect the reward. In one such case reported by DuBois, the alleged delinquent was held incommunicado in the local jail for four days on bread and water, then taken to Camp Gordon, Georgia, and inducted.[15]

Another serious form of discrimination was practiced on many black professional men when they registered for the draft. At a time when the army was seeking doctors and dentists, black men in these professions were being turned down for commissions; later they were drafted as privates. DuBois entered an official protest for the NAACP. Col. R. B. Miller of the Medical Corps replied: "The Surgeon-General directs me to say that colored medical officers have been supplied to all colored organizations with colored line officers. Colored medical officers will not be assigned to units in which the other officers of the organization are white." [16] Even this policy, although discriminatory in itself, was not applied in the 92d Division when it was organized; there were black line officers, but the divisional medical staff was white. Assistant Secretary of War Frederick P. Keppel informed a group representing the Federal Council of Churches that the chief reason for not taking more black doctors was that the medical profession did not rank the colored medical schools very highly.[17] In any case, opposition to commissioning black officers of any sort was so powerful that Keppel's explanation is not convincing.

The next step was assigning the black draftees to training camps. There were so many problems and protests surrounding this issue, especially after the Houston mutiny, that Chief of Staff Gen. Tasker Bliss, buying time in which some answers might be found, simply delayed calling the black draft.

Much of the opposition to black conscription had revolved around the issues of where blacks should be trained and whether or not they would be trained with white units. Secretary of War Baker specifically informed a Southern congressman, in hearings on the Selective Service Act, that the policy of the War Department was (and would remain) to organize blacks into separate units based on race. This policy, he said, had been adopted as necessary to preserve discipline.[18] Herbert Seligmann wrote that the War Department met with strong objections to stationing black troops in the South, or even to accepting them for service [19]—although the records show the conflicting evidence that Southern draft boards were reluctant to exempt blacks.

In the press, the *New Republic* declared that the South was not opposed to the recruitment of black men as such but feared the mobilization of large numbers of undisciplined blacks.[20] The *Columbia* (S.C.) *State* proposed that if most of the Southern colored troops were sent to Northern camps, the major Southern objections to their conscription would be resolved and the colored men would be happier and safer. The *Chicago Defender* also made the point that they would be safer. The *Montgomery* (Ala.) *Advertiser* took the practical view that, in fairness to white men, blacks too would have to be conscripted. The *Savannah* (Ga.) *Press* concurred, adding that the Negroes would be better trained and disciplined if encamped in Northern states, and that those states would get some valuable discipline of another sort from the experience. The *Arkansas Gazette* was less facetious and expressed soberly the general Southern opinion that the black man could be best trained and disciplined by Southern whites: "In spite of the rantings of writers who know nothing of the negro, there is a bond of sympathy between the Southern white man and the Southern negro that is very strong and that can be used to good advantage." [21] Here the *Gazette* was assuming that only Southern blacks would be trained in the South, not men from other sections who might not be chained, or might not wish to be, by the bond of sympathy.

A committee composed of black leaders and concerned white people suggested to Secretary Baker that the South could not legitimately object to the stationing of its own black citizens within its borders.[22] Baker did not commit himself on this question, but the War Department's burdens would have been lighter if it could have stationed all black draftees within the borders of their home states. Another War Department policy, however, implicitly forbade this by requiring the maintenance in each camp of a "safe ratio" of whites to blacks, one that would minimize racial disturbances. Still shaken by the Houston mutiny, the department defined a safe ratio as two whites to one black.[23] If Southern black draftees were all put in camps in their home states, where there were large black populations, the white advantage in those camps would be less than the required two to one; so some of the black draftees had to be sent to camps in the North with small indigenous black populations.[24]

Obviously, the policy of maintaining the ratio created vexing administrative difficulties. Because the number of whites would establish the allowable number of blacks, white troops had to be called up and assigned first, and then black troops could arrive in the proper number. Then other difficulties would arise. The black draftees were to be assigned to separate sections of the cantonments, but since the original building plans had not called for special black areas, these would have to be built before the colored troops could be called.[25] Presenting an additional problem was General Crowder's order that trains carrying recruits to camp would also have to be segregated.[26]

Tensions inherent in segregated black camps near hostile cities could have been alleviated by the volunteer organizations that took it upon themselves to serve soldiers. These organizations provided sorely needed recreational facilities and gave the tired, homesick soldier a chance to relax, to talk to sympathetic women, to exchange gripes or laughs over a cup of coffee; in short, to blow off steam. They were tremendously important and could have relieved the atmosphere of discrimination in which the black soldier found himself. But instead, in stateside camps and later in France, the facilities of the biggest of these organizations, the YMCA, were almost always strictly segregated—which aggravated, rather than relieved, the tensions.

A major function of the Y was to provide for the recreational, educational, and religious needs of soldiers, and with white soldiers it was an outstanding success. But almost every YMCA "hut" was segregated, and segregation was strictly enforced. Sentries patrolled the white Y areas and kept blacks out. Often there were no huts at all for the black soldiers, sometimes a leaky tent. Despite official disclaimers, facilities for blacks were in almost every case inferior. Where there was no black hut, a black soldier or officer could not buy so much as a postage stamp in a Y hut meant for whites. White women volunteers who staffed the huts refused outright to serve blacks. In France, the commanding officer of a black regiment built his own hut for his soldiers when YMCA units in the area refused to sell them cigarettes.[27] Ralph Tyler, the only accredited black war correspondent in France, wrote: "The only discrimination a Colored man from the states, or any other country, encounters in this land of liberty is at the hands of the Y.M.C.A., and most regretfully, Colored soldiers who have been at the fighting front, who have wounds to prove they have been in battle, and whose Croix de Guerre, decorating their breast was the proof that they had performed some act of valor for their country are the victims of the Y.M.C.A.'s undemocratic discrimination. . . . Too many Y.M.C.A. people over here accord Colored soldiers treatment due a pariah rather than a patriot. . . ."[28]

One of the most vital services of the Y was to provide a chance for soldiers to talk to women, the women volunteers who gave the huts a homelike atmosphere. This meant so much to the soldiers, especially in France, that as one man said, just to look at the women was enough; "we can fill up on that."[29] But the black soldiers had little of this gratification, because very few black women volunteers were accepted by the Y. When they were, it was because the army needed them, as at Romagne, in

France, where black labor troops reburying war dead became so restive that black women Y workers were sent in the hope that their companionship might keep the troops from rebelling against their horrid assignment.[30]

The Knights of Columbus and the Salvation Army had a much more liberal racial policy and did a good job, within their limited means, of providing recreation for black soldiers. There was never any friction in their integrated huts, black soldiers in the camps reported.[31] The powerful Red Cross, too, generally treated the black soldiers fairly in its hospitals and in towns they were passing through. Still, it was a very white Red Cross; the organization did not welcome black volunteers and was most reluctant to use black nurses. In this matter of nurses, however, the chief stumbling block was probably Surgeon General William C. Gorgas, who would not grant permission for black nurses to go to France.[32] The War Camps Community Service helped black soldiers a little, but it was late in building recreational facilities (segregated) for blacks and had trouble raising money for black programs.[33] The Federal Council of Churches was more successful in its efforts, but its work was limited almost entirely to arranging for black chaplains for the black troops.[34]

A service that the average black soldier would probably have appreciated much more was that provided by the Hostess Houses. These were centers of recreation and relaxation for the men and their female visitors to camp, places where a woman could spend the night and get a meal. Although the Hostess Houses were built on government land with government materials and labor, they were staffed by local volunteers—and were strictly segregated. It would be more correct to say that they were for whites only until April 1918, when the first Hostess House for blacks opened, a whole year after the nation went to war. Other black Hostess Houses followed, but there was so much hostility between black and white women volunteers, so much discrimination against black women visitors, and so much official foot dragging in providing the necessary facilities that black soldiers got little benefit from an institution that made army life more bearable for white soldiers.[35]

If the patriotic service organizations had done a better job for the black soldiers in camps, tensions in nearby towns would have been eased and the men themselves would have been less likely to seek recreation in those towns, which was often the start of trouble. But almost no one cared enough to make the black man's soldier days less dreary, frightening, and lonely. The favored solution to racial tension was to give the black man less, rather than more; to have segregated camp areas, "safe ratios," and a citizenry alerted to expect trouble from the black man.

Inseparable from the problem of where to train black troops was a corollary: for what were they to be trained? Racist suggestions were freely offered. Senator Vardaman warned about "the negro's lust for blood." A magazine writer said: "The negro is not a white man with a black skin; he is a different race at a different stage in evolution. . . . That fact . . . should throw light upon the white man's program for the negro." [36] Top military men voiced their opinions that blacks had inherent character weaknesses, were cowards, and increasingly showed a tendency toward moral worthlessness.[37] Military authorities were pressing strongly to have the black troops serve primarily as laborers, a use for which their peacetime occupations specially fitted them.[38] Colonel Anderson highly recommended such a course to the War Plans Division.[39]

As early as August 1917, Chief of Staff Tasker Bliss had proposed six alternative plans for the employment of black draftees:

Plan 1: they might be stationed with whites from the same area, but in a segregated section of the camp;

Plan 2: one regiment of Negro combat troops might be organized at each of the sixteen National Army cantonments, with the remaining black troops to be used as military laborers; this plan would have put 48,000 black men in combat units;

Plan 3: black troops might be stationed at separate facilities at least a mile from the regular camps to prevent racial mixing;

Plan 4: two Southern camps might be created for all the black troops;

Plan 5: black troops might be given a minimum of training at the eight Northern camps, after which they should be shipped to France where they would receive final training, with weapons;

Plan 6: the calling of the black draft might be delayed, and at last, after minimal training at the camps nearest their homes, the men would be sent to France and used exclusively as service troops.[40]

Bliss gave his personal endorsement to Plan 6 and explained his objections to the first five plans. Sending black and white draftees to the nearest camp meant that both groups would be trained and armed in the same manner, and furthermore, in some Southern camps, blacks could conceivably outnumber whites. If, as in Plan 2, a regiment of blacks was to be organized at each army cantonment, some of the Southern blacks would have to be sent North to make up the unit. The creation of separate facilities at each camp, as called for in Plan 3, would cost around $16,000,000. Bliss's objection to putting all black troops in two special camps as in Plan 4 was that such a concentration of armed blacks would present a grave danger to the nation. Plan 5 would require the complicated logistics of moving the great mass of blacks from the South to the North. The advantages of Plan 6, Bliss pointed out, were that the blacks need not be moved, would receive no training with weapons before sailing for France, and would serve their most useful function—as labor troops.

Such persistent rumors were abroad that blacks would be given only labor assignments that black leaders put the question to Secretary Baker. In December 1917, more than three months after he had approved Plan 6, Baker told DuBois that no attempt was being made to deprive blacks of the same training and employment as white troops. He said that 30,000 blacks would be trained for combat, and 50,000 would be put in depot brigades which might serve as either labor or combat troops. According to this promise, better than 35 percent of black soldiers would be fighting men.[41]

The use of black troops continued to be debated throughout the war. By the time Colonel Anderson's study for the War Plans Division was made in 1918, many thousands of black troops were already overseas. In the absence of clear policy, individual commanders tried to convert combat troops into labor troops at every opportunity. By the end of the war, despite Baker's pledge to DuBois, 80 percent of the black troops overseas were assigned to labor duties, and only 20 percent ever saw combat.

When "every rag and bone and tin can" of a man is accepted into a group, the group's average performance is obviously going to be lower than that of a second group selected according to a higher standard. Almost superfluously, military planners were supported in their opinion that black troops were meant to wield picks and shovels by the bulk of scientific thinking of the war period, which held that the black American civilian was neither physically nor mentally capable of performing the duties of a combat soldier. The cream of the race had been skimmed off, it was believed, by the four Regular regiments and the National Guard units.

In World War I, intelligence testing was a new tool of the new science of psychology: in fact, the massing of men for war gave psychologists their first real chance to develop and validate the tests. Today, the limitations of intelligence tests are acknowledged; the pioneers of World War I were making mistakes that would be obvious now to any beginning student in psychology. Still, reputable psychologists did not hesitate to generalize from the tests—imperfectly framed and administered, and given to unequally chosen groups—that the mental age of the average white draftee was 13.15 years, and that of the average black draftee only 10.1 years. A moron was defined as any adult whose mental age was between seven and twelve. Those who opposed equality for black people exploited these figures.[42]

George O. Ferguson, a University of Virginia psychologist, was probably the foremost authority in the field of black intelligence. Although he was careful to note the areas in which evidence was inconclusive, he nonetheless published some unsubstantiated conclusions. For example, he pointed out that "as yet comparatively little of a scientific nature has been accomplished in investigating the mind of the Negro." But such lack of scientific evidence did not prevent him from speculating: "While there is thus no difference of well established significance between the brains of the two races, it is not unreasonable to suppose that the great differences in physique and features between typical Negroes and whites are accompanied by correspondingly important neural differences. Unless there are such corresponding neural differences the situation is probably unique among biological phenomena." There is, of course, a great difference between "not unreasonable to suppose" and "reasonable to believe," but the first was easily metamorphosed into the second because that accorded with ingrained white opinion. [43]

Before the war, Ferguson had made a study of school children in three Virginia cities—Richmond, Newport News, and Fredericksburg—which yielded the unsurprising results, considering educational opportunities, that city children were more literate than those from rural areas, and that white children were more literate than colored. Further, Ferguson established an arbitrary "figure of eminence," a level of intellectual attainment which he claimed only one out of every 4,300 persons was capable of reaching. In Ferguson's own list of living Americans who met his arbitrary standard, he named 4,464 American whites, 6 mulattoes, and 2 blacks; by population, he calculated that 99 mulattoes and 397 blacks should have made the list if the races were equal in intelligence. [44]

With America's entry into the war, Ferguson became involved in the development and administration of intelligence tests for the army. Two tests were used, the Alpha and the Beta. The Alpha test, a forerunner of present standardized tests of the Stanford-Binet type, required a degree of literacy. Black recruits tested were from Virginia, West Virginia, and Pennsylvania, with a few from the Carolinas and the District of Columbia, and were accepted as literate on their own statement that they could read and write; they scored significantly lower than the companies of white troops from the 80th Division. [45] In the Beta test, designed to test illiterates, the median scores for whites and blacks were so similar that they indicated no significant racial differences in intelligence. These results were believed to invalidate the Beta test, so it was discarded in favor of a revised Beta which reflected the same degree of racial differences as the Alpha test—an action of dubious scientific integrity.

Ferguson's racial theory was not shaken by the very high correlation between performance and years of schooling; what that proved, he claimed, was that those with the most innate ability remained longest in school. "It is also worthy to note," he wrote, "that Northern Negroes obtained higher average scores on a given test than the Southern, and that urban blacks attained higher average scores than the rural." [46] The obvious inference from the high correlation between education and performance on the intelligence tests was similarly accounted for by another psychologist of importance, William McDougall, who said: "Does not common experience teach us that, where schooling is difficult to obtain, the brighter boys who find themselves making good progress in school are those most likely to continue at school? Is it not possible that the brighter boys are the sons of the more intelligent parents and are more likely to enter school than the dullards and the sons of unintelligent parents?" [47]

N. D. Hirsch, who made tests on both black and white recruits, suggested a reasonable modification of McDougall's theory: "The difference between the literates and the illiterates is partly due to innate differences, partly to education; but the difference is much greater in whites than in coloreds. If we assume that the attraction of schools works selectively in equal degrees on whites and coloreds, and this seems a fair assumption, then it follows that the higher the level of innate capacity, the more it is improved by education." [48]

Unfortunately, almost all these studies of black intelligence show starting assumptions that guided the work to predictable results. They generally ignored differences in social and economic levels, and in educational opportunity and quality. For instance, in a further test Ferguson made of rural and urban blacks from Virginia, the median scores of city dwellers was 53; of rural dwellers, 40. [49] Although this would further indicate the tests reflected culture or school quality rather than intelligence, Ferguson did not pursue this line of thought. It was axiomatic to him and other psychologists that intelligence was what the intelligence tests tested, and other factors were ignored.

By 1918, both the Alpha and the Beta tests had been revised. Also, a reading test was required to establish literacy for the Alpha, instead of the unsupported assertion of the man being tested that he could read and write. The median for the new

Alpha was 51 for whites, 17 for blacks; on the Beta, 33 for whites, 16 for blacks. In other words, black performance was "scientifically" established as about one-third as high as white on the Alpha, and one-half as high on the Beta. It was, therefore, disconcerting that when draftees at Camp Lee were tested in August 1918, some companies of black Northerners scored considerably better than some companies of Southern white mountaineers.[50] A number of explanations were offered for this result, one of the more interesting being that the large number of blacks in the South had depressed the intelligence of those whites among whom they lived. At any rate, none of the findings shook Ferguson's belief in the validity of the tests.

Ferguson's racial conclusions were reinforced by Carl C. Brigham of Princeton University, who acknowledged his indebtedness in treating the race question to two popular racist writers, Madison Grant and Prof. William Z. Ripley. Brigham's analysis, perhaps the most complete at that time, used the army tests extensively. Though he recognized that Southern schools were likely to be poor, he concluded that "it is absurd to attribute all differences between northern and southern negroes to superior educational opportunities in the North, for differences were found among groups of the same schooling, and differences are shown by Beta as well as by Alpha." (One must remember that Beta was revised until it showed those differences.) Instead, Brigham explained the higher scores of Northern blacks by a higher proportion of racial mixing, coupled with cultural factors which tended to draw the more intelligent blacks out of the South—the theory of "selective migration." In 1930, Brigham recanted the conclusions of his earlier study, calling them "pretentious" and "without foundation" and saying that "comparative studies of various national and racial groups may not be made with existing tests. . . ." But the damage done by his tests and analysis could not be undone.[51]

Col. Robert M. Yerkes, of the U.S. Army, who wrote a flattering introduction to Brigham's early report, collected and collated the data obtained from all these tests, publishing the results in the early twenties. His conclusions so angered important Southerners in Congress and some of his superiors in the army that this study remained relatively unknown. Yerkes pointed out

TABLE 1
ALPHA TEST SCORES FOR SOUTHERN WHITE AND
NORTHERN BLACK DRAFTEES

| *White* | | *Black* | |
STATE	SCORE	STATE	SCORE
Tennessee	44.0	Ohio	45.7
Texas	43.4	Illinois	42.2
Oklahoma	42.9	Indiana	41.5
Kentucky	41.5	New York	38.6
Alabama	41.3	Pennsylvania	34.7
Mississippi	37.6		
Louisiana	36.1		
Arkansas	35.6		

SOURCE: Yerkes, ed., "Psychological Examining in the United States Army," *Memoirs of the National Academy of Sciences* 15 (1921):690–91, tables 205, 206, reproduced in Ashley Montagu, *Man's Most Dangerous Myth* (New York, 1964), p. 389.

that Northern whites outscored Southern whites, and Northern blacks outscored Southern blacks; and furthermore, that black draftees of some Northern states did significantly better than white draftees of some Southern states (see table 1). Neither Yerkes' findings nor Brigham's later recantation had any mitigating effect on military opinion of the intelligence of black soldiers.

Findings on the health and physical fitness of black draftees are subject to the same invalidating circumstance as findings on their intelligence: draft boards accepted blacks with disabilities which would have disqualified whites, so black draftees were bound to have lower medians than whites in both physical and mental fitness. All that can be drawn from the results of physical examinations is information on the physical condition of black draftees, which cannot meaningfully be compared with the physical condition of white draftees, nor accepted as an index of black health and physical fitness in the entire black population, because draft boards in different areas had different standards for black draftees.

Given the "rag and bone and tin can" directive for the black draft, it was predictable that complaints would be heard that black draftees were an inferior lot physically. Depressed social conditions among blacks resulted in their having more health problems than whites; yet draft statistics clearly show that local boards put a greater proportion of black than of white registrants in Class I. Black writers cited draft figures as proof of black physical fitness, but an army source maintained that 100,000 white registrants would provide 1,240 more soldiers than an equal number of black registrants.[52]

By official statistics this was an overstatement, unless the army source was referring only to combat soldiers. Two army doctors, A. G. Love and C. B. Davenport, made a careful study of the physical condition of both white and black recruits, based on examinations of 530,000 whites and 15,000 blacks.[53] They found that among the white troops there were 974 sick reports per 1,000 men per year as against 1,155 sick reports for blacks, which indicated that the average black was 19 percent more likely to be sick than his white counterpart.

Love and Davenport classified reported diseases in four categories: (1) diseases against which blacks were less likely to have been immunized, (2) diseases for which there appeared to be a difference in natural immunity between blacks and whites, (3) venereal diseases, and (4) other diseases. For diseases in the first category, army medical personnel found higher rates in blacks than in whites and usually more acute forms. Chickenpox, for example, was eight times as common; smallpox was about nine times more fatal. In the second category, tuberculosis was from two to two and a half times more prevalent among blacks; lobar pneumonia was four times as fatal, bronchial pneumonia three times as fatal, and the rate of both types of pneumonia was two to three times the rate among whites. Addiction to drugs was more common among blacks, and they seemed more susceptible to neuralgia and hemorrhoids. Also in category 2 were diseases to which black troops seemed to have greater natural immunity: skin diseases of all types, including skin cancers; diabetes, ear and eye diseases, nervous instability; also diphtheria, scarlet fever, German measles, polio, and influenza—even at the peak of an influenza epidemic, the rate for blacks was only half the rate for whites. No consistent dental pattern could be found, some black recruits showing no sign of tooth decay and others showing no sign of teeth. The investigators concluded that blacks were naturally more resistant to dental decay organisms, and that where there was massive tooth loss it was probably attributable to the effects of mercury, then widely used in the treatment of syphilis.[54]

Love and Davenport claimed that in the camp whose health conditions they were analyzing physical examinations and sanitary conditions were identical for white and black troops. If this was true, the camp was so atypical as to make any generalization worthless. But it probably was like most others, with conditions far from identical. Although the surgeon general had promised equal recreational opportunities, medical inspection and treatment, instruction in hygiene, and clinical and hospital facilities for venereal patients, the promises were not kept.[55]

In addition to these inequities, and to the significant fact that many chronically ill blacks were accepted by draft boards, there are several other plausible explanations for the higher rate of sickness the investigators found among black soldiers. For one, a sickness might linger or become acute because white officers, almost unanimously of the opinion that blacks were natural malingerers, would not authorize sufficient medical treatment to effect a cure. Accounts of desperately ill men who were denied medical attention are all too common.[56]

Even more significant in relation to health differences between black and white soldiers were the poor clothing, housing, feeding, and working conditions of black troops, especially in the South. The only Southern camps reliably reported as giving blacks good treatment were Bowie and Meade.[57] At camp after camp, black troops were not provided with suitable wearing apparel until almost the end of the war. They worked outdoors in November without winter clothing, sometimes wearing only what they had had on their backs when mustered into the service in September. At Camp Pike, 2,500 of the men had only overalls and summer underwear at a time when the temperature averaged 39 degrees.[58] In general, black troops got used clothing of inferior quality; it arrived at one camp significantly ticketed for the "current colored draft." [59]

Shelter for black troops often consisted of tents without the flooring or boxing usually provided for whites housed under canvas, and sometimes without stoves in winter weather. Near Baltimore, 300 blacks were crowded into a barracks equal in size to one occupied by thirty-five white soldiers. The black area of a camp might be situated on the edge of a swamp, or it might have no sewers. Conditions did not improve until after the Armistice, when black troops moved into housing evacuated by demobilized white troops.[60]

Mess halls were so inadequate that many men had to carry food to their tents. An open shed might serve as a mess facility. Food was bad, the meat scarce and sometimes unfit to eat. In some camps the cooks were venereals who were adjudged unfit for heavier work. Water was commonly scarce in the black area; there might be only enough for one bath per man each week, if that, and there was often no water in the latrines during the day. Black troops worked outdoors long hours in all kinds of weather, whereas white troops usually had indoor recreation provided for them on inclement days. Sickness did not always excuse a black man from work, and many of the chronically ill died.[61]

Conditions in the camps around Newport News were particularly atrocious. These facilities served both for regular training and as a major collection point for stevedores and others who were shipping out for France. At Camp Lee, under the command of Gen. Adelbert Cronkhite, men reporting for sick call were summarily given a dose of castor oil and dismissed. Venereals were not segregated from men with other ailments as they were among white troops. The men at Camp Humphreys still had no mess facilities by the middle of 1918; they ate in the open and were marched down to the Potomac River for their weekly bath. By far the worst of all was Camp Hill, where no provision had been made for the 6,000 black draftees who began arriving in October 1917. On arrival, the lucky ones had unfloored, unheated tents; others stood around fires all night or slept in the woods under trees. Very few had blankets. From October until January their only clothing was what they had worn when they came, and no bathing facilities were provided during that entire time. These men ate outside regardless of the weather; one group of 500 had only 150 mess kits among them. Their hospital was a floorless tent, and doctors ordered sick men to work without treatment. Eventually, some shelter was provided, with twenty to thirty men in each sixteen-foot-square tent. Every day was a workday, including Sundays and holidays.[62]

There is overwhelming evidence that, despite the assertions of Love and Davenport, the facilities and treatment of colored troops were far from equal to those of whites. Under the circumstances, it is scarcely necessary to adduce malingering as an explanation for the large number of sick reports. Indeed, if black soldiers had been permitted as free access to needed medical care as whites, the sick reports would certainly have been even more numerous. There had to be an extraordinary amount of illness among blacks, especially with venereals and other sick men set to hard labor and the preparation of food.

In regard to venereal diseases, there were higher incidences of syphilitic, chancroid, and gonococcal infections among black soldiers than among whites. Again it must be noted that blacks were accepted for war service with venereal conditions which would have excused whites, because draft boards shared the general belief that most black men were venereals, so if there was to be a black draft it would have to take them, diseases and all. In addition, the army was in part to blame for the high venereal rate, because although for white troops the foulest red-light districts were posted as off-limits, black troops were not thus restricted and protected.[63]

There were no accurate national statistics on civilian venereal rates; but white authorities assumed so many blacks had venereal diseases that almost nothing was done to prevent their spread. In the South especially, black women were not afforded the same legal protection as white women. There was an almost complete lack of civilian facilities for the diagnosis and treatment of such diseases; public health facilities for blacks were practically nonexistent in the South, and so were educational programs. The absence of recreational facilities for blacks added to the magnitude of the venereal problem.[64]

Studies of venereal incidence among civilians produced inconsistent data. One study of the syphilis rate among poor people in Galveston, Texas, showed a prewar rate of 25 to 30 percent infection among blacks, and the same among whites. In an analysis of 1,000 female black patients in a charity hospital of a large Southern city, only 16.6 percent were reported as syphilitic, whereas it was generally claimed that better than 60 percent of Southern blacks were infected. Another study calculated the incidence of syphilis among civilians as about 5 to 6 percent for blacks, 3 to 4 percent for whites; among soldiers, 3.2 percent for blacks, 2.2 percent for whites. The last figures come close to the results of studies at the hospital of Johns Hopkins University, where it was computed that blacks had a syphilis rate about one and a half times that of whites. But Davenport and Love reported the civilian venereal rate for blacks as four times that of whites for syphilis, four and one-half times that of whites for chancroid venereal diseases, and two and one-half times that of whites for gonococcal infections. Ignoring the lack of educational, recreational, and health facilities, the investigators attributed the much higher black rates to two factors: the difference in social pressures on the races, and the general inability of blacks to control their sexual appetites—a belief as general as it was unsubstantiated.[65]

War Department statistics show that venereal diseases hospitalized 63,586 servicemen in 1917, of whom 59,503 were whites and 4,083 were blacks. This represented a rate per 1,000 men of 109.1 for the white troops, and 310.5 for the blacks. The same report shows that in treatment for venereal infections blacks got from 10 percent to 30 percent fewer days of hospitalization.[66] From these figures the surgeon general concluded that venereal diseases, particularly gonorrhea, ran a less serious course in blacks than in whites, ignoring the probability that blacks were less likely to receive hospitalization and more likely to be discharged earlier from treatment.

The same report showed that background and social class were closely related to the rate of venereal disease, implying the importance of information and of opportunities for early treatment. In the National Army, men from urban areas had an incidence rate of 10.2 per thousand; men from rural areas, 21.5 per thousand.[67] As further evidence, in the National Guard, where most men came from a higher economic and social level than did draftees, the rates were substantially lower in both urban and rural men; 8.5 per thousand, urban; 14.4 per thousand, rural. It is also probable, although no geographic breakdown is available, that the incidence of venereal infection was higher in the South because there were more rural poor and fewer urban concentrations and services in the South than in the North. There is evidence that the mortality rate for all causes was higher in the South, even in urban areas, than in the North; the 1910 rate for Charleston, South Carolina, was 18.9 deaths per thousand for white civilians, compared with the national rate of 13.7; 39.3 per thousand for black civilians, compared with the national rate of 21.9.[68] Such figures must be taken into account in weighing the incidence of venereal diseases among American blacks in the army, because they were preponderantly draftees, Southern, rural, and poor.

Military officials insisted that only nonvenereals be sent to France. Nevertheless, 2.5 percent of the black troops were found to be venereal on arrival, and one study alleged that the rate of infection then rose to between 4 and 6 percent "owing to the ease with which the colored soldiers could associate with the lower type of French women." [69] Where officers commanding black units showed concern, the venereal rates decreased. One group of 1,800 men reported only two cases in a month; another unit of 700 did not have a single case in a two-month period. At first, officers withheld passes and denied other privileges to entire units if the venereal rate was too high; this practice was later prohibited as unfair, but conscientious officers required prophylaxis for all black troops returning from leaves.[70]

By the last year of the war, the strenuous efforts of military authorities had reduced the venereal rate to 35 per 1,000 among the troops, black and white combined. "Considering that 71 percent exposed themselves with highly infectious women," said the official report, "the result is extremely gratifying." [71] The very high exposure figure of 71 percent is unsubstantiated, and seems questionable for 1918 when involvement in combat must have limited contacts between soldiers and women. But it seems fair to point out that, if the figure of 71 percent even approaches the truth, its magnitude should shake the myth that it was the black race which was unable to control its sexual drive.

There were too few black troops to justify holding them mainly responsible for that impressive percentage.

Related to this is another myth-shaker. At one point, military officials declared French houses of prostitution off-limits to all American troops. Very quickly, the white rate of venereal disease fell from 240 to 26 per 1,000 men; the black rate fell from 625 to 100 per 1,000. When the off-limits restriction was lifted, the white rate began to climb again; but the black rate, because of compulsory prophylaxis, continued to drop until it reached 30 per 1,000.[72] This seems clear proof that the higher incidence of venereal infections among blacks resulted not from uncontrollable brute sexuality but from ignorance or negligence about prophylactic measures.

But myths, especially when they serve a useful purpose, are not easily shaken. The purpose here was to put the black draft into labor units rather than combat units. Army planners used the available information on the physical conditions of black soldiers for this purpose, occasionally exaggerating certain aspects of the medical reports to justify their actions. When Gen. John J. Pershing, commander in chief of the American Expeditionary Forces (AEF), complained that black troops were arriving in France with "tuberculosis, old fractures, extreme flat feet, hernia, venerial [*sic*] diseases, all existing prior to enlistment," Colonel Anderson of the War Plans Divisions answered that these men were the pick of the Negro draft.[73]

4. The Problem of the Black Officer

I met some junior officers who said they were not keen on saluting Negro officers. They would not feel that way if they understood the spirit of the salute. If one of them came from a town where there was an old Negro character, one of those old fellows who do odd jobs and is known to everybody, he'd at least nod his head and say, "Howdy, uncle." Now suppose through some freak of nature this old Negro should be transplanted into an officer's uniform; the salute would be merely saying to him, "Howdy, uncle," in a military way.

Instructions reportedly given by Gen. Adelbert Cronkhite, commander of Camp Lee, to his subordinates.

NO AMOUNT of education or ability could make a black man white; and so long as he was black he would be odd man out in the U.S. Army no matter how able or educated he might be. The problem the army created for itself by this attitude was hydra-headed. There sprang from it not only the vexing question of what to do with the black draftees, largely Southern and lower class, but the equally or perhaps more vexing question of what to do with the middle-class, college-bred, often non-Southern black man who if he were white would be welcomed as officer material.

An unofficial Officer Training Camp, white, had been started by preparedness-minded citizens at Plattsburg, New York, before the United States entered the war. Immediately after war was declared more such camps were established until there were fourteen in operation. Not one of them was open to black men despite Secretary Baker's insistence that there would be no racial discrimination in the army.[1]

Joel Spingarn, a white intellectual who was the first president of the NAACP, and his NAACP associate James Weldon Johnson, the gifted black writer, requested Baker to have blacks admitted to OTC, but Baker said this was something he could never persuade the bureaucracy to agree to. He was more optimistic, however, about the next NAACP suggestion, that a separate black OTC be created—provided a sufficient number of candidates could be found. The segregated facility had been proposed by Gen. Leonard Wood, leader of the preparedness movement.

At once the black community set about meeting this challenge. Students from Howard and other black colleges toured the country soliciting applications for officer training.[2] Most black civilian leaders supported the effort, although the more radical ones ("radical" at that time meaning an uncompromising integrationist) opposed the suggestion of a segregated facility. Spingarn defended the idea thus: "The army officers want the camp to fail. The last thing they want is to help colored men to become commissioned officers. The camp is intended to fight segregation, not to encourage it. Colored men in a camp by themselves would all get a fair chance for promotion. Opposition on the part of Negroes is helping the South, which does not want the Negroes to have any kind of military training. . . ."[3] There is little reason to doubt that Spingarn knew what he was talking about. He was a privileged, upper-class white scholar of considerable note, who after a brief but distinguished academic career at Columbia University dedicated himself to the black cause.

Howard University, whose "flying corps" of students had produced a petition for officer training signed by 1,500 black college men, offered its facilities for the training course, but the War Department chose to establish the black OTC at Des Moines in Iowa, a state that had an excellent record in racial matters. A new difficulty arose, however, when the army announced that candidates must be between the ages of twenty-five and forty; all the black applicants were under twenty-five. A new drive was made, and applicants in the prescribed age group were found. When Congress finally authorized the Des Moines OTC, Speaker of the House Champ Clark of Missouri declared it marked "an epoch in American history and a new day for the Negro."[4] A black spokesman called it the "one constructive movement for the Negro since the passage of the Fifteenth Amendment." [5] DuBois said that Baker in creating the camp had done more for the black race than any other member of the Cabinet. In the black community as a whole, the news of Des Moines was hailed with excitement and hope. [6]

Considering all the hard work and enthusiasm black people expended to make Des Moines a fact, it is disheartening to see what the army's attitude was and how the decision to train black officers was negotiated. As Spingarn said, there was in the army profound hostility to the idea of a black officer group, and a firmly rooted assumption that blacks were incapable of military leadership; there is evidence that some highly placed army people actively worked to justify the hostility by proving the assumption. Their attitude was explained by one observer in these words: "The official personnel of a fighting unit is of the first importance for military efficiency, and, unfortunately for the Negro, in his present level of culture, not many men of his color can be found who are qualified for positions of command. . . . The Negro race in increasing numbers may be expected to develop men of this type, but as yet they are rare, and difficult to discover. . . ." [7] This gloss on the military view of blacks seems calmly reasoned, but the evidence shows quite plainly that when the army did find black men who were "qualified for positions of command" it resorted to every means to disqualify them.

That some blacks were selected to serve as officers was not a military decision so much as a political decision, achieved by Secretary Baker and accepted by Congress and Wilson's administration chiefly because of fear of black disaffection if there were no black officers for the black troops being drafted. The military reconciled itself to the decision with certain reservations: (1) that no more than 2 percent of officer candidates should be black men [although 13 percent of the draftees were black]; (2) that few colored officers would ever be utilized [in fact, they would make up only about 0.7 percent of officer strength, although they formed 2 percent of officer candidates]; (3) that these few should be washed out as quickly as they could be charged with incompetence; and (4) that there should be no black officers of field rank [major and up]. [8]

Fortunately for their morale, the black officer candidates who hurried to Des Moines were ignorant of these negotiations on the policy level. They were under enough emotional strain as it was. The horrible lynching of Ell Persons took place just before they assembled at camp, and the violence at East St. Louis and Houston occurred during their training period. These events were sensationally covered in the press, and such reading can hardly have made for a serene and studious frame of mind.

The OTC at Des Moines opened in July with 1,250 candidates. Of these, a thousand had been drawn from the civilian population; the others were noncommissioned officers from the four regiments of black Regulars. Gen. Charles Ballou was transferred from his post as second in command of the 24th Infantry to head the Des Moines camp. The general told his men that success required "strong bodies, keen intelligence, absolute obedience to orders, unflagging industry, exemplary conduct, and character of the highest order." [9] The instructors were twelve West Point graduates, but much of the training and paper work was assigned to the Regular noncoms among the officer candidates. [10]

The trainees followed a rigorous schedule: 5:30—reveille, then breakfast; 7:30—infantry drill (without weapons); 8:30—calisthenics; 9:00—rest period; 9:15—infantry drill; 10:45—morning hike; 11:45—dinner and rest period; 1:30—practice at rifle range; 2:30—training in communications; 3:00—care of equipment; 4:30—supper, followed by instruction in regimental organization. From time to time the men had bayonet training, dug trenches, and learned the basics of map making and maneuvers. All their training was specifically for infantry officers, with no instruction in other arms and branches of the military service. [11]

In what free time the men had, they gave drill exhibitions and concerts for the public and visited within the small black community of Des Moines. In general their conduct was highly praised. [12] Some whites and a few blacks, too, feared that the officer candidates might be too "pushy" for Iowa, where racial equality, although guaranteed by law, was not consistently honored. The Houston mutiny must have made a great many people nervous. General Ballou said he had a few trainees who overreacted to every real or imagined slight, although he made every effort to insure that the Iowa laws were enforced.[13]

Near the end of the scheduled ninety-day course at Des Moines, military authorities announced without explanation that training would continue for an extra month. To the candidates, the humiliating implication was that they were too slow or stupid to learn the course in the usual time, and no one disabused them. The actual reason was that, because of the Houston mutiny and such problems as lack of camp facilities for black troops, the call-up of the black draft had been postponed, and so there were as yet no berths for new black officers. Still, once these officers should be commissioned, they would go on the army's payroll, although they would have no work to do. Newly commissioned white officers could not always be immediately assigned, either, but they were in any case commissioned at the end of their ninety-day training. At Des Moines, however, graduation was thriftily set ahead.[14]

Embarrassing as the delay was to the trainees, some of them benefited by the extra month's training. Unlike most white officer candidates,[15] black candidates did not have to be college men, and many of them had had only some secondary education in inferior Southern schools. As for the noncoms from the Regular regiments, they qualified more by experience than education. So it appears that General Ballou was not given the best available men for officer training. As he later bluntly put it: "For the parts of the machine requiring the finest steel, pot metal was provided."[16] Probably if black men in the eighteen- to twenty-five-year age group had been accepted at Des Moines, Ballou would have gotten many more college students or recent graduates; as already mentioned, the first 1,500 who applied for officer training were college students. But making the age requirements for blacks twenty-five to forty eliminated most of the men young enough to have enjoyed the benefits of the northward migration: Northern schooling, and the money and opportunity to go on to college. Those advantages had also given the younger black men a sense of their own value which older Negroes had not had a chance to develop, and perhaps this was part of army thinking in not taking the younger men. One very embittered officer of the 92d Division later claimed that the "ignorant" Regulars and the "passive" Hampton Institute men got the highest commissions to insure that the black division would fail.[17]

There was always a difference in terms for blacks and whites. Ballou thought this sometimes gave the black man an advantage: "When the War Department prescribed as a condition to entering the Colored Officers' Training Camp less stringent terms and an intellectual equipment inferior to that required for entrance to a white camp, it *gave* the colored man something better *because he was black*. When it limited him to certain grades in the 92d Division it *deprived* him of something *because he was black*. Both acts were wrong." [18] General Ballou's thinking shows an extraordinary sympathy for the black officer, and it would be very convincing if there were not such clear indications that the War Department could have found better qualified candidates if it had so chosen. There is too much evidence that both circumstances Ballou cites were designed to guarantee the failure of black men to advance in the army, as Spingarn had pointed out.

By the end of the extra month at Des Moines the army was organizing the black draft into an infantry division, and camps were being prepared for them. Graduation at Camp Des Moines was held on 15 October. The 639 commissions granted to those left of the original 1,250 candidates were: 106 captains; 329 first lieutenants; and 204 second lieutenants.[19] Most of the captains were the former noncoms in the Regulars. They seem to have been selected for the highest commission granted at Des Moines on the basis of experience rather than for intelligence, education, or potential. An important element of their experience was the learning of their role in relation to white officers; obviously, they would not have achieved noncommissioned ratings nor have been recommended for Des Moines by their white superiors if they had not learned their role well and practiced it consistently.[20]

The graduates, after the customary furlough, were assigned to various units of the 92d Division. Occasionally one of the white commanders in the division expressed himself as satisfied with his black officers, but a greater number did not find them prepared for their duties. The harshest criticism was leveled at the black captains, who in most cases were declared inadequate to the duties of company commanders.[21]

Like other complete infantry divisions, the 92d had, in addition to four infantry regiments, such auxiliary arms as machine-gun and signal battalions, engineers, and field artillery. The Des Moines graduates who had the hardest time were those assigned to the auxiliary arms, in which they had had no training. Those assigned to field artillery were the only artillery officers in the entire army who had not completed training at regular artillery schools or been certified by elimination boards. Officers of the 349th Field Artillery started the course, but before they could finish it they were sent with their regiment to France. So black officers in the auxiliary arms had only on-the-job training in their unfamiliar duties; they studied at night what they were to teach their men the next day. Predictably, their regular duties suffered, especially the required reports and other paperwork. In some instances the men were temporarily commanded by white officers while their regular black officers were being instructed, but this too was unsatisfactory because the black officers had no chance to get to know their men before going overseas.

After seven months, white commanding officers declared all their black artillery officers inefficient. The General Staff recommended that all of them be replaced by whites until they had completed artillery school, after which they might be used as the need arose. A War Department inspector went so far as to recommend that all black officers be replaced. In the course of time practically all black captains were replaced, which gave the status of fact to the army prediction that blacks did not have the makings of company commanders.[22]

There was no second graduating class at Des Moines, although only about half as many men had been commissioned in the first class as would have been used to staff a white division. Camp Des Moines was closed, and the War Department announced that future black candidates would attend regular officer training facilities. No large number ever did.[23]

Those who did found themselves severely handicapped. At Camp Meade, ninety-six potential artillery officers trained for a week; they were then sent to Camp Taylor, Kentucky, where their barracks were changed six times, giving them just long enough in each one to clean up the area before turning it over to white troops. The camp commander frankly told the black candidates that he did not want them on his post. At the end of the course he recommended commissions only for the blacks who qualified for battery service, the most dangerous and fatiguing duty, although white graduates were recommended also for combat trains or as replacements, depending on their performance. Again, this sounds reasonable when one considers that of the ninety-six black candidates only forty-four graduated, which does not indicate a high average of competence; but what of the fact that of the ten honor men in the 2,500-man camp, six were black? It raises the question whether individual performance in blacks would win them the same rewards as performance in whites, and the answer here appears to be negative.[24]

Artillery officer candidates who trained at Fort Sill also had a rough time, and of the twenty-four who were accepted for the course (all from the Regular regiments) only six completed it. They had been messed and housed separately from the white candidates. At the Fort Sill aviation school the four black men who were admitted were treated with extreme discourtesy; three requested transfers back to their units, and the fourth washed out two days before graduation. At other camps black candidates were treated more fairly and did better. Of fifty-six who trained at Camp Hancock, Georgia, to be machine-gun specialists, forty-three completed the course. There the camp commander insisted on courteous behavior, the local newspaper took a friendly attitude, and the instructors were French and British officers.[25]

As the war proceeded some blacks were trained as replacement officers at camps Upton, Meade, Sherman, Dodge, and Travis, where they were decently treated, and at Funston where they were not. In Puerto Rico black and white officers trained together. Some black noncoms received officer training in France, and a large percentage of them won commissions. Also, in the course of the war a way was opened at last for young black college students to achieve commissioned or noncommissioned status through the Student Army Training Corps, a program of military training instituted at both black and white colleges; but the war came to an end before many of these student officers saw active service.[26]

There were many complaints of discriminatory treatment of

black officers after they were commissioned and assigned. Commenting on one such complaint, Col. W. F. Clark of the General Staff advised the chief of staff that it need not be answered because it referred not to the army alone but to the social system of the entire country. "That social distinctions did exist in the United States was a condition, not a theory," Clark said.[27] The War Department took the attitude that its function was to win a war, not to solve the race question.[28]

As in training, black artillery officers had perhaps the hardest time of all in being assigned. There was a prevailing conviction among general and staff officers that although blacks might do an adequate job in infantry and cavalry, they could never perform acceptably in such an intricate branch of the service as artillery. Gen. William J. Snow, chief of artillery, who was of this mind, pointed out that black officers had received only infantry training and that no effort had been made to find officers whose interests or aptitudes would suit them for the larger guns. None of the officers graduated from the Fort Sill school of fire (only six out of twenty-four candidates) had had much formal schooling, nor had they been consulted before their appointments. Nevertheless, the six were sent overseas with their regiments on orders from the War Department.[29] Gen. Leonard Wood, formerly army chief of staff, urged that these officers not be assigned to labor battalions, because if they were they would be in command of the white noncoms of those battalions; indeed, if they performed well and were promoted, they could easily outrank some of the white officers. Obviously, black artillery officers presented a problem to the army, but Gen. Frank McIntyre proposed a solution for the future: "In order to prevent a recurrence of cases of this nature, it would seem advisable not to commission colored men in the Field Artillery as the number of men of that race who have the mental qualifications to come up to the standards of efficiency of the Field Artillery officers is so small that the few isolated cases might better be handled in other branches."[30] When prejudice made the black officer a problem, the simplest solution was to say he was inferior and close the field to him.

The fear of having blacks outrank whites was an underlying cause of discrimination against black officers. It was army policy to avoid having white and black officers of the same grade serve in the same unit, where they would be in a competitive situation. The common means of preventing this was simply to replace the black officers, and the easiest excuse was inefficiency due to their "race and culture." [31] This happened in the 93d Division as well as in the 92d. In one regiment of the 93d the five original black officers were replaced over the protest of their commander on orders from the office of General Pershing; the same policy was to be followed in another regiment, but the war ended before it could be fully implemented. The commander of the 317th Engineers tried several times to have all his black officers replaced, both during training and later in France. [32]

Inevitably, discrimination in high places against blacks was reflected in discourtesy farther down the chain of command. White junior officers were disinclined to salute a superior if he was a black man, despite General Cronkhite's explanation that it was just a military way of saying "Howdy, uncle." Gen. John B. Castleman insisted as a matter of military discipline on proper signs of respect toward his black officers, although he took pains to explain that white men would be saluting the uniform and insignia of rank, not the man who wore them. Other white officers were more lax in enforcing or themselves observing proper military courtesy. Col. James Moss of the 367th Infantry told his black officers not to require salutes from whites. Des Moines graduates at Camp Meade for artillery training were issued enlisted men's clothing and told that they were still only officer candidates and would therefore have to salute all white officers including those inferior to them. Commissions were sometimes withheld from noncoms who completed officer training. Discrimination followed the black officer to France, where at a training facility they had to wait for whites to be seated before they might enter the classroom; and where after the Armistice they were deprived of the privilege granted white officers of enrolling for courses at French and British universities. [33]

Much of the discrimination against blacks occurred because the military authorities subscribed to the clichés that only the white Southerner really understood blacks, that "black still naturally turns to white for leadership," [34] and that "a colored man does not obey readily and willingly a colored superior." [35] Even the exceptionally fair-minded General Ballou agreed that to the mass of black troops "a *colored* officer was simply 'a stuck up' nigger," although black sources do not corroborate this. [36] An inadequate black officer may have been regarded with contempt by his troops, and certainly, from what we know of the selection and training of black officers, there must have been some incompetents among them, as of course there were among whites also; among both black and white officers there were individuals who had sought commissions not from aptitude or leadership but for the status and pay of officers and to avoid the draft. Add to this the discourtesy and disrespect shown black officers by white superiors and subordinates, and it is obvious that the black officer was tremendously handicapped in commanding the respect of his men.

Because of the cliché-dominated thinking of the army, many black units of the 92d Division were under the command of white Southerners who brought all their inbred race prejudices into the service. In the 371st Regiment of black draftees, for example, the officers were almost solidly white Southerners. It is also a fact that, although military officials frequently said it was crucial for the black regiments to have only the most experienced white officers, all the white junior officers in the 92d were recent graduates of OTC without any experience whatever. General Ballou objected vehemently to their low caliber, claiming that the division "was made the dumping ground for discards, both white and black." [37]

Ballou's primary concern seems to have been the proper one of building an efficient organization. There are indications, however, that many other white military officers and officials wanted black officers to fail regardless of the effect on the organization, and that they therefore did not make the best use of the men best qualified by their natural talents and education. [38] The most flagrant and irresponsible example was the involuntary retirement from active service of the outstanding black officer in the Regular army, Col. Charles Young of the 10th Cavalry Regiment.

Young had been the third black graduate of West Point and was the only one remaining in the service at the outbreak of

World War I. He had met discrimination throughout his career but was apparently such a dedicated, competent, and generally well-regarded officer that he managed to win promotions. Perhaps another reason for his advancement is that the government found it useful to have a black officer of field rank when there was a need to send a United States military aide to Haiti or Liberia. Young served in both places. In Liberia he contracted a severe tropical fever, and was returned to the States in 1915 with high praise from the Liberian president for his services. When he recovered, he rejoined his regiment on the Mexican border, training some of his men to become officer candidates when a black OTC should be established.[39]

Colonel Young was sixth on the promotion list of colonels in 1917. With the rapid wartime expansion of the military, it was certain that he would come up for promotion to brigadier general that year and thus be eligible for a high post such as assistant divisional commander in a black division. Young's Selection Board recommended him for promotion, and he went on 23 May 1917 to the military hospital at San Francisco for his physical examination. The doctors there reported that he was suffering from high blood pressure, and he was retired from active service the day before many colonels were advanced to brigadier. Young protested that he was not sick, his physician certified that his blood pressure was normal for a man of middle age, and in a dramatic effort to prove his fitness Young rode on horseback from his home in Chillicothe, Ohio, to Washington, D.C. But his protestations gained him nothing, and he became inactive as of 30 July.[40] His loss as a potential commander of black soldiers in the war stirred anger, protest, and deep disappointment in the black community, which felt sure he had been railroaded out of active service.[41]

The papers of Secretary Baker throw further light on the story of Colonel Young. While Young was having his physical in San Francisco, Senator Williams of Mississippi, one of President Wilson's strongest supporters and an outspoken racist, forwarded to the President a complaint from a young white lieutenant in the 10th Cavalry. Wilson passed the message on in a letter to Baker, informing him that the lieutenant wanted to be transferred because he found it "not only distasteful but practically impossible to serve under a colored commander," [42] and asking Baker what could be done about it. Although Baker had small patience with such complaints, he consulted with Chief of Staff Gen. Tasker Bliss [43] and wrote the President that Young would be in a hospital under observation "for the next two or three weeks to determine whether his physical condition is sufficiently good to justify his return to active service." Baker added: "There does not seem to be any present likelihood of his early return to the Tenth Cavalry so that the situation may not develop to which you refer." [44] Three days later, Wilson wrote to Senator Williams that Young "will not in fact have command because he is in ill health and likely when he gets better himself to be transferred to some other service." [45] How Wilson could know something to be true *in fact* that Baker said *might happen* after two or three weeks is a disturbing question to which the only logical answer seems to be that a decision had been reached prior to the medical observation on which the decision was allegedly to be based. [46]

The Colonel Young affair indicates redundantly that decisions about black officers in the armed forces were political rather than military and casts doubt on the reliability of criticism of the ability of black officers in World War I. It is perhaps the clinching evidence that the military did not want black officers who might succeed. If Young had been promoted the army would have had to assign him as second in command in a black division; the morale and performance of junior black officers would almost certainly have been better under Young's firm leadership, and Young would probably have won acclaim. But the political decision to oust Young had been made, quite possibly before Senator Williams's letter to Wilson. And so neither of the black divisions that were reluctantly assigned for combat, that suffered insult and privation throughout their superficial training, was to benefit by the experienced command of the outstanding "race man" in the army.

The profile of the typical black officer or noncom of the 92d Division which emerges from all the evidence is that of a traditional kind of Negro, past the stage of youthful daring and initiative, short on education, without self-confidence or any reason for it, poorly selected and inadequately trained for his army job, ridiculed by whites, uneasy with his men and perhaps not entirely trusted by them; and convinced by all his experience that the way to survive in the army was to avoid "causing trouble," to agree with the white man and not try to make decisions of his own, and to employ whatever devices would protect him from the unjust, illogical, irrational hostility of the white army. Such a man might have bars put on his shoulders or stripes on his sleeve, but those symbols alone would not imbue him suddenly with the skills and commanding presence needed to lead men in battle.

As General Pershing later wrote, the lower-ranking black officers (and there were none of high rank) of the 92d Division had been recruited and trained too hastily, had not the required competence for their tasks, and had had little experience in the handling of men. Their white superiors, he said, for these reasons did not feel that the 92d Division would accomplish much.[47] Such prophesies have a way of fulfilling themselves.

5. Two Black Fighting Outfits

Again, the Ninety-second Division of Negro troops was established by the Secretary of War and approved by President Wilson over the protest of the General Staff; but no effort was made to secure for this division certain necessary persons of technical training. . . . *The permission to make such transfers has been denied by the War Department.* Unless this decision is reversed, the Ninety-second Division is bound to be a failure as a unit organization. Is it possible that persons in the War Department wish this division to be a failure?

W. E. B. DuBois, the *Crisis*, May 1918.

THERE were eventually two black fighting organizations, the 92d Division and the 93d Division (Provisional). As in decisions about black officers, here, too, decisions concerning the formation, assignment, and training of over 30,000 black combat troops were governed by political and administrative considerations rather than by military needs.

The 93d was tagged "Provisional" because it never achieved full divisional strength. It consisted solely of four infantry regiments, of which three were composed almost entirely of National Guard units and the fourth of black draftees. All three National Guard units had originally been ordered to train with divisions formed from their state's white guardsmen, but the white divisions rejected them. The black guard units were a problem, therefore, because there was no place for odd infantry regiments in the military organization. The army's solution was to tack on a fourth regiment, composed of draftees, and call the combined organization the 93d Division (Provisional).

The black guardsmen numbered between 5,100 and 5,600 men commanded by about 175 officers, of whom 125 were black.[1] When called into federal service, the 15th New York Regiment had 2,053 men and 54 officers, and the 8th Illinois had 1,405 men and 42 officers. The other guard units were far below regimental strength. The First Separate Battalion of Washington, D.C., had 950 men and 55 officers; the 9th Separate Battalion of Ohio had 650 men and 15 officers; and the guard companies of Tennessee, Massachusetts, Maryland, and Connecticut averaged 150 men and 2 officers.[2] Some units had been recently and hastily recruited and were untrained, while others had been at practically full strength for some time; the 8th Illinois had seen actual combat service on the Mexican border. Black officers staffed some units, while others had white or both black and white officers. What they had in common was that all were volunteers; as such they enjoyed considerable status in the black community and were considered by the military (and by themselves) far superior to the black draftees.

The 15th New York (which was eventually to become the 369th Infantry Regiment of the 93d Division) had been organized in the fall of 1916 by William Hayward, a prominent white New Yorker who was appointed colonel of the regiment. Hayward's command consisted of ten companies of about 65 men each, all of whom had previous military experience. In the spring of 1917, authorized by the government to recruit to wartime strength, the 15th quickly expanded to 1,378 men and about 47 officers. Many of the officers were members of white guard units, untrained but eager to serve with the black regiment; still, throughout its active service the 15th was low in officer personnel, averaging two to a company instead of the authorized six. The additional men needed to fill out the regiment had been recruited in five days by appeals made from street corners and theater stages.[3]

Having no armory, the men of the 15th trained in the New York streets. They were never inspected by a state or federal officer, nor were they helped in their training by experienced officers from outside the regiment. They managed to get some weapons by forming shooting clubs, which by law were granted rifles by the state, but they were still short of firearms and without bayonets or sufficient uniforms to go round. One thing they did have was a great forty-four-man regimental band with a musician of note, James Reese Europe, as bandmaster, and another famous black singer-musician-composer, Noble Sissle, as drum major. Europe was especially known as arranger and pianist for the day's most popular dance team, Irene and Vernon Castle. Sissle was a stage star and celebrity. All the bandsmen were professional musicians, and their military pay was augmented from a special fund.[4]

In mid-May 1917, the regiment was ordered for training to Camp Whitman near Peekskill, New York. In order to make an impressive showing when the regiment marched to the camp, all available uniforms and rifles were issued to the men on the flanks of the formation. Setting up camp was slow and difficult for the untrained men. They had almost no equipment of their own, not even messware. Their 250 rifles, for nearly 2,000 men, were distributed among those on guard duty. Sticks substituted for rifles during drills.[5]

Soon even this unsatisfactory training ended, and the 15th was broken up into smaller units which were scattered about the New York area doing guard duty: at training camps, on interned German ships, along 600 miles of railroad, on Ellis Island, and at bridges and tunnels, not only in New York but also in New Jersey and Pennsylvania. Often the men worked under the command of noncoms in these guard duties, and in general they worked and behaved well. Civilians in the various duty areas seemed to like them and lent them necessaries to make them more comfortable in their barren quarters. In New York's San Juan Hill section, a crowded ghetto in the West Sixties of the city, some of the men got into a fight with the police. Colonel Hayward claimed the police were guilty of false arrests, but the newspapers played up the incident as a race riot.[6]

The duties assigned to the 15th precluded further training. Colonel Hayward, exasperated by official neglect of his regiment, asked that it be made part of New York's. white guard division—the 42d, or "Rainbow," Division—but the answer was that "black was not one of the colors of the rainbow." [7] In the fall of 1917, however, the War Department at last ordered the regiment to Camp Wadsworth at Spartanburg, South Carolina, for training.

Spartanburg girded itself for trouble with these Northern black men. The mayor of the city set the tone in a speech to the Chamber of Commerce: ". . . they will probably expect to be treated like white men. I can say right now that they will not be treated as anything except negroes. We shall treat them exactly as we treat our resident negroes. This thing is like waving a red flag in the face of a bull, something that can't be done without trouble." [8] The Chamber of Commerce predicted that there would be violence if these black men tried to be served in Spartanburg stores. City officials and the governor and both senators of South Carolina protested the assignment of the 15th to Spartanburg. [9]

Colonel Hayward did what he could to avoid trouble. He tried to pacify his men by explaining that the Southern attitude was based on ignorance, and asked them not to retaliate to verbal or even physical abuse. He arranged for public band concerts by Europe's regimental band, which was so admired that it was hired to play at the country club. White officers patrolled the streets at night to prevent incidents. For the first week everything seemed to be going smoothly except that the stores refused to serve the black soldiers; some of the white soldiers also training at Spartanburg so resented this that men of the 12th and 71st New York regiments boycotted the offending stores. [10]

But in spite of tight security and extraordinarily disciplined behavior on the part of the men, serious incidents occurred. Captain Marshall, who was a Harvard alumnus and member of the New York Bar, was called a "dirty nigger" and thrown off a streetcar. Uniformed blacks were pushed off the sidewalks. In one such incident, although the black soldier obeyed Hayward's injunction not to retaliate, white troops of the 7th New York beat up his assailants. One alarming incident occurred when a rumor spread through camp that two men of the 15th had been arrested and beaten by the police. Half a company, armed, marched into town and sent a delegation into the police station to check on the rumor. Hayward found them drawn up outside the police station, ascertained that the rumor was false, and ordered them back to camp; they obeyed his order, although they admitted to him that if the rumor had been true they had planned to shoot up the town. The camp commander, Gen. Charles L. Phillips, praised the men for their good discipline and obedience, but, foreseeing real trouble soon, he sent Hayward to Washington to persuade the War Department that his regiment was ready to go overseas.[11]

It was while Hayward was off on this errand that the storm broke. On an October day, ten days after the arrival of the 15th at Spartanburg, Drum Major Sissle was in town with Lieutenant Europe and some other soldiers, black and white. Sissle went into the lobby of a hotel to buy a newspaper and was told by the hotel manager to take off his hat. The drum major, newspaper in one hand and change in the other, did not comply quickly enough to suit the manager, who knocked off Sissle's hat, kicked him when he bent to pick it up, and kicked him again as he tried to leave. The soldiers were furious and ready to smash up the place, but Lieutenant Europe restrained them, although all the thanks he got from the manager was abuse. The officers of the regiment wired Hayward about the incident and persuaded reporters not to play it up.[12]

In alarm, Secretary Baker sent Emmett Scott to investigate the incident. Scott admitted that the provocations were great but warned the men of the 15th that their behavior would affect the entire race and that the nation would not tolerate another Houston.[13] The War Department decided that the safest course was to ship the regiment to France immediately. Two days after the hotel incident the 15th broke camp. Maj. Arthur Little, a white officer with the regiment, recalled their departure in these words: "Our movement was secret, and our destination unknown; but as we swung along through the camps of the Twelfth, Seventy-First and Seventh Regiments, in the course of our hike, thousands of brave New York lads of the 27th Division lined the sides of the roadway, and sang us through, to the tune of *Over There*. At the railroad siding most of the Division Staff were present to wish us Godspeed. Gen. and Mrs. Phillips remained until our train pulled out." [14] The 15th New York had trained at Spartanburg exactly twelve days.[15]

While preparations were made for shipping it overseas the regiment was again moved about, first to Camp Mills on Long Island in New York, where fights broke out with white Alabama troops—apparently not the fault of the 15th, because the colonel of the Alabama regiment apologized and punished his men—and then to Camp Merritt in New Jersey. There the 15th is reported to have been held under guard during its entire stay.[16] At last, in the middle of winter, the regiment sailed.

The sailing of the first black regiment was greeted with great enthusiasm by the black community, and presumably also by the War Department. When the regiment embarked it still bore the name of the 15th New York and carried its state flag, the only military organization to ship out without a federal designation.[17] But although it sailed as New York National Guard in December 1917, in January 1918 it became the 369th Regiment, 93d Infantry Division (Provisional).

An objective look at the performance of the 369th, even thus far, might have shaken some of the clichés of army thinking about blacks. White Northern officers could be more successful with black troops than the white Southerners who were supposed to understand Negroes so well. Black officers could be capable, reliable, intelligent, and trusted by the troops. Black troops could be hardworking and trustworthy. Such enlightenment might have made changes in the army's policies which would have improved not only race relations but the efficiency of the military organization. But no reassessment was made, and all the traditional army attitudes remained unmodified.

Meanwhile another black regiment, the 8th Illinois National Guard, was being prepared for service overseas as the 370th Regiment, 93d Infantry Division (Provisional). It was the only guard organization with a full complement of black officers, from Col. Franklin A. Dennison down, when it was called into federal service, which was a source of great pride among American blacks but just one more "problem" for the military. Dennison received mobilization orders late in March 1917. All places in the regiment had been filled by the end of May, and the organization became part of the U.S. Army in July.[18]

The 8th was sent south to Camp Logan, the regular training station of the Illinois Guard but a poor choice for this black regiment because the Houston mutiny had been launched from Logan. While an advance company was preparing the camp for the 8th, the mutiny occurred, leaving Houston tense and hostile. Chicago's black leaders urged not sending the 8th to Logan, but it was ordered there in October. The *Chicago Tribune* had this to say: "The regiment was sent into the South by an order that was not particularly notable for its wisdom, but the men went without a murmur. They were billeted in a city that was not disposed to a felicitous reception. . . ." [19]

They attracted attention all along the way. "Where are the white officers?" people asked. At train stops in Arkansas and Texas the black troopers refused to respect segregated facilities; in one incident they tore down the Jim Crow signs in a railway station, and in another they were chased out of the station by whites. When a store refused service to men from Company E, they looted it. [20]

The ultimate deployment of the regiment was still being debated. The General Staff thought they might be used for functions other than infantry, but only as all-black units, not mingled with whites. Machine-gun and train duties were proposed as possible assignments. This suggests that at one time the War Department may have considered attaching the men of the 8th Illinois to the white 33d Division, because a provisional regiment did not have these branches. Such a move would have got rid of Colonel Dennison, who would have been superfluous had the troops not served as a complete regiment. However, the 33d refused to accept the 8th because of its black officers. [21] A clerk on the headquarters staff of the 33d expressed an attitude probably typical of the whole division in saying that only cooks of the 8th performed competently; the Negro's heart was in his stomach, said the clerk, adding: "The negro likes to go to church because God gives him equality. He likes to be in the army because there he approaches nearest to that equality with the whites which he enjoys in theory but never knows in practice. And in the army he wears good clothes, eats three meals daily, sleeps in a bed at night, and at the end of the month, has a little money in his pocket." [22]

Trouble started before the 8th had been at Logan a week. First, some of the men were put in the guardhouse for getting into a fight with Houston people. Then, a policeman shot a black soldier for interfering with an arrest. Men of the regiment were barred from streetcars for refusing to obey Jim Crow rules and were backed by white troopers of the 7th Illinois. [23] Houston's tension and hostility grew. Obviously the solution was to move the 8th along quickly toward embarkation.

On the first of December 1917, the 8th officially became the 370th Regiment of the 93d Infantry Division, although the state designation of the 15th New York had not yet been changed when that regiment sailed on 10 December. The two guard regiments formed the division's 185th Brigade. In March 1918, with praise from their brigade commander, the 370th left Logan for Newport News preparatory to sailing.[24] The atrocious conditions in camps around Newport News have already been described. As for the city itself, the regimental chaplain characterized it as ". . . a place of a thousand prejudices. The people, always hateful toward the Negro, had resolved to add fuel to their hate toward the '8th.' All kinds of rumors had preceded our coming. 'Twas said that it was the '8th' that had started the trouble in Houston and that we had resolved to start similar trouble in Newport News. Not only the white civilian population had resolved to get us but our supposed comrades in arms, the white soldiers and officers, especially the M.P.'s. . . ."[25] Because of security measures taken by Colonel Dennison nothing more serious than a few brawls developed. Within a month, on 6 April, the regiment sailed for France with the heartening endorsement of an inspecting officer who said that the regiment would never be fit for combat so long as black officers were in command.[26]

Smaller guard organizations from other states had a special problem. They were not big enough to be separate military units, and no white organization would accept them. From the time America entered the war until early in 1918 these black guardsmen of various states were assigned to a number of different camps and duties.

We have seen that the First Separate Battalion of Washington, D.C., was the first guard organization to be called into federal service and that it was set to guard vital facilities of the capital city against sabotage. Black people visiting Washington were thrilled to see the black troopers on duty, and the black press praised their performance. Apparently they did their jobs conscientiously, on one occasion perhaps too conscientiously when a black private shot a white workman who ignored the command to halt.[27] But a Kentucky congressman, Robert Y. Thomas, complained to the President's secretary that the black guardsmen neglected their work: "You had better take these nigger soldiers away as guards of the tunnel and put some white men there. The nigger soldiers spend a good deal of their time socially at night, in talking to nigger women who congregate around that place. I do not know whether you know it or not; but I know that a nigger knows nothing about patriotism, love of country, or morality, and if in the Army at all, should be commanded by white officers. If they are not they are going to make trouble wherever they go." [28]

The Washington men were not the only guardsmen plagued by "nigger" haters. The 9th Separate Battalion of Ohio ran into trouble while training at Camp Sheridan near Montgomery, Alabama, when one of their number was kidnapped by white men for allegedly brushing against a white woman on a streetcar. His comrades went in pursuit. White M.P.'s arrested thirty-five black soldiers in the town and gave chase to the men who were chasing the kidnappers. The provost marshall ordered all black soldiers confined to camp, but the battalion commander demanded their release, saying that his men had a right to go into the city. [29]

It was finally decided to unite these troublesome small guard organizations into a regiment. Secretary Baker agreed to the filling of field and staff positions with surplus white officers from other guard organizations but ordered that black company officers who had entered the service with their companies were to be retained. [30] There must also still have been a possibility of higher-ranking black officers for that regiment, because about a month after Baker's order Gen. Henry Jervey expressed his opinion of such a proposal, reminding the adjutant general that "while colored men make excellent soldiers under skillful white officers in whom they have implicit confidence, the United States has not given field rank (except in isolated instances) to colored officers." [31] This is a particularly neat example of military nonsense. Aside from Jervey's illogic, if the army was so convinced that to perform well black soldiers had to have skillful white leadership, one would think it could have done better than to assign surplus guard officers qualified only by availability. Or was the presumption that any white officer was a good officer? [32]

In any case, Baker's order prevailed, and black company officers were retained. The 372d Infantry Regiment was established in January 1918 and began to collect at Camp Stuart, Virginia. It was composed of six National Guard units: Washington, D.C.—First Battalion (Companies A–D); Ohio—Second Battalion (Companies E–H); Maryland—Company I; Tennessee—Company K; Massachusetts—Company L; Connecticut—Company M. To fill out the regiment, around 250 draftees from Michigan, Illinois, and Ohio were transferred to the 372d, and more draftees were brought in later as replacements. Two white officers, Col. Glendie B. Young and Lt. Col. Albert W. Cole, headed the regiment. In accordance with army policy, all headquarters, supply and machine-gun officers were white, but in compliance with Baker's wishes the twelve rifle companies had full complements of black officers. Two of the three battalions were at first commanded by black officers, but one of them (Maj. James E. Walker of the First Battalion) was replaced by a white major on grounds of illness, although the reason was more likely the army's abhorrence of field-rank black officers.[33] The regimental historians insist that the 372d was "steeped in machinations" from its inception; that whites within and outside the organization worked to discredit the black officers. As a result, they say, when the regiment sailed for France on 30 March 1918, morale was extremely low among both black soldiers and their black officers.[34]

These three regiments were made up almost entirely of black guardsmen, but there were no more of them to form the fourth regiment of infantry necessary in a division. The fourth regiment, therefore, the 371st, had to be organized from black draftees. By War Department order, draftees from the Carolinas plus some from Georgia, Florida, and Alabama were to make up the regiment. White officers were put in command: Col. Perry L. Miles and Lt. Col. Robert M. Brambila, both of the Regular army. According to Emmett Scott the regiment was slow in forming because the black draft in the South was delayed until the cotton had been harvested, and that may have been a contributing reason. In October, 3,380 men of the new 371st were assigned to Camp Jackson for training.[35]

Most black leaders complained that the officers were typical

Southerners with traditional Southern attitudes, and about three-quarters of them were from the South, although Colonel Miles was an Ohioan. They were "arrogant and overbearing" men, wrote DuBois later, and he hinted that black soldiers had seized the opportunity to kill some of them during combat.[36] A regimental officer admitted that he and his fellow officers were inexperienced and unsure of themselves, and that most of them were not happy about commanding black troops.[37] Among black commentators, Charles Williams was alone in the opinion that many of the officers took a real interest in their men, and this may have been true of some; Williams was generally a reliable reporter and quick to see discrimination where it existed.[38] But another black writer, Monroe Mason, historian of the 371st, found that the men had had the spirit beaten out of them. In speaking of the assignment of a white chaplain to the black troops he said: "This official bit of stupidity was resented even from outside sources, but objection was useless, for the men themselves, accustomed to the whip-and-lash method of living, meekly submitted to the ministering of the Caucasian 'Sky Pilot.' "[39]

Whatever troubles the draftees may have had, they were transformed men by the end of their training period. Arriving draftees at Camp Gordon had been thus described: ". . . they were a spectacle to behold. Hundreds coming directly from cotton and corn fields or the lumber and mining districts—frightened, slow-footed, slack-shouldered, many underfed, apprehensive, knowing little of the purpose for which they were being assembled and possibly caring less—the officers but recently from the training camp received them."[40] The description would probably equally fit the draftees who arrived at Camp Jackson in October. By winter, the change was amazing: "The marching and close order drill were excellent; the manual of arms unbelievably perfect. The men took the greatest pride in their uniforms and in their equipment. Their salutes were snappy; their carriage soldierly; and we were proud, not only of our individual companies, but of the regiment as a whole."[41] There are many tributes to the appearance, marching, and drill of all black troops, draftees as well as guardsmen. How these results were achieved would depend on individual officers. Also, the most unfit two-thirds of the original 3,380 men had been weeded out and replaced. Only the best men remained, and these had undoubtedly benefited by plentiful food, instruction, and physical exercise.[42]

The warm welcome given the troops by the citizens of Greenville, so unlike the studied hostility of Spartanburg and Houston, may have accounted in part for the great improvement in the men of the 371st. Lawrence Stallings, a sensitive and informed writer, suggested that Greenville accepted these black men because they were under strict white leadership. "The different attitude toward Negroes still under white masters was one for psychologists, not soldiers, to ponder," Stallings said.[43] Perhaps because of the reason Stallings suggested, the blacks of the 371st had no serious trouble either with the white 81st Division, composed mostly of Southerners, which surrounded their encampment, or with the camp commander or civilian authorities. But what lay ahead of them was a war, not a Sunday School picnic, and the question was how well would the "whip-and-lash method of living" prepare them for the exigencies of battle.

At last, in January 1918, the War Department organized these four regiments into the incomplete 93d Infantry Division. The 369th Regiment (15th New York), which had already sailed for France, together with the 370th (8th Illinois) composed the 185th Brigade under command of Brig. Gen. Albert H. Blanding. The 371st (black draft) was combined with the 372d (miscellaneous guardsmen) to become the 186th Brigade commanded by Brig. Gen. John H. Harries. The headquarters staff of the division sailed from Hoboken on 18 February 1918.

The next problem that sprouted from hydra-headed racism was what to do with the great remaining mass of black draftees. Gen. Lytle Brown, chief of the War Plans Division, wrote thus to the chief of staff: "It is believed that organizations contemplating their service as laborers and of a noncombatant nature, would be best. However, on the other hand, they desire combat service and public sentiment, to a certain extent, demands their organization as fighting units."[44] And so, political considerations once again taking precedence over military preference, another combat division, the 92d, was created out of the black draft. Even so, there were tens of thousands of black draftees left over to satisfy those who thought they would best serve as laborers.

To avoid concentrating black troops at any one cantonment, units of the division were distributed among various National Army camps; to avoid difficulties in the South, the camps chosen were Northern. The 92d was the only American full division to be so fragmented throughout training, and it never assembled as a division while in the United States. Consequently, men sailed to France as total strangers to others in their own regiment, and to their officers, without having had an opportunity to build pride and trust in each others' units.[45]

Originally about 40,000 men were assigned to the division, of whom the 26,000 considered best qualified were retained for training.[46] Men with special skills were sought among civilians and also in the labor units, and the War Department sent 4,000 black draftees to technical schools such as Tuskegee and Hampton.[47] The effort to help capable men move upward was surely a step in the right direction, but it was constantly running head-on into the counterefforts made by the military brass to move as many black men as possible downward into labor units.

The black officers of the 92d, none higher than captain, were Des Moines graduates. They should have accumulated experience in leading their men while in training camp, but in some cases the troops were assigned as practice material to white officer candidates.[48] Again, as in the 93d Division, a number of surplus white National Guard officers were transferred to the 92d, not for their leadership qualities but because they were available and had "some experience with colored men."[49] Here, too, as in the 93d, all field and staff officers and one-third of all other officers were white. Care was taken to insure that within any individual unit no white officer was outranked by a black.[50]

General Ballou, who had headed the Des Moines school, was given command of the division. DuBois called Ballou a "timid, changeable man" and added: "Whenever any occasion arose where trouble had occurred between white and colored soldiers, the burden of proof always rested on the colored man. All discrimination was passed unnoticed and nothing was done to protect the men who were under his command. . . . His action in censuring officers in the presence of enlisted men was an act that tended toward breaking down the confidence that the men had in their officers, and he pursued this method on innumerable occasions. . . ." [51]

Ballou claimed that he did try to protect his men, saying that when he "learned that the draft would bring colored troops to many camps, I worked through channels to secure from white officers and white soldiers tolerant treatment of the Negro, especially in the matter of refraining from the more offensive epithets." [52] In forming and training his division, Ballou was constantly battling odds. Where the artillery regiments of a comparable white division, the 35th,[53] had at least one battery of guns apiece, in the 92d one regiment had no battery at all, and none of the others had more than one. The 92d had no signal or fire-control equipment except for an obsolete Battery Commander's Telescope in the 349th F.A. Throughout the division, the men got less training than white men would have because they were all in Northern camps where severe weather precluded outdoor practice during the winter. These weaknesses, plus low and fluctuating strength, large numbers of replacements just before sailing, decentralized control, and shortness of the training period were noted by Col. Alfred A. Starbird of the Inspector General's Office.[54] An additional handicap of the 92d Division was that General Ballou, unlike commanding officers of white divisions, was not given the opportunity to tour the battle front prior to his division's sailing and to modify the training program in accordance with firsthand observations of the war.

Each regiment of the 92d Division has its own war story, so it is pertinent to examine their origins and organizations. The 365th, with many men from Texas and Oklahoma, was commanded by Col. Vernon A. Caldwell. The 366th, under the command of Col. Ralph B. Parrott, came mostly from the mining districts of Alabama, and the men were described as "the worst looking lot that ever reported to any of the camps. . . ." [55] The men of that regiment spent so much time at noncombat work that they were derisively called the "fatigue [work] regiment" by the neighboring white divisions. The 365th and

366th together formed the 183d Infantry Brigade under the command of Brig. Gen. Malvern Hill Barnum, who had had previous experience with black soldiers of the 9th and the 10th Cavalry.[56]

The 367th was composed mostly of New York draftees and had as its commander Col. James A. Moss, a Southerner of long experience with black troops. He called his regiment the Buffaloes, a name given many years before by the Indians to the black Regulars and later adopted by the entire 92d Division. Of Moss's 108 officers, only 8 were white, and most were from New York.[57] Gen. George Bell called the 367th the best-drilled regiment in the camp and told the men he could lead them with complete confidence against any soldiers in the world.[58] When the regiment paraded in New York to receive a regimental standard from the Union League Club, it won general praise. One newspaper called it "a serious, stolid, soldierly regiment to the last man." [59] The 368th, which with the 367th composed the 184th Brigade, had a very different provenience, consisting as it did of draftees from Tennessee, Pennsylvania, and Maryland. Col. William P. Jackson was its commander, and he had assigned to him 97 black officers from Des Moines.[60]

In addition to the four infantry regiments, three field artillery regiments were organized for the division, the 349th, 350th, and 351st. Old army hands had consistently maintained that it was ridiculous to try to train black officers for this arm of the service,[61] and no doubt felt vindicated when, as previously mentioned, these officers were all declared inefficient and replaced after seven months. Col. W. E. Cole who inspected them admitted that these men had not received proper training, and from that drew the amazing inference that favoritism had been shown them because "they received their commissions under less exacting circumstances than any white officer." [62]

Although all commanders agreed that blacks were untrained in the intricacies of artillery duty, such as laying down a barrage, no effort was made to attach these men to artillery organizations for training until the eve of their division's departure for France—and some even later. On 30 May 1918, some men were at last sent to the 167th Field Artillery (F.A.) Brigade; on 1 June, 900 were sent to Camp Dix for artillery training; and on

20 June the last contingent of artillerymen was to arrive from Tuskegee and Howard where they had been receiving instruction. The division had begun to sail for France on 10 June.[63]

After the war, Lt. William N. Colson, a black officer of the 92d Division, charged that the army had deliberately misassigned men to various parts of the division so that it would fail; he claimed that South Carolina illiterates formed the nucleus of the 351st Machine Gun (M.G.) Battalion, while men well qualified for such technical work were put into labor regiments.[64] It was reported by another officer that men of the 350th M.G. Battalion received only standard infantry training during the winter of 1917–18, from white instructors whose outstanding qualification was previous experience with black troops, and that they were equipped with obsolete guns which they would not be using in combat.[65] In the 317th Engineers the personnel was competent enough, but the men received only rudimentary instruction in engineering because, of the black officers assigned to them, only three had engineering experience. General Ballou blamed the educational system for a situation in which "not one colored man could be found who could qualify as an engineer officer. In fact only one colored engineer of suitable age was found in the entire United States; and he was physically unfit."[66] So the black captains in the 317th Engineers were also replaced after seven months, and so were all other black officers of that regiment after its arrival in France, with the exception of the chaplain, the medical detachment, and two line officers.[67]

Various smaller specialist units completed the division. The hospital and ambulance units were approved for overseas service. The 325th Signal Battalion fared pretty well. Most of its black officers were high school or college graduates, and some had the advantage of radio training at a special civilian school which Secretary Baker supported despite the insistence of the army that it was useless to give blacks such technical instruction. Two black service companies, the 322d Butchery and the 316th Laundry, were organized on 4 June, only a few days before the division sailed.[68]

At and about Camp Funston, Kansas, where part of the 92d had trained, racial conflict was always at the bursting point. One black soldier said wryly that relations were perfect between

Funston's white and black troops—they never saw one another. "There was an amusement zone in the white section of the camp," he explained, "to which the men of the 92d never have the slightest inclination to enter, in fact they are barred." [69]

One black sergeant tried to break through the color barrier, not in camp but at a theater in a nearby town called Manhattan, thereby precipitating one of the most talked-of incidents concerning black soldiers. The sergeant tried to buy a ticket at the theater and was refused admittance, although Kansas law prohibited discrimination. When this came to General Ballou's attention he issued his Bulletin No. 35, which outraged blacks everywhere. In it the men were reminded that they had been told to avoid places where they might not be acceptable; the sergeant was chastised for starting trouble, although, the bulletin admitted, "he is strictly within his legal rights in this matter, and the theater manager is legally wrong." Nevertheless, Ballou maintained, "the sergeant is guilty of the GREATER wrong in doing ANYTHING, NO MATTER HOW LEGALLY CORRECT, that will provoke racial animosity." The general might have paused to consider how much racial animosity that statement would provoke. But instead, his bulletin proceeded: "The Division Commander repeats that the success of the Division, with all that success implies, is dependent upon the good will of the public. That public is nine-tenths white. White men made the Division, and they can break it just as easily if it becomes a trouble maker." [70]

Ballou's bulletin brought an uproar of protest, especially the patronizing if literally true statement that white men had made and could break the division if they so chose. The clear implication was that a man who tried to exercise his legal rights was a troublemaker, if he happened to be black. Black Americans everywhere were outraged. Ballou himself later agreed that his statement was perhaps hasty and ill-conceived; still, he defended his position in a letter to DuBois, asserting that a soldier's first duty was to preserve the peace, even at the expense of his own rights, but adding that he had immediately assigned a black officer to investigate the action of the theater owner. [71] In fact, Ballou asked the judge advocate to examine the case; the judge advocate recommended that the Justice Department prosecute, and the theater owner was fined.

General Ballou's first duty, as he conceived it, was the success of the division he commanded. After Bulletin No. 35 and the ensuing protests, he addressed his men, chiding the 5 percent who, he felt, overreacted to racial slights and asking the others not to push too rapidly for equality. He ended his address with these words: "I simply *will not* tolerate having the success of this camp, with all that that success means to your race, ruined by the acts of a selfish and conceited handful of men who are so puffed up by a little prospective importance that personal considerations and petty social pride and ambition have entirely obscured the great issue of demonstrating physical, mental and moral fitness for the responsibilities of commanders and leaders of men." [72]

In defending his Bulletin No. 35 to the inspector general, Ballou insisted that technically it was only a suggestion, not an order. But when the commanding officer says "I *will not* tolerate" it sounds very much like an order. Furthermore, Ballou told the inspector general that "from that hour I had thus talked with the men there was no more friction down town. It *stopped,* as I told them it *must stop.*" [73] In the same report Ballou said that no complaints had come from outside the camp, which was not entirely true. The NAACP had protested immediately, pointing out that the men had done nothing illegal but had been treated illegally, and characterizing Ballou's action as "unjust, humiliating, and inexpedient." [74]

Although Ballou probably never did understand how insulting his Bulletin No. 35 was to black people, its result was to destroy the popularity he had enjoyed among them as commander of Des Moines and now of a black division. [75] This was unfortunate, because in matters of a less sensitive and subtle kind he comes through as a much more just and decent man than most of his colleagues in the military. But his name became anathema. In an almost hysterical reaction to the bulletin, one black writer said that the selection of Ballou as commander of the 92d was "the greatest blunder in our Military History"; that Ballou was mediocre, "a disappointment to the War Department, broke faith with those who made him. He approached questions that involved the race issue with fear and trembling; his slow mind was unable to cope with the complex problems of a combat division; he was sadly lacking in ability, initiative and dynamic powers. . . ." [76]

Bulletin No. 35 was issued in mid-April 1918. The 92d Division left for France two months later. There is no doubt that the trust of the men in their commander was shattered, and it seems likely that Ballou never again completely trusted the men who, according to his lights, had so misunderstood him. These were not good auspices for the battle performance of the 92d Infantry Division, reluctantly conceived, superficially trained, and inexpertly led.

6. Laborers in Uniform

i am riten you to Day Becose you Can Do some good   We are Fair
mitty hard all so we Have a mean lutenden to us He is a Negro hater
  it is 600 men   Just same as slave is now you is not try to Have any
slaves in your army   we is now workin on Santonio and Camp Stanley
Road. . . .

> Letter from a corporal of the 445th Reserve Labor
> Battalion, 21 December 1918, to Emmett Scott,
> in Scott Papers, 115-1.

BLACK stevedore regiments, labor battalions, development
battalions, pioneer infantry—whatever these service units
were called, they were the day laborers of the army. It is estimated that one-third of all labor troops in the military service
were black; they numbered, before the end of the war, at least
160,000 black men out of the many more who had been
drafted.[1] They were Colonel Anderson's rags, bones, and tin
cans, men with physical or mental handicaps which, it was felt,
would not incapacitate them for manual labor. Although they
were the "culls" of the draft, not measuring up to the standard
for combat service, they were as clamored for as the black infan-
tryman was clamored against.

As we have seen, almost no weakness could win them exemptions from their draft boards—unless white employers inter-
vened. Did a black man have flat feet, which would have kept a
white man in civilian clothes? In the opinion of the military: "A
negro's feet are naturally flat, just as is his nose. As a conse-
quence a large number of negroes are rejected at all exemption
board hearings through every portion of the South. Most of the
negroes I have seen rejected for that reason would outwalk and
outrun easily most of the white men rejected." [2]

The General Staff felt certain that, because most black draftees had been manual workers as civilians, this was the work

proper to them and they should continue to do it for the army, in the labor units.[3] Colonel Anderson added his opinion that the "poorer class of backwoods negro has not the mental stamina and moral sturdiness to put him in the line against opposing German troops who consist of men of high average education and thoroughly trained." [4] Naturally, in wartime the army had no time to educate and train backwoods Negroes with a view to discovering their latent capabilities. Colonel Anderson pointed out that the black draft could start doing useful work around the camps as soon as they were called up, simply as work gangs and not as organized military units; he specifically advised against so organizing them until just before they were to go overseas, because until they were organized no time need be taken from their work assignments for training, which they wouldn't really need for the work they would do in France. Anderson did, however, leave the door open for the black draftee who showed aptitude for combat service, and he suggested a training company within the labor battalion for such rare promising individuals.[5]

But almost all the black draftees would serve in the military equivalent of chain gangs. In such a capacity, Anderson asserted, the black "soldier" would cause no trouble even in the South and could be assigned to camps without outraging the racial sensitivity of Southerners: "It is recommended that the question of race prejudice be not considered at all in the assigning of labor battalions to camps. These camps are mainly situated in the Southern states. The negroes mainly come from the southern states. . . . Each southern state has negroes in blue overalls working throughout the state with a pick and a shovel. When these colored men are drafted they are put to work in blue overalls (fatigue clothes) and continue to do work with a pick and shovel in the same state where they were previously working. . . ." [6]

One could not ask for a much plainer statement of the function of the great majority of black men in the army. Any lingering doubt is dispelled by another of the colonel's remarks: "While it is known that prejudice against colored troops exists more or less in southern States, it is believed, in view of the fact that these men are nothing more than laborers in uniform, that they do not have colored officers and that they came from the states within which they are mobilized, their mobilization and organization in the labor and service battalions at the points now designated should be continued." [7]

Colonel Anderson perfectly reflected the army attitude that colored men were inferior, that they must be segregated in the armed forces, and that despite a few black combat troops which had been organized for political reasons the army would remain a white man's club. "White men released by them [black labor troops] from day labor work, would be free to spend their entire time being instructed for combatant service," Anderson pointed out.[8] At the same time, Secretary Baker continued to assure the public that the War Department did not tolerate discrimination, and that he regretted "what seems to be a certain amount of overworked hysteria on the part of some of the complainants, who seem to think that only colored draftees are being assigned to duty in the service battalions." [9] Secretary Baker may have felt sincerely aggrieved by these hysterical complaints, because it was not true that only blacks were assigned to labor units. But surely his statement was to a degree disingenuous, because he must have been aware that with white draftees the objective was to make as many of them into fighting men as possible; with black draftees, as few of them as possible.

Perhaps the much-tried wartime secretary of war averted his eyes from what he could not change, but that did not alter the brutal truth: black draftees were thought of strictly in terms of how much work could be got out of them. The great bulk of military files dealing with black troops shows a carefully planned system of racial discrimination. Those responsible for the system knew perfectly well that it would, if revealed, arouse some "overworked hysteria," so it was kept under wraps. For instance, in October 1917, when the chief of staff ordered the adjutant general to create stevedore and labor companies to comprise about 70 percent of colored men in the service, he cautioned that this plan should be kept confidential.[10] On another occasion, when a staff officer proposed that black draftees be put into white divisions to perform the menial work of teamsters and drivers, cooks and kitchen police, the General Staff rejected the proposal for reasons that plainly show military thinking:

There is at present wide-spread objection in the service to the performance of duties of a menial nature, but to admit their menial quality by assigning such duties exclusively to an inferior race would make it well nigh impossible to persuade white men ever again to resume such duties.

The enlistment of men of an inferior race to do the so-called menial work is contrary to previous practice in our army and would tend to unnecessarily emphasize the inferiority of the colored race. It is not thought the War Department should go on record as proposing any such plan.[11]

The first objection to the plan was the entirely practical one that certain kinds of work would be so degraded by becoming "black work" that no white man would ever do those necessary duties. There was also objection on the political ground that such a plan would start trouble by emphasizing black inferiority, and so the War Department should not "go on record" as sponsoring it. Further, there was the historical objection that such a plan was "contrary to previous practice in our army." What is totally lacking is any moral objection to the undemocratic idea of a subject group and an élite group, or any philosophical objection to labeling a part of mankind inferior on grounds of skin color.

Late in 1917 there occurred another incident in which the army took discriminatory action which it preferred to keep off the record. In November, Quartermaster Gen. Henry G. Sharpe recommended that a special regiment of black stevedores be formed to serve in case civilian longshoremen went on strike. In reply to a warning voiced by one civilian, that using blacks for strikebreaking would add a racial dimension to labor unrest, Colonel Lochridge of the General Staff explained that white troops used for such a purpose would probably be former longshoremen and union members and would therefore not make reliable strikebreakers, whereas black stevedores would not have union connections and would therefore be more suitable. The adjutant general authorized the creation of a unit of uniformed black strikebreakers early in December, but he cautioned that no general order would ever be issued stating the purpose of these troops.[12] This was not the only instance where black labor troops, whom most unions had excluded when they were civilians, were used for purposes to which union men in white labor units might object. Gen. George W. Goethals, director of purchase, storage, and traffic, asked for black labor companies to be assigned to depots where there were labor troubles. Black troops were accordingly ordered to Canton, Ohio, despite the warning of the acting quartermaster general that violence might occur if black strikebreakers were sent.[13] It seems possible, although it was never explicitly stated, that some military officials hoped that the use of blacks as strikebreakers would divert the resentment of the white union men from the army to the black man, always a useful whipping boy.

As with the black combat troops, so with the black labor troops; there were at first indecision and confusion in organizing them. Between the summer of 1917 and the beginning of 1918, however, their role in the army gradually crystallized. The first call for black draftees in September 1917 ordered 83,400 men to various National Army camps. Earlier, in August, Gen. Tasker Bliss had authorized four stevedore regiments consisting of 2,400 black draftees with black noncoms from the 24th Infantry and 10th Cavalry and white officers and staff. The War Department authorized enlistments for these units, the remainder to be drawn from the draft on a voluntary basis as far as possible. At Camp Hill three separate regiments were being formed, but there was little unit feeling because men and entire companies were shifted from one regiment to another in order to put those best prepared into a unit that could be rushed overseas.[14]

In September, twelve black labor companies were formed in response to a demand by General Pershing for men to work in warehouses and to load and unload trucks. The War Department was still recommending that as many as possible should be volunteers for this service, and that noncoms should be blacks from the Regular regiments.[15] By January 1918 the army decided that the 250-man company was too small a unit for best efficiency, so the War Department authorized the organization of black draftees into labor battalions of 3,500 men each, without the earlier injunction to seek volunteers. By that time it was the clear and consistent military policy to make practically all black draftees "laborers in uniform." They would work on the docks, clean up ("police") the camps, haul coal, wood, and stone, dig ditches, take care of livestock, dispose of garbage, and care for animals. In some instances they were trained for more technical duties as drivers or mechanics, but they ended up loading, digging, and performing general fatigue duties.[16]

If the troops were to be laborers, their noncoms and officers would act in the unmilitary capacity of overseers. This in turn affected the original intention to make use of black noncoms from the Regulars, along this line of army reasoning: "Non-commissioned officers assigned to this battalion will act in the capacity of overseers and foremen of certain kinds of engineering work which makes it desirable in the opinion of the Chief of Engineers to have white men. White non-commissioned officers will be messed and quartered separately." [17] But here, too, policy was somewhat haphazard at first, except for the separate messing and quartering. Some black noncoms were assigned to labor battalions, often over protests like that of Lt. Col. U. S. Grant, a descendant of the liberating general of the Union army fifty-odd years before: "Everyone who has handled colored labor knows that the gang bosses must be white if any work is to be done." That policy, the lieutenant colonel said, had been established for the Quartermaster Corps and should not be changed so as to deprive any other corps of what had been adjudged necessary—white noncoms. Indeed, change of military policy was in general repugnant to Lieutenant Colonel Grant, and fresh ideas merely a source of confusion and irritation. He said:

> After a policy has been adopted by the War College Division, approved by the Chief of Staff, and put into effect, it should not be changed or overturned without experience having shown conclusively that the change is required for the good of the service. Changes resulting merely from the personal theoretical ideas of a changed personnel are bound to cause confusion and irritation. Confidence in the good judgment and reasonableness of our predecessors, until practice or experience has shown them to have been in error, is a necessary condition for the retention of the confidence of the service at large in the trustworthiness of the General Staff.[18]

Grant was sounding off in response to a report by Colonel Lochridge in which he complained that white noncoms who volunteered to serve with black labor battalions were mostly undesirables; that they required separate housing and messing; and that if noncoms were all to be whites, the black troops would have no incentive to work well because they would be cut off from advancement. Lochridge thought enough educated black men could be found in the draft to provide the noncommissioned personnel; and in any case the officers, who would certainly be white, could maintain proper discipline. Lochridge concluded: "It is admitted that 'gang bosses' for negro laborers are necessary in some walks of civil life, but this is not believed to be the case with the service. About the only argument that can be advanced for approving the request of the Chief of Engineers in this respect is the fact that five such battalions have been so organized." [19]

The conflict of opinions continued throughout the war. Although there were some black noncoms with the labor troops, army resistance remained firm. Colonel Anderson, with his simple confidence in white superiority, suggested that physically unfit whites could be used as noncoms in black labor units.[20] Gen. Lytle Brown told the chief of staff: "Colored foremen for colored troops is not logical. A colored man, unless he be one who has trained as a non-commissioned officer in the Regular Army for a number of years, is utterly incapable of handling men of his own race. These labor companies are expected to work." [21] If a plan put forward by Gen. Henry Jervey for allowing both black and white noncoms in the same unit were implemented, General Brown said, the result would be an undesirable degree of racial mixing.[22] Colonel Anderson pointed out that the noncoms should not only be whites, but forceful whites, because they would have to deal with the "culls" of the black draft; and he therefore recommended the type and class of men who, as civilians, had been overseers of black work gangs, "the class of men who can get work out of the colored men." [23]

By March 1918 the conflict about black noncoms had been settled by limiting them to the grade of corporal. Usually an order to change over to white noncoms asked for "white men who have had experience in handling colored labor." [24] It was not easy to find enough such white men. One black writer has claimed that some were recruited through advertisements in

Southern newspapers for "men who know how to handle Negroes." [25] Many "nigger-baiters" were said to have been recruited from their jobs as gang bosses on turpentine farms, plantations, and public works projects. [26] Black leaders, who had earlier received assurance from the War Department that eventually every type of assignment would be open to black men in the service, [27] were now reassured that "only a small proportion of the non-commissioned grades in colored organizations are reserved for white soldiers," although actual figures show as many white as black noncoms; only the ranks above corporal in labor and reserve labor battalions, they were informed, and positions on the stevedore battalions and regimental staffs were closed to black men. [28] Since it was considered unacceptable to have black noncoms serving alongside whites of the same or a lower grade (the army circumlocution for this was "difficulties of administration"), it would in effect be impossible for any black man to rise above the lowest noncommissioned rank unless all, or almost all, white noncommissioned personnel were removed.

It is noteworthy, in the light of the then prevailing trend, that an occasional officer expressed himself as preferring black noncoms. The commander of the 505th Engineer Service Battalion found that housing white noncoms separately, as specified, meant that they were quartered apart from their men and that consequently it was difficult to maintain order and discipline in the barracks at night; furthermore, said this commanding officer, "it has been found that some of the better type of colored men possess more ability to direct work and exercise control than do many of the [white] noncommissioned officers assigned to the organization." [29] Gen. Daniel W. Ketcham of the War Plans Division agreed with that statement. Gen. W. W. Atterbury of the Transportation Department wanted useless white men replaced by blacks; Gen. Frederic Abbott did not go quite so far but suggested that at the corporal level whites be replaced by blacks as soon as the battalions were organized. [30] The white officers of the 519th and 520th Service battalions were reported to have found enough competent blacks within their units to justify replacement of all white corporals. [31] Late in 1918, the commanding officer of the 406th Reserve Labor Battalion asked for black sergeants because they "make more efficient duty sergeants in colored labor battalions." [32]

With War Department approval, policy was changed for a time to permit black sergeants, but it was later modified by the requirement that all noncommissioned personnel of a unit be of the same race. That meant a renewal of the color bar in promotions, because few officers were willing to lose all their white noncoms in order to keep a few black sergeants. Some officers found a way of getting round the regulations by allowing black men to function as noncoms, but without the rank or pay that went with the job. In some units there was actual appointment of "acting corporals" who never got permanent warrants for their positions.[33]

Because of the clear if unpublicized understanding in the army that almost all black draftees would be laborers, only the small number assigned to combat regiments received any significant amount of military instruction; all white draftees, whatever their eventual assignment, received basic training. Basic required about forty-three hours of training a week, including physical drill, infantry drill, marching, and work with rifles. For the black units, training was sketchy or nonexistent, haphazard and varying from camp to camp. Those at Camp Meade spent a reasonable amount of time on military drills and work with rifles; those at Camp Humphreys had only two half-days a week of such training.[34] At Camp Wadsworth an inspector, Col. James G. Hannah, reported: "This battalion in excellent shape—and camp very clean and orderly. Is used all day on labor work and has 1 hour drill after recall. Is for labor purposes, and *drill*, except for discipline, not believed essential." [35] But in a report on Camp Greene, Hannah did not give unqualified approval to the absence of training: "The Bns [battalions] are used for *work* at the camps I visited and actual drill and instruction was as best it could be arranged. 422nd Bn was drilling 1 hr. per day *after day's labor work was completed.* Unless Camp Cmdrs are limited to a certain % of strength for *work* details no schedule etc. is going to be carried out. They are seemingly looked on as *laborers* to save combatant troops the details and are being used as such." [36]

In September 1918, an official questionnaire sent to the battalions revealed that, though one-third of the units had training companies for men considered to have combat aptitudes,[37] in only one battalion was the training company permitted to train instead of work; only two battalions had rifles, and those two had only a few.[38] The 438th Reserve Labor Battalion was luckier; while it was being organized the men were permitted to drill for six hours a day, performing only the labor details essential for their own camp.[39] But this was an unusual case.

The inconsistency of conditions among the black battalions can be explained mainly by the differing attitudes of officers. Some gave their men as much training as possible (though without weapons) and organized group sports. Another officer trained his men only in military courtesy.[40] A black observer noted that at Camp Lee whites in the depot brigade were being trained but blacks in the same brigade were not. They were not only laborers in uniform but entertainers in uniform, he observed: "All that is necessary here is to be able to sing for the officers and salute them properly when you meet them, and that with going on 'detail' constitutes the training." [41] One of the black men at the camp said the white officers treated black soldiers as a Roman tribune might have treated conscripts of a vassal race.[42]

In other white units training suffered because of an unwieldy number of men or a scarcity of officers. The 419th Reserve Labor Battalion had only eight officers for 1,900 men—and from time to time an additional 2,000 or more men might be temporarily assigned. Also, where the commanding officer was only a captain, he could not pull enough rank to get what was required for proper training, however good his intentions.[43]

Part of the training time was to be spent in school work, and this also varied widely from camp to camp. Labor and stevedore units at Camp Greene (about which Colonel Hannah seemed dissatisfied) had no schools at all. At Camp Lee some troops got three hours' instruction each day in English, with the purpose of improving verbal communication. Camp Custer permitted only sick men who could not work to attend schools, but lessons were taught by members of the group, not by formal instructors. At Camp Tyler, 2,500 black troops were given two hours of instruction each day in reading and writing, and two hours of verbal instruction; the men were reported to be interested and making good progress, and all of them learned to write at least their names.[44] In schooling as in training there was a striking difference in the treatment of whites. At Camp Sevier, for instance, over 80 percent of white illiterates were permitted to attend school, but only 27 percent of black illiterates could be spared from work for instruction.[45]

Finally, a determining factor in the skimpy schooling and training of black labor units was the rush to organize them and send them overseas where they were urgently needed. The usual amount of time between forming a unit and shipping it to France was about a month, which was in line with Colonel Anderson's admonition not to organize labor units until just before they were sent overseas.[46]

In a somewhat more favored position than the labor battalions were the regiments of the pioneer infantry, which were organized in the summer of 1918. In a typical regiment, white officers would have under them a nucleus of skilled noncoms from the black Regulars, assisted by such specialists as mechanics, horseshoers, grooms, and carpenters who had trained at various black technical colleges; the rest of the men were draftees considered a cut above those put in the labor battalions. Theoretically, these pioneer troops were trained for work just behind the front—somewhat more technical work than was contemplated for the labor battalions—and, also theoretically, they were given standard infantry training so that if necessary they could be used in combat.

There were both black and white pioneer infantry regiments. For the black units, however, the military does not seem to have seriously contemplated combat service; the pared-down infantry training they were given indicates rather that their true function was work. As with the labor battalions, training varied from one P.I. regiment to another, usually depending on officer attitudes. The 63d P.I. was given standard infantry training except for gas-defense drills and target practice. An army inspector reported that "no technical training is contemplated. It is not believed that the regiment will be in condition to qualify for combat service." [47] The 64th had no gas-defense practice either, but in a fourteen-week course it was trained in shooting weapons, tactical defense, open-position warfare, and field fortifications and received engineering instruction in technical matters such as bridge and railroad building, laying barbed-wire entanglements, demolition, and digging trenches. The 801st P.I. was issued rifles and instructed in their use but never actually fired them; it, too, had no gas-defense drills, and it received no technical engineering training.[48]

Whatever practical reasons there may have been for skimping on the training of black working troops, whether lack of time, lack of officers, lack of officer interest, or lack of facilities, the underlying cause was army belief that the proper function of the black draftee was labor. "They do not regard us as free citizens of the Republic, in the national army for the defense of our country and the principles of democracy," wrote the black man from Camp Lee.[49] Reports of investigators officially document the bitter complaints made by black men in personal accounts and letters in which they describe the humiliation, mistreatment, and outright brutality they suffered in the army. Sick men, including venereals, were often forced to work without medical treatment; if they worked unsatisfactorily they were handcuffed with cow bells attached to their chains; if they claimed they were too sick to work, they were chained to posts. Records of black troops were likely to be incomplete or lost, so that they sometimes went for long periods without pay or allotments. White M.P.'s made it almost impossible for black troops to go into town for recreation except by stealth, and no recreational facilities were provided for them in camp. Surgeon General Gorgas insisted that medical treatment should be fair and equal in military hospitals, but Jim Crow attitudes sometimes led to racial strife in which, in one instance, white patients attacked black patients with knives and forks for not yielding their places in the mess line. In at least two instances white noncoms shot black prisoners under their charge.[50]

Perhaps the most outrageous misuse of black draftees was the practice of some white officers of hiring them out to work for civilians, often to the financial gain of the officers. Men of the 430th Reserve Labor Battalion cut wood and dug potatoes for civilian contractors near Richmond, Virginia, hired out to the contractors by Capt. Charlie Boyd, who, the men of the battalion claimed, said that the only way to get work out of Negroes was to work them three days and whip them three days.[51] A battalion from Camp Meade was hired out to build roads for a civilian contractor. At Camp Sevier officers were accused of pocketing the pay of men whom they hired out for work, and similarly at Camp Beauregard where officers allegedly hired out a jazz band formed by their men to play for $20 a performance—and kept the money. It is still more shocking to find in the official records that the government in at least one instance lent itself to the irregular practice of hiring out soldiers. On that occasion the War Department authorized a three-month furlough for 1,500 black troops to work as civilian laborers in the construction of a chemical plant. It may be that the plant was thought essential to the war effort, and certainly labor (especially cheap labor) was scarce at the time. But there is an unpleasant smell of conscious wrongdoing in the instruction given the camp commanders of these troops by the General Staff: "They are not to be allowed to work in their uniforms. These men will work for a private contractor, who will take whatever men are given him." [52]

With all the abuse that black labor troops suffered, it would have been extraordinary if they had not tried at some time to strike back. Some of them did, in a serious incident during the summer of 1918. The 328th Labor Battalion, scheduled soon to ship out, was sent into Pisgah National Forest to cut fuel wood for Camps Wadsworth, Sevier, and Greene. While they were at this work the supply system broke down and no food arrived. After several days of hunger the men rebelled. A delegation of about a hundred of them confronted the officers and told them the men would not work until they were fed. The leaders of the uprising were put in the guardhouse, and three of them were later tried by a court martial "for attempting to create this mutiny and for threatening the lives of a Captain and a Lieutenant." The three were sentenced to death, but their terms were commuted to discharge and ten years in prison. [53]

Their aborted gesture of defiance accomplished nothing for the black laborers in uniform, who continued to be, both in stateside army camps and after going overseas, "just same as slave is."

"Yes, of course I want colored men," General Pershing is reported to have said. "Aren't they American citizens? Can't they do as much in the line of fighting and as much work as any other American citizen?" [54]

The first American troop convoy sailed for France before the end of June 1917. It did not carry any black troops, but there were aboard between 400 and 500 black stevedores, still technically civilians but subject to military rules because their employers were under contract to the army. Although not soldiers, they wore uniforms, some surplus Union Blues from the Civil War, which a quartermaster officer had dug up. They were sent to help speed the unloading of American ships on arrival in France. These men, like the tens of thousands of black laborers who would follow them, drew the worst berthing aboard ship and had no mess facilities. Many ate and slept on deck in all weather, rather than in the hot, airless lower holds assigned to them. The few black officers who accompanied them were not permitted in the white officers' mess, although black men were recruited for service there as mess boys and stewards. [55]

All the white soldiers in that first convoy were moved quickly inland, combat troops to their training centers and labor troops to set up bases and supply lines. The few hundred black stevedores were kept on the docks to unload, but there were not enough of them and the call went out for more. [56] One American civilian contractor, who took another 1,500 black laborers to France, had this to say about them: "They are the finest workers you ever saw. One Negro can do four times as much work as any other man, and have fun doing it. The French stevedores stand by and watch with amazement at my hustling gangs. The way they handle a 100-pound crate makes the Frenchman's eyes bulge." [57]

The Services of Supply (S.O.S.), as the black labor battalions were to be called toward the end of the war, soon took the place of the civilian laborers. They manned three main divisions that supplied the front: the base sections, the intermediate sections, and the advance sections. The base sections, nine in all, were areas surrounding the great ports. The last one to be established, No. 9, around Antwerp and Rotterdam, would serve American occupation troops in Germany after the Armistice. In terms of the number of troops and the amount of supplies involved the most important base sections were No. 1, St. Nazaire, and No. 5, Brest, both on the Atlantic coast. Supplies unloaded at the base sections were speeded inland to the intermediate bases, distribution points from which material was moved up into the advance sections just behind the front, and from there to the front itself.[58]

The black one-third of the S.O.S. men were organized into forty-six engineer service battalions, forty-four labor battalions, twenty-four labor companies, fifteen P.I. regiments, three stevedore regiments and two stevedore battalions, and two butchery companies. Practically all army stevedores were black men, organized into work gangs; the gangs that moved the material from below decks were commanded by corporals, those that received at the hatches by sergeants. These noncoms were white, because although blacks were often found more satisfactory as gang bosses than whites, the barriers to the promotion of blacks existed overseas as in stateside camps. So although the black gang bosses were acting noncoms they did not get noncom pay; the only titles they earned were such jocular ones as "Chief Travelling Stevedore." [59]

Stevedores "packed and unpacked the American Expeditionary Forces in a manner never attempted since Noah loaded the Ark," wrote one commentator.[60] Their work started the moment the ship docked, and they unloaded for a week or more until the ship could return and they could proceed to their assigned shore stations. The 331st Labor Battalion, which had handled all fatigue details on shipboard, worked for a month on the docks after landing at Brest, meanwhile quartered in the primitive, dirt-floored tents called shelter halves. Even P.I. regiments when they landed might be commandeered for stevedore work; one P.I. unit was sent back out to sea to fight a fire on an incoming ship.[61]

The work was massive and continuous. On a single day, stevedores brought to shore 42,000 men with their portable gear and unloaded 5,000 tons of cargo. Irvin S. Cobb, a white, Southern-born journalist who became an admirer of the black servicemen, wrote: "Five thousand tons in one day, when those Continental wiseacres had calculated that by employing to their utmost all the facilities provided by all the docks in sight, we might move 6000 tons in a month!" He went on to say, "The victory that we are going to win will not be an all-white victory by any manner of means." [62]

The stevedores accomplished these amazing feats by working day and night, sometimes in shifts and sometimes in sixteen-hour stretches, in all kinds of weather. They unloaded a ship's cargo of coal in eighteen hours. A group at Brest unloaded 1,200 tons of flour in nine and one-half hours, and then, to break their own record, averaged 2,000 tons a day for five days more. At Bordeaux the stevedores docked almost 800,000 tons of material in the month of September 1918, averaging over 25,000 tons a day. Black stevedores landed everything from bales of hay to 90-ton naval guns, and often they sang as they worked, with black pacesetters establishing a fast tempo, black song leaders maintaining it, and black "jolliers" keeping the men in a good humor. By work gangs handled in that way, the great ship *Leviathan*,[63] largest vessel afloat, was completely unloaded in only fifty-six hours by Company A of the 301st Stevedores.[64]

Not all the black laborers were stevedores. They were also responsible for building warehouses, sheds, and supply dumps near the ports and at related railroad facilities. They built barracks at the bases and temporary housing as troops moved toward the front. A number of labor battalions felled and brought in wood for fuel and for building docks, the men in one unit cutting an average of thirty-five trees per man per day. The 335th Labor Battalion in 20 days cut over 1,000 cubic meters of wood and a quarter of a million poles and dragged it out of the forest with sling ropes. The 331st cut over 40,000 cubic meters of wood in 108 days, stacking part of it and moving the rest over a long distance to a railroad siding. While on such details, the foresters were housed in floorless tents and ate in the rain and mud.[65]

Other black units quarried stone for building and road repair, and built or rebuilt railroads. One of the worst details was Graves Registration, to find, record, and rebury the dead. In addition to the regular day's work, the men might at any time be asked to perform some emergency job: "Upon one occasion an order came in for a hurry-up shipment of flour for the French army. It was at the close of a boiling day in August and the negro labourers—those smiling darkeys from the cotton plantations of the South—were 'all in.' . . . The Director of Labour assembled his men (it was just after supper), told them of the emergency, and called for volunteers. Every man responded. In exactly fifty-five minutes those black negroes had loaded 700,000 pounds of flour in sacks, and ten minutes later the special train was on its way. . . ." [66]

S.O.S. men with previous experience on Pullman cars as porters, cooks, and waiters pulled lighter details serving on the private trains of general officers, including Gen. James C. Harbord of the S.O.S. and General Pershing himself, and on special trains running between American bases which were reserved for officer use.[67] Even the combat outfits were tapped for specially qualified men, as when the 369th Infantry Regiment was requested to supply two personal orderlies for General Pershing.[68] One firsthand observer noted that the "black boys on the 'America Special' " were just as efficient and cheerful as civilian porters although they did not get tips. "The tipless porter therefore is one of the rare exhibits of the war!" he wrote.[69]

The black P.I. regiments in France were virtually labor troops, although usually they worked at the somewhat more technical jobs for which they had been trained. Generally they were just back of the lines, and often under fire. One regiment, for example, probably the 805th P.I., was rushed in to repair a road near Varenne which had been so damaged by German shelling that ammunition could not be moved forward nor could the wounded be evacuated. By working through the night the pioneers made the road passable, and apparently they sang as they worked, with the shells still falling near, because one account of the incident records that "the lilt of darky voices was ever in our ears. . . ." [70] Similarly, when the 808th Pioneers had to build a railroad within range of enemy fire, one officer reported: "We cannot understand their makeup, for under hardest conditions they hold themselves together and are able to raise a song." [71] This unit lost between 150 and 200 men in the unsanitary Pontanezen Barracks during the peak of the influenza epidemic.[72]

Not all the pioneers came that close to combat. Most of them worked at less dangerous details as engineers, stable and veterinary personnel, and mess men. Nevertheless, seven of the seventeen black P.I. regiments were entitled to wear combat ribbons, whereas in the white P.I. regiments only eight out of twenty earned that right.[73]

All this labor, prodigious and dangerous as it often was, could not dispel the pall of discrimination under which the black men worked. Overseas as back in stateside camps, the black laborers were inadequately fed and housed, and clothed in fatigues or reclaimed uniforms held unfit for combat troops. Black stevedores rarely got passes when their day's work was done, a circumstance they found particularly galling. In the case of 12,000 black troops at a base in an advance section, troops with an excellent record for work and conduct, the base's standing orders read: "All colored enlisted men of this camp are hereby confined to the limits of the Camp and Depot until further advised." [74]

An endless series of examples could be cited of discrimination in one way or another against the black laborer in uniform. Here is a summing up of their condition by one of the foremost black historians of the period, Carter G. Woodson: "Abusive language, kicks, cuffs, and injurious blows were the order of the day in dealing with the Negroes impressed into this branch of the service. As there were in these camps no Negroes in touch with the outside world except the Young Men's Christian Association secretaries, and the slave driving officers succeeded in displacing some of these, there was no one to whom these Negroes could take a complaint. . . ." [75] As one black officer put it, briefly and bitterly: "The spirit of St. Nazaire is the spirit of the South." [76]

There are enough patronizing tributes to "smiling darkeys," cheerful "black boys," and the "lilt of darky voices" so there can be no doubt that many labor units did herculean jobs quickly and well. Just as undoubtedly, some must have loafed, and surely that is not surprising in the light of the abusive treatment they got whether they worked or not. Doing as little as one can get away with has always been such a feature of army life that we call it "soldiering," but when a black soldier soldiered it was somehow more reprehensible than when a white soldier did the same thing. Many officers raised outraged voices about black soldiering and the inefficiency of black labor troops. "Every ef-

fort was made to appeal to their sense of duty without avail,"
wrote one officer, "and every form of legal punishment had been
administered to the miscreants without success." [77] General Atterbury, who had advised replacing inefficient white noncoms
with competent blacks, now seemed blind to the possibility that
the leadership might be at fault when he reported:

> A number of these negroes are so lazy that they perform very
> little work; there have been cases of men flatly refusing to
> work. Fining them and putting them in the guardhouse is
> very little punishment to them, and to be dishonorably dis-
> charged and sent home is just what they desire. It is requested
> that authority be given to weed this class of men out, form
> them into disciplinary companies and use them on road or
> quarry work near the front. . . . Inasmuch as going any-
> where near the front is the greatest punishment that can be
> extended to these negroes, it is believed that it will have a
> very beneficial effect on the work of the entire force. [78]

Atterbury's proposal was approved by AEF authorities in
March 1918, but later in the year the experiment was reported
by Pershing's inspector general, Col. H. K. Taylor, to have
been a failure. Taylor said that front-line units had neither the
staff nor the facilities to train and discipline these "incorrigi-
bles." He laid the problem right in the laps of the officers: "If
the officers in charge cannot control the negroes under them, the
officers themselves should be removed and replaced by officers
competent to maintain discipline. The burden of controlling in-
corrigibles should not be passed from one command to another
because the first is unable to handle the matter." [79] There were
reasons beyond their control, Taylor granted, for the poor performance of these men; they had been recruited in haste, sent
abroad with little training, and there put to work without any
further training or discipline. But basically, he opined, the problem was created by the nature of black people: ". . . the enlisted men are negroes and have all the vices peculiar to the Ethi-
opian race. Their average mentality is that of a child of ten and
they have a controlled enthusiasm for work." [80] From this one
must conclude that Taylor thought they needed the kind of
officer who would bring the spirit of the South to St. Nazaire.

Among the more important critics of black laborers of the S.O.S. were two general officers in that service, General Harbord and Gen. Johnson Hagood. Like Taylor, Hagood laid most of the blame on the officers, who, he said, often just stood around to see that the men did not loaf while black boss stevedores actually directed the work: "In riding over a road alongside of which a railroad was being constructed, I counted ninety per cent of the negro hands resting. In the warehouses and on the wharves gangs of several hundred negroes would be sitting down waiting for some job that was not quite ready for them; and in one warehouse I noticed fifteen or twenty lying around asleep." [81] Although he had no high opinion of black workers, Hagood was fair enough to admit extenuating circumstances: often the work assigned to them was nonproductive; units were sent on details too far from their posts, so that time was wasted getting them to and from work. Further, Hagood pointed out that "in other cases they are not properly fed, the Sick Report is too high, and, in general, the labor is not properly officered." [82] These are damning admissions to be made by a commanding officer, more convincing than any number of complaints by the men themselves of mistreatment and discrimination.

General Harbord said the only thing the black labor troops wanted was to go home, so the best way to motivate them was by organizing a work contest in which the reward for the most efficient company would be to leave France first when the Armistice was signed. [83] Harbord was much concerned about black troops mingling with white women. In his book on the war he implied that a number of blacks were court-martialed and hanged for rape, [84] which could not be true because a Senate investigation showed that fewer than a dozen American soldiers were legally executed for all causes. [85] The general was not alone, to be sure, in his fear of relations between black men and white women. Everywhere in France, talking to a white woman or entering a French home were the most serious offenses a colored soldier could commit. To prevent social contacts most cafes and other public places were off-limits to blacks, and any black soldier who broke the regulations could expect violent abuse from the M.P.'s and severe punishment.

The low opinion of black laborers held by senior officers was reflected all down the chain of command and by the men in the ranks. A popular song among the combat troops was: "Mother, Pull Down Your Service Flag, Your Son's in the S.O.S." The laborers in uniform were men you could ridicule or take advantage of and get away with it. Officers were reported to have appropriated money the men had given them for safekeeping.[86] M.P.'s were protected in their abuse of blacks. An M.P. sergeant arrested Corp. William Fauntleroy of the 804th Labor Company for drunkenness; later Fauntleroy was shot "while trying to escape," and the sergeant was court-martialed. Fauntleroy's commanding officer testified that the black soldier was not a drinking man, and an autopsy showed no traces of alcohol, so the reason alleged for the arrest seems to have been a lie. Because one witness testified that Fauntleroy had given a false name when arrested, one of the white captains in the unit told the men: "Well, he has been shot, and we should be careful and not lie to Officers or be fresh." The sergeant was acquitted.[87]

Black spokesmen tried to point out that the color bar to promotion deprived blacks of any incentive to excel.[88] Pershing maintained that they could be promoted to corporal, and that this opportunity "affords excellent means of discipline." [89] The chief of engineers gave his opinion that deserving blacks could eventually be promoted to sergeant in labor units. One wonders if these officers were being sincere. What of the order designed to prevent "administrative difficulties" by barring blacks from positions equal or superior to those of whites in their units, and the inflexible rule that blacks and whites must have separate messes and quarters? Both virtually locked the black man into the ranks; or, at least, promotion for blacks was too remote a possibility to serve as an incentive.

One proposal for raising the morale of black laborers came from General Harbord. As reported by Lawrence Stallings: "He [Harbord] pleaded for any sort of emolument: a button or an emblem that he might bestow on some great black man from the Southern swamps who put in many a thirty-six hour stretch at a back breaking job because he knew his countrymen in the North would lose their war if he let them down. . . ." [90] Military authorities, however, did not see the virtue of Harbord's suggestion, and no such award was ever approved.

Another idea, proposed quite late in the war, would, the War Department believed, have the same salutary effect at a nominal cost. "Labor Battalion" had acquired the unsavory reputation of being a euphemism for a disciplinary unit, an organization to which men were assigned as punishment. So what Pershing proposed and the War Department approved was to change the name "Labor Battalion" to the more "dignified" title "Services of Supply." This was expected to remove the stigma and presumably keep the "darky voices" raised in song and the black backs bent in cheerful labor.[91]

Apparently no one bothered to analyze why the labor battalions were regarded as penal institutions, or to change the conditions of endless boring work, miserable living, kicks, curses, and isolation which indeed made a labor battalion the worst sort of jail; no more did anyone observe that when the men of the battalions were called on for their best, as in competition or emergency or danger—in short, when they were appealed to as *men* to accept a challenge—they responded like men and performed prodigious feats. The change of name took none of this into account. It was purely semantic, not substantive. And it failed. "Services of Supply" at once became shortened to the distress signal "S.O.S." The black laborers in uniform found no alteration in their conditions of work, their treatment by noncoms and officers, or their reputation as the rags, bones, and tin cans of the army.

1. Court martial of men of the 3d Battalion, 24th Infantry, U.S. Army, charged with mutiny and murder at Houston, Texas, on the night of 23 August 1917. Thirteen were hanged three days after sentencing. (U.S. War Department General Staff No. 165-WW-127-1 in National Archives Building [hereafter NA].)

2. West Pointer Charles Young in 1916, then a major leading U.S. troops in Mexico under Pershing's command. Two years later he was fighting to stay on active duty, but lost that battle. (Adjutant General's Office No. 94-UM-204046 in NA; reproduced by permission of Underwood & Underwood.)

3. Black "laborers in uniform" performed incredible feats unloading vital supplies in France. Here, men of the 301st and 303d Stevedores form a chain to empty a lighter at Brest. (U.S. Signal Corps No. 111-SC-18315 in NA.)

4. Men of the 342d Labor Battalion cut and haul from the forests of Haute Marne, France, wood for fuel and building. (U.S. Signal Corps No. 111-SC-49553 in NA.)

5. Lumber processed at this portable mill at the rate of 21,000 feet per day was used to build docks, barracks, railroads, and bridges in France. (U.S. Signal Corps 111-SC-51963 in NA.)

6. This blacksmith of the 365th Infantry was a very important man in a horse-powered army. Hampton and Tuskegee institutes helped train black soldiers in such skills. (U.S. Signal Corps No. 111-SC-25939 in NA.)

7. On the running board of a salvage truck, a soldier briefly takes the weight off his feet and the war off his mind. (LC-USZ62-26640 in the Library of Congress.)

8. Mess stevedores at Base Section No. 5, Brest, France, fed the AEF as it passed through that port, coming and going. (U.S. Signal Corps No. 111-SC-31940 in NA.)

9. Kitchen engineers—KP's of the
518th Engineers peeling spuds at Base
Section No. 6, Marseilles, France.
Luckily or unluckily, potatoes were
plentiful. (U.S. Signal Corps No. 111-
SC-36516 in NA.)

10 & 11. Three stars top two: Lt. Gen. Robert L. Bullard, *on the left*, commanding officer of the 2d Army, AEF, had a poor opinion of the black 92d Division, which was part of the 2d Army, and also of its commander, Maj. Gen. Charles C. Ballou. This conflict at the top level affected the treatment and chance for advancement of every black officer and soldier in the division. (U.S. Signal Corps No. 111-SC-50133 and U.S. Signal Corps No. 111-SC-88256 in NA.)

12. Lt. Col. Otis B. Duncan of the 370th Infantry, *center*, highest ranking black American officer in France at war's end, with two other decorated officers, Maj. J. R. White, *at the left*, and Lt. W. J. Warfield. (U.S. War Department General Staff No. 165- WW-127-9 in NA; reproduced by permission of Underwood & Underwood.)

13. Lt. James Reese Europe, leader of the famous 369th Infantry band, with some of his bandsmen. They played concerts in more than twenty-five cities on a 2,000-mile tour of war-torn France, and the French went wild about them and their music. (U.S. War Department General Staff No. 165-WW-127-41; reproduced by permission of Underwood & Underwood.)

14. The 369th Infantry during one of its 191 days in the front lines. Helmets, gear, and weapons are those of the French army, to which the regiments of the 93d Division were attached. (U.S. Signal Corps No. 111-SC-11914 in NA.)

15. *Above,* the raw material of the army: new arrivals at Camp Meade, Maryland, responding to the draft call. (U.S. War Department General Staff No. 165-WW-127-45 in NA.)

16. *Below,* some of the draftees who landed in Company A, 321st Labor Battalion, setting off along a French road to collect and rebury battlefield remains. Even the sun hid its face. (U.S. Signal Corps No. 111-SC-36192 in NA.)

17. A battalion of the 368th Infantry, 92d Division, advancing along a camouflaged road at Binarville, France, during the great September offensive, 1918. They ran into trouble. (Free Library of Philadelphia.)

18. Among the few recreational centers open to black soldiers was this club run by women of Newark, New Jersey. These men were probably back from overseas, the two with canes apparently wounded. (U.S. War Department General Staff No. 165-WW-127-49 in NA.)

19. February 1919: men of the 369th Infantry who were fortunate enough to get home alive march in their victory parade past New York's Flatiron Building. The massed phalanx formation they had learned from the French. (U.S. War Department General Staff No. 165-WW-127-26 in NA.)

20. The "unknown soldiers" greeting the Statue of Liberty as they sailed into New York harbor, home from the war to make the world safe for democracy. These happen to be New York's own, the 369th Infantry, formerly the 15th National Guard. (Courtesy of Arno Press.)

7. The 93d Division in France

There are no American troops anywhere near us, that I can find out, and we are *"les enfants perdu"* [*sic*], and glad of it. Our great American general simply put the black orphan in a basket, set it on the doorstep of the French, pulled the bell, and went away. I said this to a French colonel with an "English spoken here" sign on him, and he said, "Welcome leetle black babbie."

Maj. Arthur Little of the 369th Infantry
Regiment, 93d Division.

THERE was as much confusion about what to do with the black soldiers once they got to France as there had been stateside.

The proud former 15th New York National Guard, on arrival in France in December 1917 (after being hustled off following its bad experience at Spartanburg), found itself merely the 369th Infantry Regiment of the incomplete 93d Division and was set to work at once alongside S.O.S. troops laying railroad track from the port to supply dumps.[1] As for further combat training to supplement its meager three weeks in training camps at home, a member of the regiment summarized it as "four days' drilling and a haircut."[2] Colonel Hayward complained that they "never saw their rifles except by candlelight."[3]

During the first two months of 1918 cables shot back and forth across the Atlantic as General Pershing and Gen. John Biddle of the General Staff debated what to do with the black combat troops of the 93d, whose other three regiments were to arrive in April. Early in the discussion Pershing cabled to Washington that he intended to use the black combat regiments in the S.O.S. for a time (as the 369th was already deployed), after which they would become pioneer infantry.[4] This was an outright breach of promise; the 93d had been organized and trained with the understanding that it would be combat infantry. The

111

369th, 370th, and 372d appear to have been the only former National Guard troops the army tried to employ as laborers. In February, Biddle cabled back that since the 93d was to serve in the S.O.S. it would not need replacements as combat regiments did; in any case, Biddle explained, there were no replacements: "There are no more negro regiments here except the 92d Division and it is not desired to organize more." [5] By that time Pershing had changed his mind and had decided to turn over the four regiments of the 93d to the French, to whom he had promised four combat regiments; he would therefore, he told Biddle, need replacements. Biddle then offered him two regiments of the 92d for that purpose, because it was still considered undesirable to organize any more black infantry regiments. Later on, said Biddle, when the rest of the 92d Division was shipped, Pershing could reverse the situation and use the 93d as replacements for the 92d. Pershing ended the discussion by saying he did not care what the War Department did about black combat troops so long as he had four infantry regiments to give the French army.[6]

Later Pershing wrote in his war memoirs that the regiments were only lent to the French temporarily, "with the provision that they were to be returned for the formation of the 93d Division when called for. Unfortunately, they soon became identified with the French and there was no opportunity to assemble them as an American division." [7] There are no cables in the War Department files supportive of this statement of Pershing's. The regiments were apparently not lent but transferred to the French army, and forgotten until after the Armistice. They were the only American regiments completely integrated into the French army. The French had for some time been pressing for American regiments to serve as replacements in their own badly decimated divisions; but Pershing's position was that American troops should be organized into divisions, not the smaller units of regiments, and that, although Americans might train with the French or British, they would eventually be formed into an autonomous American army, holding its own sector of the front.[8] It is safe to assume that Pershing's image of his American army was white in color.

In the midst of this debate on the deployment of American

troops, the black combat regiments began to arrive. General Pershing cabled the War Department that a General Hoffman of the 93d Division had arrived, and what was he supposed to do with him? [9] Washington responded that the 93d existed as a division only on paper, and would actually contain just four infantry regiments. [10] The prospect of getting four unaffiliated regiments must have seemed to Pershing a perfect solution to his problem with the French, who were clamoring for American troops. The troops in question happened to be black, which was in itself a problem to the American army. Giving them to the French, who had their own black colonial troops and labored under no tradition of race prejudice, would nicely settle two problems with one stroke of the pen. Pershing delivered his four regiments, as promised.

To integrate the 93d into the French army presented administrative, if not racial, difficulties, because the French regiment was differently organized than the American regiment. Furthermore, French equipment was different from what the Americans were accustomed to. Their Springfields had to be exchanged for the Lebel rifles used by the French, because available ammunition fitted only the Lebels. These ancient weapons had zero firing accuracy but were adequate as mountings for bayonets on which the French colonial troops chiefly counted in infantry attacks; they employed artillery to accomplish what Americans expected of their Springfields. One American observer thought the French system would bring out the best in Negro soldiers, who "simply doted on cold steel. . . ." [11] This was to equate, in a typically racist way, American blacks with French colonials simply because they, too, were black; that the two groups had totally different cultural backgrounds was ignored. There are reports of Senegalese, Moroccan, and other French African troops who preferred the bayonet and the knife to squeezing a trigger, but there are no such reports of Afro-American troops. But whether the American troops liked them or not, all articles of gear and even helmets were French; only the American uniform was retained. This created its own particular difficulty; the French overcoat had generous pockets for stowing away small items of gear, but the American overcoat did not, and many men jettisoned gear which they would have had to hand-carry or hang from their persons—not very convenient in a combat situation. Some American officers chose to interpret this discarding of encumbrances as a panic action.[12]

The men's rations were French, and this, too, was a source of trouble. Soup, however hearty and good, was not a meal to men accustomed to more solid food, although the French soldiers loved it. The French ration of two quarts of red wine a day caused a lot of trouble. Some Americans, instead of making the unaccustomed wine ration last all day as the French did, drank it off the moment they received it, which would, of course, make anyone drunk. This was remedied by cutting off the wine ration for the black American troops and giving them extra sugar instead, although their white officers continued to draw the wine ration.[13]

To the dismay of American military officials, the integration of the black troops with white French troops was all too complete, without social or other discrimination. Treating blacks as equals was considered to have the most sinister implications for the future, when the black soldiers went home to the states. Colonel Linard of AEF Headquarters explained this to the French in a document called "Secret Information Concerning Black American Troops," telling the French how American blacks must be treated and why.[14] It was distributed to French officers who were likely to come into contact with American blacks, and to civilian officials in towns where black troops were likely to go.

In his "Secret Information" Linard explained that the French people must understand the position of blacks in America, whether or not they agreed with it. No use arguing this matter which some call "prejudice," Linard said; it was the unanimous opinion of white Americans on the "Negro question." The document went on to explain that the approximately 15 million Negroes in the United States presented a threat of race mongrelization unless blacks and whites were kept strictly separated. Since the danger did not exist in France, the French people were accustomed to being friendly and tolerant toward blacks; but such behavior deeply offended Americans as an attack on their national beliefs and aroused the fear that it might give American blacks intolerable pretentions to equality—and have an adverse effect on American public opinion (presumably, about aiding the French). White Americans considered blacks to be lacking in intelligence, judgment, and civic or professional morals—vices which presented a constant danger and required severe reprimand. Therefore, Linard said, it was necessary to avoid any intimacy, beyond civil politeness, between French officers and black officers; the French should not eat with them nor shake hands with them, nor visit or converse except as required by military matters. And while it was all right to recognize their services in moderate and realistic terms, they should not be lavishly praised, especially not in the presence of white Americans. Try to persuade the French people, Linard requested the authorities, "qu'elles ne gâtent pas les nègres"—not to spoil the Negroes. Americans are outraged by any intimacy between white women and blacks; and in any case such familiarity between the races would diminish whites in the eyes of our colonials. Military authority cannot directly intervene in this matter, Linard said in closing, but it can influence the people through their civil authorities.

When this document was read in the French National Assembly in July 1919, it drew exclamations of disapproval. M. René Boisneuf, the indignant member who presented it, appended examples of mistreatment of black troops by white American soldiers and M.P.'s, cases where blacks whom the French had decorated for bravery had subsequently been abused, beaten, and even murdered. M. Boisneuf proposed that the French government make formal amends, paying reparations to the families of men killed in such frays. In response, the French Chamber of Deputies immediately and to loud applause passed a resolution declaring loyalty to the immortal principles of the rights of man; condemning prejudice based on religion, class, or race; affirming the absolute equality of men in enjoyment of the benefits and protection of the law; and expressing confidence that the French government would require everyone to respect its laws and would punish any infractions committed within French territory no matter who the perpetrators or who the victims.[15]

Despite all the difficulties, somehow the black American infantry regiments of the 93d Division became part of the French army and shared in the fight to make the world safe for democracy for others.

The 369th had its battle baptism in the Argonne and went over the top near Chateau-Thierry and at Belleau Wood—all major and bloody fights. Other regiments of the 93d came later and so saw less action, but in the big fall offensive that finally shattered German resistance, all the black regiments were engaged. All of them, it seems from the individual regimental records which follow, did well enough to satisfy any commander; the commanders admitted that they did well.

The 369th, first to land, was the first to join the French. After many weeks of S.O.S. labor, with no chance for training, regiment morale was low. It had even lost its great morale-building band, which had been detached for a thirty-seven-day, 2,000-mile concert trip through France.[16]

At last Pershing "lent" the outfit to the French, and the regiment was given marching orders. It broke camp at St. Nazaire on 13 March 1918 and moved up to Givry-en-Argonne to become part of the 16th Division, 8th Corps, 4th French Army, commanded by General Gouraud. In mid-April the regiment was given responsibility for a four-and-one-half-kilometer sector; although the 369th comprised less than 1 percent of American troops in France, it held 20 percent of all territory then assigned to the American army.[17]

Late in May an incident occurred that made the 369th famous and singled out a black sergeant as the first American to win the croix de guerre. One night, Sgt. Henry Johnson and Pvt. Needham Roberts were manning an observation post in "no-man's land" when they heard suspicious noises. A German raiding party, after cutting its way through the barbed-wire entanglement, suddenly attacked them. Both men were wounded in the opening moments; but with grenades, rifles, and a bolo knife they beat off the Germans, inflicting losses that from documents later captured seemed to have numbered four enemy dead and thirty-two wounded. Roberts suffered such crippling wounds early in the fight that most of the action fell to Johnson, who thus won his decoration and a great deal of glory for the regiment.[18]

Journalists strove to visit with "les enfants perdus," as Colonel Hayward called his men. And they found he had not exaggerated. One wrote: "Being encased in the French Army to a greater degree than any other American contingent—they are the only doughboys supported by French artillery—these chocolate soldiers are temporarily in a state of splendid isolation so far as the remainder of the American expeditionary force is concerned. . . ." [19] Irvin S. Cobb was among the correspondents who got through to the 369th. He was impressed with the men, but concerned that they were not being given enough combat training: "Perhaps this was because we had grown accustomed to thinking of our negroes as members of labor battalions working along the lines of communication—unloading ships and putting up warehouses and building depots and felling trees in the forests of France. . . ." [20] After the heroism of Johnson and Roberts, Cobb said, "n-i-g-g-e-r will merely be another way of spelling the word American." [21] Cobb was unaware of Colonel Linard's admonition not to spoil the blacks.

The Germans launched their spring 1918 offensive. Americans thrown into the line near Chateau-Thierry helped stop them by the beginning of June, and then were assigned with some French troops to clear the enemy out of Belleau Wood. On 6 June, the 369th went in with the French under such heavy fire that a French officer suggested to Colonel Hayward that he pull his men back to a less exposed position. "My men never retire," said the colonel in the way of colonels; "they go forward or they die." [22] So they went forward. A few days later another black sergeant, Bob Collins, earned his croix de guerre for the effective handling of his machine gun under punishing fire. [23] In the same action, Pvt. Jefferson Jones, manning an advance observation post, came under heavy rifle fire and sent this cool message to his company officer:

> I am being fired upon heavily from the left. I await your instructions. Trusting these few lines will find you the same, I remain,
>
> Yours truly,
> Jefferson Jones [24]

On 4 July, the 369th was sent to strengthen the 161st Division of the 4th French Army in anticipation of a German drive. During the trip to their new sector, facing Butte de Mesnil near Minancourt, the men were exposed for about six miles to heavy enemy bombardment, but they marched to the cadence of a newly coined motto: "God Damn, Le's Go." They made it to the front and, on 15 July, replaced a weary regiment of Moroccans.[25]

General Gouraud had advançe information of an impending heavy German attack. His strategy was to evacuate his front-line trenches except for a few small patrols, and in the second- and third-line trenches to leave behind only a small number of men who were to fire signal rockets when the Germans approached their positions. The device worked. A preparatory German bombardment fell on the virtually empty front line; the rockets enabled Gouraud to aim his artillery fire at the massed German troops just behind the front line; and rifle fire from the second- and third-line trenches combined with the artillery fire to prevent the enemy from breaching the Allied line. Among those left behind to fire the signal rockets were men of the 369th. Sixteen men of the regiment were among the volunteers who had stayed to man the front-line trenches; they endured five and one-half hours of shelling, miraculously escaping without casualties. General Gouraud made special mention of the courageous work of the 369th in a congratulatory message after the victory.[26] As Colonel Hayward proudly described the engagement: "The first thing I knew all there was between the German Army and Paris on a stretch of front a little more than four miles long was my regiment of negroes. But it was fair enough at that; all there was between us and Berlin was the German Army. They tried pretty hard to get by, but they never did. No German ever got into a trench with my regiment who did not stay there or go back with the brand of my boys upon him." [27]

The attack repelled, Marshal Foch ordered a counterattack on the enemy in the Marne bulge. The 161st Division was assigned to wipe out one of the remaining German salients in the 4th Army area, their chief stronghold at Butte de Mesnil. This was the first major advance in which the 369th took part, and it was successful. Capt. Charles Fillmore, one of the regiment's few black officers, was commended for his calm leadership. The Germans subsequently made a counterattack on the 369th in this area, hurling 9,000 shells at the regiment in a forty-five-minute period; but they were repulsed. A large number of Mauser rifles was captured, and many men of the regiment swapped their old Lebels for the German Mauser, which was much like the American Springfield; but, alas, when the captured ammunition was exhausted, the Mausers were useless.[28]

In mid-August the 369th was relieved for a week's rest after 130 days in the lines. When the regiment returned, it officially became part of the French 161st Division instead of being merely attached to it. So as part of a French division the black Americans participated in the first American offensive of the war, in late September.

General Pershing had gained time in which to organize and battle-test the American army by Gouraud's smashing victory in the German attack of July and the subsequent French counterattack. By mid-September the Americans were ready to undertake a major advance of their own in the Argonne Forest, across ground that the Germans had held and fortified since 1914. The country was generally rolling, but cut through by many ravines and covered with heavy timber. For four years German engineers had been increasing the natural defensive strength of the region with formidable barbed-wire entanglements and machine-gun replacements. Pershing would attempt to advance through the forest, his right flank covered by the French 17th Corps, and his left by General Gouraud's 4th Army as it advanced through the plain of Champagne. All black troops took part in the offensive, the 93d Division with Gouraud in the Champagne, and the 92d with the other Americans in the Argonne itself. D Day was 26 September 1918.

In the front line with the French 161st for the initial assault, the 369th dodged machine-gun fire from one shell hole to another in a wave formation and drove out the enemy with grenades and rifles; the Moroccans on their left charged into the guns in a mass and killed with their knives. By nightfall of the first day of the assault the regiment had advanced about four kilometers, at a high cost. The 3d Battalion, which had started the day with twenty officers and 700 men, ended it with seven officers and 150 men; it took 125 prisoners, twenty-five machine guns, and two 77-mm. guns.[29]

As the offensive continued, the 369th turned in a good account of itself in heavy fighting, sustaining severe losses. Part of the regiment was at the capture of Bellevue Ridge and the taking of the strategic railroad junction of Sechault.[30] Casualties were numerous. A machine-gun company became a German target as it tried to get through enemy wire entanglements and was almost completely wiped out. At one point the regiment advanced faster than the French troops who were supposed to support it on right and left, and so both its flanks were unprotected; also, there was a shortage of rations for two days until a volunteer, Sergeant Major Marshall, made his way to them from headquarters with food. By the time the 369th was pulled back for reorganization, it had advanced fourteen kilometers through severe German resistance.[31]

By this time the 1st Battalion was down to three officers and 100 men, the 2d to ten officers and 300 men, and the 3d to seven officers and 137 men. Casualties included 125 killed in action and 36 who later died of their wounds; and 636 wounded seriously enough to require hospitalization. Stallings wrote of the regiment: "During the September 26 offensive, the 369th Regiment was in the line nine consecutive days as a regiment in a French division. They never lost a foot of ground on defense, and they failed in only one attack, this their final one when they went forward against concrete naked of any barrage, the French artillery having failed to come up. . . . This failure, of course, gave rear area critics a chance to carp." [32] One example of rear-area carping is the charge in an official report that "the men quickly became demoralized after the loss of their officers which was not from cowardice, but rather lack of confidence and lack of experience under the leaders who remained." [33] The accusation, although not very serious, is unsubstantiated by any evidence; and the report neglects to mention that the normal limit for a regiment under sustained attack at the front was three to four days, as against the nine days endured by the 369th.[34] What may have looked like demoralization was probably pure exhaustion.

At last, in mid-October, the regiment was moved back to a

quiet sector in the Vosges Mountains for a period of rest. It was still there on 11 November, the day of the Armistice. Six days later the 369th made its last advance, and on 26 November it reached the banks of the Rhine, the first Allied unit to get there.[35]

The regimental officers had no complaints about the 369th. According to Colonel Hayward, it had been in combat 191 days, longer than any other regiment in the AEF, after the shortest combat training of any regiment.[36] Major Little wrote:

> Of my knowledge I can testify that the impression so frequently expressed to the effect that the colored man cannot or will not stand physical hardship is just buncombe.
>
> If our men believed that going without food was unavoidable, they would never complain of hunger. If our men were satisfied that new shoes were unavailable for issue they would march all day (and cheerfully) with their bare feet touching the ground through the broken soles of their old shoes.[37]

Like the laborers in uniform who could accomplish such work feats when they were appealed to as *men*, not forced to as *black* men, the fighting black soldier put up with whatever he had to if he was convinced that he was made to suffer not because he was black but because the means of relief were simply not available. In the 369th, he was treated like a man and responded in a manly way.

The entire regiment was awarded the croix de guerre for the taking of Sechault, and about 170 officers and men received individual croix de guerre. The 369th was the regiment that most impressed and pleased the French; one thing that gave them particular pleasure was that many of the black troops had learned to speak the French language. Secretary Baker was reported to have called the 369th the all-round most serviceable regiment sent to France.[38]

By the time the medals and kudos were handed out, all the regiment's original five black officers had been replaced by white officers. Captain Fillmore, who had won praise at Butte de Mesnil, and Lieutenants Lacey and Reid were transferred to the 370th Regiment;[39] Captain Marshall was sent to the 365th Regiment (92d Division). Lieutenant Europe had also been transferred but was later returned to the 369th so that the famous regimental band he led could maintain its excellence.[40] Stallings wrote of the regiment: "The general impression of Americans was that the colored soldier was mainly a comic figure, incapable of undergoing danger over long intervals. The Harlem boys were the first to wipe out that impression. As for being comics, they were natural humorists gifted by God Almighty, deliberately sending their officers into gales of laughter; but the loss of fifteen hundred men in 191 days in the zone of fire was not a laughing matter." [41]

The rest of the division arrived in France in April, almost five months later than the 369th.

The 370th Regiment almost immediately began to lose its black officers, and the process continued throughout its war career. First to go was Colonel Dennison. The colonel was said to have been in poor health before he sailed for France; less than three months after landing in France he was relieved of his command, allegedly too ill to perform his duties, and was ordered to report to AEF Headquarters.[42] Dennison may indeed have been ill, but, recalling the fate of Colonel Charles Young, one is inclined to skepticism.

In the case of Dennison, the real reason may have been not illness but a damning report on the regiment submitted by Capt. George Marvin, an American liaison officer with the French army. Marvin reported poor liaison between the 370th and the French. The black officers, he said, could not speak French and were bewildered by their assignment; the men disliked their French equipment and threw much of it away. In addition, Marvin said, the supply system had broken down because the black officers didn't know what French supplies were available, how to get them, or how to transport them from depot to post. Therefore, Marvin said, the training program to which the 370th was assigned to prepare them for going to the front had ground to a halt. He admitted that the regiment had had problems—instructors and equipment were changed three times in three weeks, a German offensive was in progress during their training period, and they were thrown into the line prematurely. Nevertheless, Marvin concluded his report thus: "From all of the above it is clearly evident that this regiment is unavailable for service at the front now and, in my opinion, will not be fit for two months to come, if ever. It was plainly evident that there had been a serious loss of morale throughout the entire command." [43] Marvin's report is dated 14 June; Dennison was relieved of his command on 12 July. There is scarcely a chance that the two events were unconnected.

Whatever justification there may have been for Marvin's complaints, the change of command was deeply resented by the men. The man who replaced Dennison, Col. T. A. Roberts, was the first white officer in the twenty-four-year history of the 8th Illinois National Guard. The regimental chaplain, William S. Bradden, in his history of the regiment, called Roberts the "arch enemy, vilifier and traducer of the Negro soldier, the one who delighted to sign his private mail as coming from the 'White Hope in a Black Regiment!' " [44]

Bradden's hatred for Colonel Roberts was so intense and unchaplainesque that one wonders how objective he could have been in his *Under Fire with the 370th*. Bradden says that after Dennison's removal, Roberts "trailed our regiment like a vulture seeks the offal" [45] in carrying out orders from headquarters to remove all high-ranking black officers; that Roberts told a black officer he had *not* asked to have his black officers replaced by whites, while that black officer had in his pocket a copy of a telegram from Roberts to Pershing asking just that.[46]

Although no evidence of such a telegram has been uncovered, some replacements did occur. Before long, three black captains and a black major were transferred. This intensified the men's dislike for their new commander. It was reported by DuBois that they shouted: "Blue eyes ain't our Colonel; Duncan's our Colonel," [47] referring to Lt. Col. Otis Duncan of their regiment, who after Dennison's removal became the ranking black officer in France.

If Roberts was at first as antiblack as Bradden claimed, the colonel seems to have become much better disposed to his regiment within a remarkably short time, as evidenced by this report of his to headquarters in August: "Please don't think that after a month I am convinced that I have a world beater of a regiment—it hasn't gone that far with me yet; but there is a lot of excellent material that is not doing as much for the cause as it is capable of doing; the men are willing and as apt in most ways as most troops that I have seen; the officers are generally good as far as I have been able to observe them. There are some weak spots that I have under observation and as soon as I am reasonably convinced that I am right, changes will be recommended. . . ." [48] These are scarcely the thoughts or words of an "arch enemy, vilifier and traducer of the Negro soldier"; in fact, for an army colonel at that time there is a remarkable absence of racist content in Roberts's report. While it is perfectly understandable that the regiment was upset by the loss of Colonel Dennison and his replacement by a white man, by the time of the Armistice there were only three white officers in the 370th Regiment.

The 370th saw its first action in July in the Argonne area during the unsuccessful German summer offensive. On 16 July, Lt. Harvey Taylor sustained six wounds during a raid, thus earning a croix de guerre. [49] In an August drive against the German lines the 370th distinguished itself by taking almost 1,900 prisoners and capturing four cannons, forty-five trench mortars, and 200 machine guns.

It was soon after this attack that Colonel Roberts reported on his regiment, and although he said he wasn't sure yet that it was a "world beater" he was obviously pleased with its performance. But he was concerned about the eventual effect on morale if the regiment remained an isolated unit. In the same report he said that "if the idea takes root that the regiment will never belong anywhere all the good intentions in the world will not advance it beyond a certain point." He suggested that the four regiments of the 93d Division be united, supported by French artillery, and thus be able to function as a full division. Being divided and constantly shifted about was damaging the regiment, he said, and if conditions did not improve "the angel Gabriel would have his hands full in trying to make anything of them—the same would apply to a white outfit." [50]

But Roberts's suggestions got nowhere. During the summer of 1918 the 370th was shifted about among four French divisions: the 73d, 10th, 34th, and 36th. Early in September, attached to the French 59th Division, they were on the Soissons front and joined in the attack. Sgt. Matthew Jenkins was awarded both the croix de guerre and the Distinguished Service Cross for taking a fortified German tunnel with some men of Company F and holding it under fire, without food or water, for thirty-six hours.[51] Soon the regiment took over a full sector of the front in preparation for the big American offensive in late September. On 27 September the 2d Battalion went into combat, and the next day it captured Ferme la Jolie through the heroism of a black lieutenant of a mortar platoon who penetrated the German lines and located the machine-gun nests. Bradden says that Roberts called his men and officers cowards during this attack because they didn't yell when they went "over the top," but that he as chaplain presided over the burial of forty men who had died in the assault; when he told that to Roberts, Bradden says, Roberts answered, "Well, that's what soldiers are for, to be killed and wounded." [52]

On the last day of September the regiment performed less satisfactorily. Its mission was to attack a well-fortified German position on the far side of the Aisne-Oise Canal. In the fighting, some units became confused and lost. Bradden claims that, in order to discredit black officers, Roberts signaled for the charge at nine in the morning although he had ordered it for nine that night; thus Lieutenant Colonel Duncan's battalion had to attack across the canal in broad daylight. This is not consistent with Roberts's expressed concern for his regiment. Bradden also claimed that Roberts, after moving forward with the troops as the attack began, then retired for the rest of the day to the safety of a bunker.[53]

The official explanation of what happened to the 370th and why it happened is no more convincing than Bradden's explanation. A War College report quotes General Rondeau, commander of the French 59th Division, as stating on 30 September that the 370th was useless in combat and needed complete reorganization. Rondeau is quoted as saying: "This is due to the fact that barring the Colonel, Regular Officer (white) of the American Army, all units, battalions, companies and sections are commanded by black officers of pronounced inefficiency. They are vain strap-wearers [*porte-galons*], of no military knowledge and showing a lamentable lack of conscientiousness in their work. . . ." [54] The general charged, furthermore, that during combat all the black officers of certain units stayed behind in the battalion command post.

One circumstance may disqualify the damning testimony of General Rondeau, and that is that he was most likely not in command on 30 September when the attack across the canal took place. General Vincendon, regular commander of the 59th Division, went on leave on 6 October, and Rondeau relieved him; but presumably Vincendon was heading the division on 30 September, not Rondeau as implied in the War Department document. The testimony of General Vincendon, delivered when he returned from leave in December, is full of praise for the regiment as a whole and for the performance in particular of two black officers, Duncan and Patton. Vincendon is quoted as having said: "The 370th R.I.U.S. [Infantry Regiment U.S.] has contributed largely to the success of the 59th Division, and has taken in bitter strife both cannon and machine guns. Its units, fired by a noble ardor, got at times even beyond the objectives given them by the higher command; they have always wished to be in the front line, for the place of honor is the leading rank. They have shown in our advance that they are worthy of being there." [55]

It is true that Vincendon's statements about the 370th's having gone beyond its assigned objectives might be interpreted as a generous way of saying that the units lost their way and outran their goals. This would be borne out by the findings of Maj. L. R. Fredenhall, who inspected the regiment on 5–6 October and reported that most of the black officers were unable to read maps and thus locate their positions. Fredenhall recommended "That this regiment be taken away from the French; that with the exception of four or five colored officers to be designated by Colonel Roberts, all of the officers be replaced by white officers; that it be trained for two weeks thereafter. It will then be a good regiment, as the men only require to be intelligently led." The men, he reported, were doing a workmanlike job, without signs of panic or demoralization; and the 400 who were listed as missing had probably not fled the fight but had simply become lost in the difficult terrain (in which he himself had got lost, the major said) and had joined nearby French units.[56] So, apparently, it was excusable for the men to lose their way in battle; it was excusable for the inspecting officer to lose his way after the battle; but it was inexcusable for the black officers to lose their way in the same territory in the heat of an attack under heavy fire.

What this conflicting testimony seems to boil down to is that the regiment, especially the officers, suffered from too many shifts in organization, too little and too inconsistent training, and, probably, a lack of trust in the white man who had suddenly replaced their Colonel Dennison. Roberts himself felt that the French did not appreciate the true worth of his regiment, although it had performed all its assignments as a combat unit. "The regiment was not as efficient as the French regiments," Roberts said. "A marked improvement was manifest as the operation progressed, but the fact remains as above." [57]

On 6 October, the 370th was withdrawn from the front. Casualties since mid-September numbered 450 to 500 killed and wounded. [58] One black battalion commander, Maj. Rufus Stokes, was shifted to the regiment's combat and supply trains and replaced in the battalion by a white officer, Maj. John T. Prout. [59] During the last week of the war the 370th was back in battle, pursuing the retreating Germans. Prout's battalion captured a German battery at Val St. Pierre; Duncan and his men took the town of Logny. The regiment had advanced into Belgium before news of the Armistice caught up with it. Is it possible that the 370th simply had too much dash, wishing, as Vincendon said, always to be in the front line because that was the place of honor?

Although the regiment as a unit was not awarded the croix de guerre, seventy-one individuals received it, and another twenty-one were decorated with the Distinguished Service Cross. The croix de guerre with palm was presented to Company C for an action of conspicuous bravery. [60] This does not come up to the record of the 369th, certainly, but it is not a bad record either. The 370th was probably not as sinning as General Rondeau said, nor as sinned against as Bradden insisted. Colonel Roberts seems to have been a conscientious commander, but black soldiers had so many strikes against them that to do their best they needed something more than that—they needed officers who believed they were great. The 369th had such officers; the 370th didn't.

The 372d, like the 369th and the 370th, was a National Guard regiment, made up of small guard units from various parts of the country and led by a combination of black officers and surplus white guard officers. It had worse leadership problems than either the 369th, with almost all white officers, or the 370th, with almost all black officers.

The colonel of the regiment was Glendie Young, a white officer who aroused racial tension as soon as the 372d arrived in France by permitting white officers to curtain off the larger portion of the barracks for themselves, leaving the smaller portion for the black officers.[61] Although Colonel Young was soon replaced, the new colonel, Herschel Tupes, furthered the demoralization of the regiment by almost immediately asking for the transfer of all his black officers. In justifying his request to General Pershing, Tupes wrote:

> *First.* The racial distinctions which are recognized in civilian life naturally continue to be recognized in military life and present a formidable barrier to the existence of that feeling of comradeship which is essential to mutual confidence and esprit de corps.
> *Second.* With a few exceptions there is a characteristic tendency among the colored officers to neglect the welfare of their men and to perform their duties in a perfunctory manner. They are lacking in initiative also. These defects entail a constant supervision and attention to petty details by Battalion commanders and other senior officers which distract their attention from their wider duties, with harmful results.[62]

Tupes requested that no additional black officers be sent to the 372d, and that efficiency boards be used to dispose of those who were incompetent.

The colonel's action destroyed what little morale remained in the regiment. Black officers and men felt that they were the victims of a deep-seated intrigue on the part of their white comrades-in-arms. The situation became more tense when three black officers were placed under technical arrest for insubordination. One observer said, "The French liaison officers could not understand why Americans should treat one another so harshly and cruelly when it was momentarily expected that the division would be plunged into battle." [63]

A court of elimination, composed of white officers of the 371st and the 372d Infantry, was created to pass on the efficiency of the black officers. It declared unsatisfactory twenty of the first twenty-one who appeared, and recommended their removal. Tension rose to a dangerous degree. The circulation of a rumor that white noncoms would be assigned to the unit raised feelings to such a peak that some white military policemen were sent in to maintain order, and white regimental officers were ordered to carry sidearms at all times. At least one soldier was shot by a white officer, which convinced the troops that these officers were ordered to shoot on any provocation. [64]

Perhaps some of the officers of the 372d were inefficient and useless; no military unit in history has been without such personnel. But the mass condemnation of black officers was more destructive of morale than a few incompetent officers could possibly have been. One white observer said: "The inference is that its [the 372d's] standards were sub-par. But it is difficult to justify on any grounds such a flagrant shock to the morale of a unit. It is such instances of tactless handling of colored troops, isolated though they may be, which brings down on the services the condemnation of the Negro press." [65]

Through all this time of change and stress the regiment was supposedly being brought to fighting form. It proceeded toward the Champagne front as it trained. During the opening days of the American September assault the 372d moved into the communications trenches, making its first attack the morning of 27 September. The men helped clear the enemy out of Bussy (or Busey) Farm, advanced toward Ripont, and were in the fighting at Sechault; then they were pulled back to Bussy Farm. In these actions they captured sixty of the enemy, and equipment including several artillery and antitank weapons. On 30 September they relieved the 371st at Trières Farm, which they were ordered to fortify and hold, and in the next week they mopped up at Monthois. Then the regiment was withdrawn from the front and replaced by the 70th French Regiment at the end of the first week in October. [66]

During these actions, the 1st and 3d battalions suffered such heavy losses that they were combined into a single battalion. A young white lieutenant said the casualties were heavy because the men refused to surrender or retreat. Gen. Mariano Goybet, commander of the crack French 157th Division, congratulated the whole regiment, and there were many individual instances of great courage. Corp. Clarence Van Allen cleaned out a machine-gun nest single-handed, killing four men and capturing three; the same corporal captured a trench mortar battery and its crew. These exploits earned him the croix de guerre with palm, the médaille militaire, and the Distinguished Service Cross. In all, the French awarded fifty-two croix de guerre and four médailles militaires to members of the 370th.[67]

In the relatively quiet Arnould sector in Alsace, to which the 372d was sent with the 157th French Division, the regiment had only thirty-three casualties, killed and wounded, in a month. Four days before the Armistice, a patrol of six men won the Distinguished Service Cross for penetrating deep into an enemy position.[68] After the Armistice the regiment was moved into Granges-sur-Cologne where the regimental band was enthusiastically received. Although white officers tried to prevent fraternizing, the townspeople were very friendly toward the black troops who had helped save their country.[69]

All the while, black officers continued to be transferred and replaced by white officers. Ralph Tyler, the black correspondent, complained about the transfers to Emmett Scott, Secretary of War Baker's special assistant in matters concerning blacks. Scott forwarded the message to Secretary Baker, adding that from the reports of the efficiency boards which he had seen, he did not believe black officers were being discriminated against. Could Baker give him some official confirmation of this, Scott asked, "so that I may dispose of statements which are filtering back to the States through letters, etc., that injustice has been meted out to colored officers."[70] Whether or not Scott really believed that the black officer was not discriminated against, the first point in Colonel Tupes's request for replacement of all his black officers was on grounds not of inefficiency, but of "racial distinctions" which presented a "formidable barrier" to comradeship among the officers; and the second point spoke vaguely of a "characteristic tendency among the colored officers" to neglect their men's welfare, to be perfunctory in their duties, and to lack initiative. Whether Scott sincerely believed black officers got a fair shake, or whether he was doing a job of pacifying the black community, everything about the treatment of black officers in the 372d cries out *discrimination*.

The amazing thing is that, with all the tension and hostility, the 372d managed well enough in combat to win a unit croix de guerre with palm, the highest regimental decoration conferred by the French government, with a citation praising "a superb spirit and an admirable scorn of danger." [71] In addition, forty-one officers, fourteen noncoms, and ninety-seven privates received individual croix de guerre; and two officers and nineteen men, the Distinguished Service Cross. Granting that the French army may have handed out medals generously to American soldiers as a way of showing its gratitude, it would not have cheapened for its own regiments the most coveted of unit decorations and the best it had to offer its own men for heroism. Assuming, then, that the awards were significant, how did the 372d manage to collect such a large share of them in the light of their brief training, the difficulties of fighting in a foreign land, the distrust shown by their commander in the black officers who led them, and the inevitable reflection of that distrust in the rank and file? What is the explanation? Could the black officers who survived Tupes's purge have been extraordinarily competent? Could the men have been exceptionally courageous? There must have been some such reason, and what balm it would have been to outraged feelings if only some highly placed American had officially said so. No one did.

The fourth regiment of the division, the 371st Infantry, is put here out of numerical order because it was of significantly different makeup than the three guard units. The men of the 371st were not of the élite, as guardsmen considered themselves and were generally considered by others. The men of the 371st were draftees, almost all fresh from the cotton fields of the Carolinas, and, right from the start, all their officers were white. Its performance might be expected to differ as much from that of the guard regiments as its origins differed. But, in fact, it differed very little; and that little seems to have been for the better.

Perhaps because of its humble background, the 371st was practically ignored in the writings of black commentators of the time; there were no poets to sing the praises of Carolina "darkies." The regiment is not often mentioned by white observers either, because they tended to focus on poor performance by blacks, and the 371st gave little opportunity for that. At war's end, the regiment as a unit was awarded the croix de guerre with palm.

The regiment sailed for France in April, at the same time as the 370th and the 372d. Upon landing, it was ordered at once to join a depleted French division at Rembercourt, much to the surprise of its commanding officer Colonel Miles. Miles is reported to have phoned AEF Headquarters in some pique and to have said, "This is the first information I have had that I am to obey any French Army officer I happen to find at a railway station or anywhere else." [72]

Rembercourt, about eighteen miles from the fortress of Verdun, had been damaged by shells and bombs and was so near the front that artillery could be heard from quarters. German planes flew over frequently. So, the green regiment was immediately thrown into a combat atmosphere and there received training with the French, with the usual difficulties of new equipment, communication, strange officers, and so forth. [73] After two weeks of this, the regiment had the honor of being inspected by General Pershing, who sent this message back to Colonel Miles through an aide:

> General Pershing asked me to write and say that in the rush of getting away he did not have an opportunity to tell you that he was very pleased with the appearance of your Regiment at inspection yesterday.
> He was particularly struck with the attitude of your men and feels that you have in your hands material with which to make a regiment that will be a high credit to the American Expeditionary Forces. [74]

In June the 371st was sent to the Verdun area, along with the 372d and the 333d French Infantry Regiment, to fill out Goybet's badly depleted 157th Division. The division, famous for its heroic defense of Verdun in 1915, wore a red hand as a shoulder patch and called itself the Red Hand Division. Miles's men adopted the shoulder patch and proudly called themselves the Red Hand regiment. Irvin S. Cobb visited the 371st at that time and reported that Colonel Miles was extremely gratified by the drill and training of his men, and that a major of the regiment said: "I'd take my chance of going anywhere with these black soldiers at my back. So would any of the rest of the officers. We haven't had any actual fighting experience yet—that'll come in a week or two when we relieve a French regiment that's just here in front of us holding the front lines—but we are not worrying about what'll happen when we get our baptism of fire. . . ." [75] Another officer said, "We were a little dubious about them. We did not know whether they would stand fire or not. But they did . . . and they were splendid fighters." [76] The French, too, had words of praise. Col. Augustine Quillet, commander of infantry of the Red Hand Division, issued this statement: "At the 371st the military honors are perfectly paid. It is very agreeable for me to make this statement and publish it." [77] The translation may be murky, but the message is loud and clear.

Although the officers admired their men as soldiers, the color line never wavered. Worried about the mingling of the men with French people of nearby towns, Lt. Ernest Samusson, the regimental intelligence officer, issued this dispatch:

It is requested that the civil authorities concerned take steps to co-operate toward the prevention of these harmful relationships by enlightening the residents in the villages concerned of the gravity of the situation and by warning them of the inevitable results.

The question is of great importance to the French people and even more so to the American towns, the population of which will be affected later when the troops return to the United States. It therefore becomes necessary for both the colored and white races, that undue social mixing of these two, be circumspectly prevented.[78]

Lieutenant Samusson's dispatch drove home again the message of Colonel Linard's "Secret Information Concerning Black American Troops."

Action for the 371st during July, August, and most of September consisted chiefly of patrols and raiding parties to take prisoners, plus one surprise attack with the rest of the division on the German lines. In that attack, Colonel Quillet reported that the men acted with great coolness, but General Goybet was not entirely satisfied with the competence of some of the younger officers—white, as were all officers of the regiment. Goybet commented that they were not familiar with the position of their machine-gun support, and that those temporarily acting as battalion commanders did not know the disposition of their men.[79] So, apparently, the staffing of the 371st with all white officers did not entirely solve the problem of incompetent leadership, but efficiency boards were not set up to judge the qualifications of the white officers who were said to perform poorly.

In late September the regiment was moved to the Champagne area to take its place among those massing for the big American offensive—including the three other regiments of the 93d Division. At the beginning of the attack the 371st was in reserve, but two days later it was thrown in to fill a gap between a French and a Moroccan division. Lacking artillery support, the men of the 371st attacked German machine-gun emplacements with the bayonet. Fighting was bitter, and the regiment advanced only 500 yards that day. Then it moved more swiftly, taking part in the reduction of Bussy Farm and other German strongholds. Resistance was strong. An officer reported: "We literally waded through the enemy. At one point we forded a small river and crossed a flooded area some four hundred yards in width." [80] Company K, finding itself isolated, took and fortified a strong advance position, capturing thirty-five prisoners and a 77-mm. cannon. Meanwhile the regiment had reached Trières Farm, outrunning its artillery support, and was forced to a halt by heavy German bombardment. Colonel Miles claimed the Red Hand Division advanced so rapidly that the Germans tried to slow them down by strafing; three of the enemy planes were shot down by his riflemen.[81] On 28 September, according to Lt. John Smith, the regiment advanced a full seven kilometers, and: "The next day we were subjected to a terrific counter-attack. The enemy used artillery and gas, and airplanes, and rushed us with infantry and machine guns. We held our ground for seven hours, fighting part of the time with our gas masks on. It was as severe a test as any soldiers ever had, but our men never faltered once, although our casualties were very heavy that day. No soldiers could have behaved any better under adverse circumstances." [82]

In the first week in October, the 157th Division was relieved and sent to the relative quiet of the Vosges rest area, where it stayed until the Armistice. In the 371st, four officers and 109 men had been killed in action, and 13 later died of wounds; forty-one officers and 873 men were wounded. They had captured three German officers and 90 men, and weapons including eight trench mortars, thirty-seven 77-mm. guns, and forty-seven machine guns. [83]

There were the usual rumors that a number of black troopers had deserted during combat, but a regimental report filed later produced evidence that the missing men had either been separated from their units and joined others, or had been evacuated to hospitals, or were among the killed and wounded. Almost every one of the alleged AWOLs was accounted for. [84]

Perhaps the rumors were part of the German propaganda effort to get American soldiers, black and white, to desert. Leaflets dropped from the air into the lines of the 371st urged Americans to "live and let live" and promised deserters good treatment in Germany until the war was over.

The wonder is that black troops did not desert in numbers, not so much because of the horrors of trench warfare as because of the hopelessness of their situation as blacks in a white army. Official warnings, such as Linard's and Samusson's, must have closed many French homes to them. Public places of recreation were likewise closed to the black soldier, as by the order of General Goybet (probably in response to the Linard "Secret Instructions") that "the entrance of inns and the sale of wines or spirits are strictly forbidden to the American colored troops of the division at all times and hours in the whole sector." [85] Any black soldier found drunk, or absent from his post after seven in the evening, was arrested. The curfew was not only unreasonable, it was cruel, because, as the regimental historian pointed out, "our enlisted men had enjoyed no real rest and absolutely no leaves whatever while we had been in France." [86] And where would they have gone if they had been given leaves as white soldiers were? All of France was off-limits to the black man, including, more often than not, the YMCA "huts." It is a wonder that they did not run away or crack up under the unrelieved strain of battle. Perhaps Love and Davenport were correct in finding black draftees less subject to nervous instability than whites.

Rejoining the American army was no cause for rejoicing in the 371st, because the men were at once ordered to remove the Red Hand shoulder patches they had so enjoyed wearing. But the extraordinary bravery of the regiment was rewarded with the croix de guerre with palm, and General Goybet said: "They have scattered their dead without counting and the view of the battlefield is more eloquent than any report." [87] In addition, sixty officers and 124 men were awarded the Distinguished Service Cross or the croix de guerre—more and higher honors than any other regiment of the 93d Division. Were the Southern draftees more docile under white leadership, less resentful of hardship and injustice, than the black guardsmen of Northern states? Were their white officers, taken as a whole, better trained and more accustomed to leadership than either the black officers who had had such a thin time of it at Camp Des Moines or the surplus white guard officers? Perhaps all these circumstances contributed to the excellent performance of the 371st Regiment; or perhaps they were more generously treated and their performance was better received and rewarded because of their humble origin in the cotton fields of the Carolinas.

During the front-line service of the 93d Division its casualties were 584 men killed and 2,582 wounded. The total figure of 3,166 represents about 32 percent of the division.[88] Beyond question, this black division had contributed its share of blood and suffering.

8. The 92d Division in France

It was my misfortune to be handicapped by many white officers who were rabidly hostile to the idea of a colored officer, and who continually conveyed misinformation to the staffs of the superior units, and generally created much trouble and discontent. Such men will never give the negro the square deal that is his just due.

> Gen. Charles C. Ballou, commander of the 92d, to
> Assistant Commandant, General Staff College,
> 14 March 1920, quoted in Dowd,
> *Negro in American Life*, p. 102.

THE 92d Division, composed of black draftees, officered up to company rank by Des Moines graduates, fought under all the same disadvantages as the 93d Division: discrimination, brief and poor training, efforts to get rid of black officers, separation of its regiments, and so on and on. But the 92d had an additional handicap, which was on such a high level that the division could never, by any feats in battle, by any excellence of men or officers, overcome it. A reconstruction of its battle narrative must take into account this special obstacle: an apparently bitter feud between Gen. Robert Bullard, who became commanding officer of the American 2d Army, and General Ballou, whose 92d Division had the misfortune to be included in Bullard's command.

During stateside training Ballou had showed himself reasonably fair to his black soldiers, although not without prejudice; or, at least, his Bulletin No. 35 indicated that he conformed completely to the American attitude that the black man must content himself with an inferior place in the army as in the society as a whole. Still, the 92d was *his* division, and if only for the sake of his own career he must have been determined to make it as good as possible, and to defend its virtues and recognize its

137

successes. Bullard, on the other hand, seems to have been a thoroughgoing Negro hater, and in addition it suited his purposes to exaggerate the shortcomings of black soldiers in order to discredit Ballou. Ballou reported that Bullard approved of the 92d only for the way it cared for its animals, and that this competence was accounted for by Bullard only because "A niggah just likes a hawse," as Ballou quoted him.[1] Bullard confided to his diary, "Poor negroes! they are hopelessly inferior," but he observed that even they could have performed better but for Ballou, of whom he said: "I'm inclined to think he will have to be 'S.O.S.'ed,' and I'll have to get this done."[2] To be "S.O.S.'ed" presumably, was to be transferred to a labor division, which for a combat general would be the equivalent of being sent to Coventry. Perhaps because of the misinformation Ballou said was conveyed to superior officers, Bullard was ready to believe Ballou's black men guilty of rape or any other infamy on mere suspicion. To Bullard, a black officer was incompetent by virtue merely of his color. Ballou was known to complain that some of his black officers were incompetent, but he claimed that his division was used as a dumping ground for incompetent whites as well as blacks; and he was not so prejudiced that he could not recognize and reward competence in a black officer. To Bullard it was fantastic to expect any black man to perform at the same level as whites, and he wrote piously that "all this constructive equality I regarded as an injustice; it is not real."[3] Like many other officers in the army at that time, Bullard seems to have retained intact the attitudes instilled during a Southern childhood.

Not surprisingly, many white officers took a stand close to Bullard's. Ballou's chief of staff, Col. Allen J. Greer, was a man who either because of the blinders of bigotry or through plain sadism circulated derogatory and untrue stories about blacks of the division—perhaps he was one of those Ballou referred to as spreading misinformation to the staffs of superiors. With enemies like Bullard and Greer, and a weak advocate like Ballou, and a career competition going on between them, the 92d Division did better than anyone could reasonably have expected. Perhaps, indeed, it did better than anyone knows, although the evidence that survives indicates that it did not do so well as the 93d. It was called a failure.

There was the usual flap about what to do with the black 92d when it should arrive in France. Pershing had decided to assign it to the British army for training, but the British wanted none of it. Pershing insisted, however, that these men were American citizens and said, "I cannot and will not discriminate against these soldiers," who, he claimed, were in a good state of training—an expedient lie.[4] Viscount Milner, a member of Lloyd George's war cabinet, protested that the 92d was not on the list received from Washington of divisions to train with the British and said: "I am rather hoping that this difficult question may not after all be going to trouble us." His wistfulness would not have changed Pershing's mind, but Washington decided not to offend the British. The division would instead train with the more permissive French.[5]

On 2 June, a few weeks after these high-level discussions of its future, the division assembled at Hoboken for shipment overseas. According to the divisional interpreter, a French-speaking black captain, M. Virgil Boutte, when the black officers went aboard ship they were given berthing tickets marked X which assigned them to second-class cabins and mess. The division boarded, however, and its various units arrived at French ports before the end of the month.[6]

At Brest, arrangements had been made for the white officers of the Headquarters Company to be billeted at a local hotel and the black officers at an unfinished barracks lacking beds.[7] Captain Boutte's diary tells the story that the white officers, unwilling to be accompanied by their black interpreter, went to the hotel by themselves but could not communicate and were turned away; Boutte then took the black officers of the company to the hotel and procured for them the rooms set aside for the white officers.[8]

The infantry regiments training with the French had fewer problems than the artillery regiments. These arrived in France with virtually untrained officers whom they scarcely knew. Much of their equipment was late in coming, and the men badly needed it to acquire experience in firing shells, which had been forbidden them stateside. The 167th F.A. Brigade was provided with only one horse for every ten it needed, and only 36 trucks instead of 200.[9] The 349th F.A. Regiment, part of that brigade, never had more than half the number of mounts it needed. Fire-control equipment was provided for training, but the brigade when it moved on had to leave that behind for the next comers.[10] A month or more after landing, the 351st F.A. Regiment had never yet fired its howitzers. The 349th and 350th had the severe handicap of officers who had not yet finished artillery school at Fort Sill when they were summoned to sail with their men; some of them continued their course at a school in France, but the colonel of the brigade said the artillery could not be ready for combat until some time after all its equipment arrived—which, as matters turned out, was not until after the Armistice.[11] This summary of artillery problems is particularly interesting in the light of the artillerymen's later performance in battle.

It has been mentioned that a study of the black 92d Division, in which the white 35th Division was used for purposes of comparison, was made for the Army War College. Col. A. A. Starbird of the Inspector General's Office made the study. Starbird pointed out that, although the two divisions were similar in length of training (fifty-seven days for the 92d, sixty-six days for the 35th) they were basically different in that the 92d was a draft organization with no previous training as a unit, whereas the 35th was a National Guard division whose initial strength "consisted of previously organized units from the same locality, partially trained as such, under their own officers and noncommissioned officers. . . ."[12] This was truly a radical difference, particularly since the 92d trained under seven different and unfamiliar commanders, with whom General Ballou had no communication except by dispatch or telephone.

The Starbird study made these other telling points: the 92d, like other black units, was limited to Northern camps where training was hampered by cold weather, while the 35th trained in Oklahoma where the climate permitted outdoor drill all winter; units of the 92d differed each from the other in equipment and clothing, according to what their commanders and the local base authorities wished to and were able to supply; the commanding general of the 35th Division toured the front five months before his men sailed and so was able to make realistic modifications in their training program, whereas Ballou never saw embattled France until he landed with his troops. Colonel Starbird concluded his report on the stateside conditions of the 92d with this statement: "Summarizing all conditions we find that although a certain amount of discipline was instilled in the division, *only rudimentary training was given in the United States,* by reason of a) the unfavorable type of the bulk of the personnel, b) low strength, c) fluxuations [*sic*] in strength, d) large number of recruits received just prior to embarkation, e) lack of proper equipment, f) impossibility of central control, g) adverse climatic conditions, h) shortness of the training period." [13] The War College's comparative study followed the two divisions to France. There, the black division had nine days less training than the 35th. The report noted: "From the viewpoint of this study, it is held that the preparatory training in France of these two divisions, being entirely too brief under the circumstances, could have accomplished little more than to emphasize the deficiencies in their basic training, particularly in that of the 92d Division." [14]

General Pershing was not satisfied with the progress of the 92d during training in France, but for reasons different from Starbird's. He held responsible the "lower capacity" and lack of education among blacks, and the "superficial" training of the black officers. "It would have been much wiser," he later wrote, "to have followed the long experience of our Regular Army and provided these colored units with selected white officers." [15]

It would have been wiser still to give the black officers a chance to complete their training on arrival in France, but that was not provided. The 317th Engineers, an outstanding example of lack of training, spent their first week in France not learning engineering but doing manual labor: building a pier at St. Nazaire, constructing barracks, and heaving baggage. In July, the 317th went to a training base at Bourbonne-les-Bains for what was to be four weeks of "intensive" training, but instructors and needed equipment were slow in arriving—by August, 30 percent of the necessary items were still lacking—so again they put in part of the precious training time in constructing facilities which would be useful to later (white) trainees. Such S.O.S. duties gave the black officers no opportunity to learn or practice engineering skills, but when they (for that reason, most likely) appeared incompetent their incompetence was laid to their color, and divisional headquarters kept trying to have them replaced by white engineering officers.[16]

Although training was sketchy, the 92d at the beginning of its stay in France did enjoy a marked degree of social freedom, more than was ever permitted the 93d. The men were allowed to go to nearby towns in their free time, to visit with local people, even to have a drink of wine or beer, although hard liquor was forbidden. At camp there was an occasional vaudeville show or ball game.[17] But the off-base freedoms were soon curtailed. In the 367th Regiment, the men were ordered to stay out of French homes under penalty of twenty-four hours on bread-and-water followed by an eighteen-mile hike with full pack.[18] On the Fourth of July some men of the division and a number of the local people celebrated Independence Day in the town square. A white officer took this unsuitable occasion to instruct troops and citizens in American *mores* concerning blacks. The soldiers were told they must treat French women as they would treat white American women—which meant, of course, that all contact was prohibited. The French were informed that blacks were inferior to whites, and that in the States they were therefore not permitted to ride in the same railway cars with whites or to live in white neighborhoods.[19] The same sort of lecture was read in other places where parts of the division were stationed, which was not surprising because General Ballou feared that social equality, "the dominant idea with many," would cause thousands of blacks to be "very much set up by this new and agreeable condition."[20] One would have expected more fairness from Ballou; possibly he was afraid that a push for equality would antagonize white officers in the division, or, possibly, he himself could not stomach the idea of social equality.

White officers saw to it that black officers got no encouragement in such subversive ideas as equality. There was the usual mess segregation; in one instance black officers had to eat outside the mess hall in a part of the yard set aside for that purpose.

As a matter of course, white officers appropriated the most desirable railway facilities, and black officers were sometimes assigned to boxcars. It was reported that Captain Boutte, the interpreter, who was a graduate of Fisk and Illinois universities and a member of the Tennessee National Guard, was singled out for special discrimination. Because of his proficiency in French he was for a time billeting officer at Bourbonne-les-Bains, but the contact he necessarily had with French people in doing his job could not be tolerated by the white officers. He was returned to his machine-gun battalion, the 350th, and was placed under arrest on charges of twenty-three violations. At a hearing before an efficiency board Boutte was cleared of most of the charges; the battalion commander was shown to have acted from prejudice and was relieved.[21] This is a most unusually happy ending, and, if the report is accurate, the verdict was probably more a tribute to Captain Boutte's talents as an interpreter than to the quality of justice meted out by efficiency boards.

What lay behind most army fears of black pretensions to equality—what is so easily gleaned from the Marvin report and Linard's "Secret Instructions"—was the neurotic terror of sex relations between black men and white women. What lay behind that terror, and whether it was real or trumped up to conceal a determination to keep the black man down, are matters for psychologists to investigate. But, for whatever reasons, black "unbridled sexuality" and black men's "lust for white women" were themes much played on by white army officers, and they produced some of the most vicious examples of discrimination.

The promulgation of orders like the following gave the impression that every black man was a potential rapist: "On account of the increasing frequency of the crime of rape, or attempted rape, in this Division, drastic preventive measures have become necessary. . . . Until further notice, there will be a check of all troops of the 92d Division every hour daily between reveille and 11:00 p.m., with a written record showing how each check was made, by whom, and the result. . . . The one mile limit regulation will be strictly enforced at all times, and no passes will be issued except to men of known reliability."[22] The day after this order was issued the men were told that Pershing would send the 92d back to the States or use it for labor "if efforts to prevent rape were not taken more seriously." [23]

The implication that rape was an everyday affair in the division was strengthened by the advice of Ballou to his black officers that they had nothing to gain by shielding men guilty of rape. He said, it is reported: "The real service would be in showing the world that the colored man had the same abhorrence of this detestable crime as the white man had, and that he could be depended upon to do justice in accordance with the accepted standards of our country." [24] Ballou could have performed the most valuable service by investigating and publishing the true facts about the incidence of rape in his division. They bear careful examination.

The first suspicious circumstance is that figures on rape vary from one army report to another. General Bullard in the late summer of 1918 reported that there had been fifteen cases of rape in the division. Colonel Greer wrote Senator McKellar of Tennessee that there had been thirty rapes, and he implied that all thirty rapists were in the 92d and that all thirty rapes had been committed in France, whereas actually eighteen of them had occurred in the States and had not in any way involved the 92d. [25]

The most accurate reports available show that ten men of the 92d were actually arrested and tried for rape or assault with intent to rape. From the evidence, it was judged in five cases that there had been assault with intent to rape, and in one case that rape had been committed. This is the only case in which a member of the division was convicted of rape during all of six months' service in France. [26]

All those rapes that were talked of but never proved were attributed by Ballou and others to the inability of black officers to control their men. Greer informed McKellar: "In these organizations where we have white company officers, namely the artillery and engineers, we have only one case of rape. The undoubted truth is that the colored officers neither control nor care to control the men. They themselves have been engaged largely in the pursuit of French women, it being their first opportunity to meet white women who did not treat them as servants." [27] Greer was right in at least one respect. His "one case of rape" was the only conviction for rape in the division, and it had indeed been committed by a man from a unit commanded by white company officers, not black officers.

In late August 1918, such matters suddenly dwindled in importance because the 92d began moving up to the front. In the St. Dié sector, not far from the German border, they were to join French troops and learn at firsthand from these experienced men what the war was all about. Then, as the French pulled out of the sector, the 92d would take it over.

But units of the division were delayed for various reasons on the way, and some men arrived only hours before the French withdrawal. Also, a German counterattack was in progress as the black troops occupied the trenches, so they were immediately baptized by bombardment and gas attack. The Germans were attacking the town of Frapelle, and the 317th Engineers were at once set to work extending the trench system so as to bring Frapelle within the Allied lines. On 31 August the black infantrymen beat back the Germans at Frapelle, and the following day they repulsed an assault on the lines near Ormont.[28] General Barnum of the 183d Infantry Brigade said that the "conduct of the officers and men were [sic] so gratifying to me . . . that I intended to express to them my appreciation of their fine conduct." [29] A word of appreciation might have made a big difference, so it is unfortunate that Barnum did not carry out his intentions until after the Armistice.

In the St. Dié sector the men of the 92d carried out an average of thirteen patrols a day, and by 19 September when they were relieved they had repulsed eleven enemy raids. Casualties occurred almost daily, but not in great numbers. Lt. Aaron Fisher and seven men of Company E, 366th Infantry, earned the DSC for repulsing an enemy raid on the night of 4 September. But the assistant divisional chief of staff was not satisfied with the results of their patrols, and he also complained that the men in the trenches were firing on their own patrol parties. With those raw troops, such mistakes probably did occur.[30]

It was at this time, as the 92d was suffering its first casualties and becoming acquainted with the wretchedness of trench warfare, that the War College, by a new table of organization, established that the 92d should have 373 white officers and 684 black officers. The proportion of black to white officers seems promising, but the table restricted so many officer positions to whites only that there was almost no chance for black promotions. Specifically reserved for whites were: divisional headquarters staff, aides to brigade commanders, captains in the field artillery and engineering regiments, adjutants, supply officers, commanders of headquarters companies, officers of train headquarters and supply officers in trains, and the adjutant of the ammunition train. The War College plan concluded thus: "The War College Division strongly recommends that no reduction from this table be made in the number of white officers assigned to this division, as this is considered the minimum with which any degree of efficiency can be reached." [31] What the plan insured without saying so was that no black officer could rise above the rank of captain regardless of ability or performance, and not many even to captain because about half the captains' positions were designated as white. Yet when Emmett Scott, Secretary Baker's adviser on black affairs, protested against this barrier to promotion of black officers, military officials assured him: "There appears to be no grounds [*sic*] for complaint that the colored soldier is not given opportunity for advancement in the ranks of our Army." [32]

The War College plan did say that capable black personnel should be recommended for promotion, even though such promotion would make them eligible for white officer positions. But this was a logical absurdity, and there is striking evidence that such promotions did not occur even when the recommendation was made by the divisional commander. General Ballou had a black officer, Lt. T. T. Thomson, for his acting divisional personnel officer. Thomson proving competent, Ballou requested that his position be made permanent rather than acting, and that he be promoted to the rank of captain which the job called for. This request "was disapproved by the War Department on the ground that the personnel officer should be white." [33] When Thomson appealed to Emmett Scott, Scott explained to him: "The Adjutant General took the position that you have not been discriminated against because under the reorganization of the 92d Division it was specified that the Divisional Personnel

Officer was to be white and that the recommendation made on April 30, 1918 for your appointment as Divisional Personnel Officer was in direct violation of the order which had been issued and it was for this reason that the recommendation was filed without action." [34]

That Secretary of War Baker did not fully concur in the army efforts to keep the black officer down is plainly shown in this communication from Col. P. D. Lochridge of the General Staff to his chief of staff: "The War College Division is of the opinion that colored officers should be limited to the grade of first and second lieutenants, as it is not believed that a sufficient number of colored men can be obtained capable of commanding companies. It is understood, however, that a number of these men have already been commissioned as captains and that it is the desire of the Secretary of War to utilize them in that grade. The organization of the division, called for by the Chief of Staff, has, therefore, been made on this basis." [35] This memo of Lochridge's, dated 20 October 1918, explains the elaborate specifications of white-only positions in the officer ranks of the 92d. It was simply another way of limiting black officers to "the grade of first and second lieutenants" without saying so and thus irritating the secretary of war, who considered himself a fair man and who, in addition, as a member of the President's Cabinet, had to take into account the political effects of alienating the black community.

There were still other handicaps for the black officer of the 92d Division who hoped to advance or even stay where he was. Pershing's policy of transferring 93d Division black officers— especially those of higher grades—to the 92d filled all vacant positions to which 92d Division officers might have aspired. Furthermore, the table of organization not only specified white-only jobs but also warned that "colored officers who are incompetent will not be retained, nor will their own estimate of their fitness be accepted." [36] It contained no such statement about incompetent white officers, although Ballou complained that he had some. As a result of these mountainous obstacles to black promotions, few recommendations for promotions of black officers were made until after the Armistice, when promotions were halted and so none of the recommendations had to be acted upon. The division, which had started out with 82 percent black officers, ended the war with only 58 percent.[37]

The effect on officer morale of the table of organization, issued while the 92d was in the trenches at St. Dié, must have been devastating; and in a few days the division would move up into the great battle of the Argonne, where morale would be of vital importance. So would the troops' trust in their officers be vital—but none of the military who complained that black men did not trust black officers ever took into account the fact that no white man in the army trusted them. The table of organization made it very plain that they were second-class citizens.

German propaganda played on this theme of second-class citizenship in cleverly worded leaflets dropped into the black lines:

Hello, boys, what are you doing over here? Fighting the Germans? Why? Have they ever done you any harm? Of course some white folks and the lying English-American papers told you that the Germans ought to be wiped out for the sake of humanity and Democracy. What is Democracy? Personal freedom; all citizens enjoying the same rights socially and before the law. Do you enjoy the same rights as the white people do in America, the land of freedom and Democracy, or are you not rather treated over there as second class citizens?

Can you get into a restaurant where white people dine? Can you get a seat in a theatre where white people sit? Can you get a seat or berth in a railroad car, or can you even ride in the South in the same street car with the white people?

And how about the law? Is lynching and the most horrible crimes connected therewith, a lawful proceeding in a Democratic country? Now all this is entirely different in Germany, where they do like colored people; where they treat them as gentlemen and as white men, and quite a number of colored people have fine positions in business in Berlin and other German cities. Why, then, fight the Germans only for the benefit of the Wall Street robbers, and to protect the millions that they have loaned to the English, French, and Italians.

You have been made the tool of the egoistic and rapacious rich in America, and there is nothing in the whole game for you but broken bones, horrible wounds, spoiled health, or death. No satisfaction whatever will you get out of this unjust war. You have never seen Germany, so you are fools if you allow people to make you hate us. Come over and see for yourself. Let those do the fighting who make the profit out of this war. Don't allow them to use you as cannon fodder.

To carry a gun in this service is not an honor, but a shame. Throw it away and come over to the German lines. You will find friends who will help you. [38]

Black men and officers of the 92d surely needed friends. But, amazingly enough, there seems to have been no significant number of desertions.

In mid-September the division moved hurriedly out of the St. Dié sector to take its position for the big American push in the Argonne. So quickly were they rushed toward the new front that they had no opportunity to rest or even take a bath. Maj. Warner Ross of the 365th Infantry Regiment, whose exceptionally sympathetic reminiscences in *My Colored Battalion* supply much information on the fall offensive, described the difficult night journey through mud and the confused traffic of a moving army; he had to produce testimony from routing officers to convince his superiors that his men accomplished the advance without straggling. [39]

Pershing's battle plan had one small flaw that determined the fate of the 92d Division. As the French and American armies advanced, their lines of attack would diverge slightly, eventually creating a gap of about 800 meters between the 77th American Division and the nearest unit of the French 4th Army. When it was realized that this gap would occur, a special brigade called the Groupement Durand (or sometimes the Groupement Rive Droite) was hastily created to fill it. Field Order No. 12 made it the responsibility of each unit in the two armies to maintain contact with the troops on its left. [40]

The Groupement Durand consisted of a dismounted French cavalry regiment and the 368th Infantry Regiment of the 92d Division. It is difficult to understand why any part of the 92d was chosen for this assignment, because the division's experience to that time had been limited to patrols. It is also difficult to understand why the 368th Regiment was picked, while the other regiments of the division were held in reserve positions for the first five days of the attack. The first tired units of the 368th arrived in the Argonne only two days before the assault began, and other units only hours before; the officers had no chance to familiarize themselves with the terrain. The men were exhausted and hungry; two black officers had got lost trying to reach their station, and their men had had no food for two days. Some of the men had traveled more than 100 miles in pouring rain on open flatcars, which crept along through the congestion of an army massing for attack. Perhaps it was assumed that these troops would do no fighting; or perhaps, as DuBois had bluntly put it, the division was meant to fail.

Whether the regiment would be called upon to fight or passively to fill the gap between units to the left and right, it was assigned an important role in the battle. According to Field Order No. 12, the 368th was held responsible for liaison with the 11th Cuirassiers on its left; the 77th was to maintain liaison with the 368th on its left. In the wooded and broken ground of the Argonne, and in the confusion of a gigantic battle, keeping contact and being where contact could be maintained was a grave and difficult task. Let it be said at once that the Groupement Durand failed. And the failure, for at least thirty years to come, would be pointed to as proof of the inadequacy of black soldiers and black officers and would prevent their rise in the army. Here, in summary, is what happened.[41]

The 368th moved into the trenches the night of 25 September and took its place in the gap the following morning when the attack began. However, the men were not supplied with the heavy-duty wire cutters necessary to cut through the extremely thick entanglements ahead of them, so they could advance only along the trench system or through weak spots in the wire. Being unable to cut their way as needed restricted lateral communication, which was essential for maintaining liaison. The regiment also lacked such necessaries as signal flares and grenade launchers, some of which they did not get until the fifth day of the battle. Perhaps the worst handicap was that for days they did not have their own artillery to support them, because the artillery regiments of the 92d had been detached and assigned to other divisions; French artillery was to support the 368th, but it did not always answer the plea for a barrage. The officers had the special problem—almost incredible except for convincing testimony in military records—that they had not been supplied with maps nor assigned specific objectives.[42]

On the first day of the offensive the 368th advanced as best it could in solitary companies or even platoons, the lack of wire-cutters preventing a mass movement. There was immediate and total breakdown of communications between units, and no liaison was ever established. The regiment got its share of German shells and machine-gun fire with no support from the French artillery. The confusion was appalling during the first day and night. Companies and platoons were ordered ahead or back without plan according to individual circumstances, often losing their way, fighting the barbed wire without proper tools. At one point units were ordered to pull back in anticipation of a friendly barrage which was never delivered.[43] During the night, orders to retreat were conveyed verbally to one company commander; he reported that he had sent a runner to battalion headquarters to confirm the order but that his query had not been answered because "the Battalion Commander had gone to bed, for the night." [44] Some isolated units stayed at the front through the first night.

On the second day, 27 September, units that had withdrawn went forward again, under the same handicaps as the day before and with just as much confusion. Somehow, by that night, elements of the regiment had taken the town of Binarville.[45]

On the 28th the regiment continued the attack, still without the ability to cut through wire entanglements and without artillery support despite repeated calls for a barrage. Confusion probably reached a peak that day. A battalion commander ordered a withdrawal without specifying where the new line was to be drawn. Enemy artillery fire was heavier than it had been; one company was subjected to a five-hour barrage. Machine-gun nests and snipers, bypassed in the advance, now harried from the rear. Some companies retreated to the support trenches after an advance of two and a half kilometers; there they were re-formed, pushed forward again for three kilometers, and once more broke and retreated. Other troops dug in for the night at the furthest point of advance.[46]

On the 29th and 30th communications were no better. One

battalion, however, managed to advance six miles beyond Binarville as the French successes in the Champagne forced the Germans to pull back out of the forest. The advance battalion found fewer obstructions as they penetrated farther behind the German lines, and so there was less confusion and the battalion units were able to maintain fair liaison with each other, although they were often out of contact with regimental headquarters now so far behind them. [47]

The 368th was finally relieved on 30 September, after five days in battle. Its casualties in the Argonne were 42 killed in action and 16 who died of their wounds; and more than 200 wounded. By the time the regiment rejoined the rest of the division everyone knew of its failure. In fact, the entire division was being called a failure, although the other three regiments, held in reserve, had not been exposed to the chaos of those first five days and altogether had only 38 men killed and wounded. [48] The reserve regiments expected now to be sent into battle, but instead, on 5 October, the entire division was ordered out of the Argonne. [49]

The battle narrative shows beyond question that, for however sufficient reasons, [50] the 368th failed in its responsibility as a liaison unit. But the vitriolic, often hysterical attacks on the black troops and their officers which followed went far beyond the shortcomings of that regiment, and comparison with the performance of and comments on white regiments shows unmistakably that the bitterness of the criticism was inspired more by the regiment's color than by its failure. Even Ballou lost all objectivity and fairness.

In describing the work of three white divisions in the Argonne offensive, a contemporaneous history of the AEF said: "Under the galling fire from the Germans, reinforced in their line of resistance, the forward units of these three divisions had retreated. Some sort of battle line was formed, but the morale of these troops was too badly shattered to permit reorganization on the field." [51] Those divisions had to be replaced. Similarly, on 29 September elements of the 35th Division broke badly. The same AEF history explained the reasons: this was the 35th Division's first battle; liaison and headquarters organization proved inefficient; food and supplies were delivered with great difficulty; so morale disintegrated, and when the lead elements began to retreat, the entire division fell back three kilometers before a line was reestablished.[52]

The matter-of-fact and exculpatory comments on white divisions that broke under fire are in marked contrast to the abuse heaped by military officials on the 92d. The comments on the 35th are especially interesting, because that was the division chosen as a control group for the War College's comparative study of the 92d. But the War College study makes no mention of the cracking-up of the 35th Division. The crumbling of morale in the 35th was not cited by any official or historian as proof that white soldiers were unable to withstand the strains of modern warfare and that white officers were unsuited for leadership, but that is precisely the construction put upon the breakdown of the 368th Regiment—to be exact, of its 2d Battalion only, the lead battalion in the attack.

Yet General Bullard labeled the entire division a failure.[53] Colonel Greer is reported as saying: "They failed in all their missions, laid down and sneaked to the rear, until they were withdrawn." [54] Gen. Hunter Liggett in his history of the AEF wrote: "This regiment twice ran away under shell fire in this battle." [55] News of the failure of black troops spread so quickly that, on 2 October, one week after the beginning of the Argonne offensive, an officer in a white division wrote in his diary that "the 92d (midnight) Division has been tried in the line and they didn't stick—labor for them hereafter." [56] Col. Fred Brown, commanding officer of the 368th, made a long if not objective investigation of the charges of cowardice and incompetence and reported the results in a paper entitled "The Inefficiency of Negro Officers." Brown concluded that all the derogatory rumors and reports were true. Two battalions disintegrated without reason, he reported, and failed to advance when ordered to do so. They fled back to the regimental command post, he said, and added: "I personally stopped the entire mob and put them in trenches near my P.C. [Command Post]. No colored officer or non-commissioned officer exercised any command at the time and could not be distinguished from the enlisted men. I wish to go on record as expressing my opinion that colored officers as a class are unfit to command troops in present day warfare." [57] This tribute to Colonel Brown's bravery occurs nowhere but in his report; similarly unique is his further statement that he went forward with headquarters' personnel (white, by the table of organization), outstripping the advance of any of the combat companies and taking prisoners and machine guns.[58] Maj. J. N. Merrill, commanding the 1st Battalion, claimed that "not a single officer of the battalion has shown any anxiety to get to close quarters with the Germans."

Merrill went on to say that the colored troops had no real interest in the war and fought only if they had a high percentage of white blood. He pronounced them "rank cowards." [59] But racial theorizing seemed to be a hobby with Merrill. In his subsequent request for transfer from the 368th, he explained: "It is a well known fact to anthropologists that the measurements of the cranial capacities and facial angles of the negroes, as depicted on some thousands of years old drawings of the Egyptian monuments are identical with those of the measurements verified upon the present day American negroes. Also, it is the expressed opinion of experts that the Negro race, as to cranial capacities and anilities has reached a state that will not improve and cannot improve." [60]

Maj. B. F. Norris of the 3d Battalion also described his men as cowards. But a black officer testified that Norris hid in a ditch during the attack, and that he even admitted later that he had. Another said Norris deserted his men under fire and returned to his command post. There was substantial evidence that Norris gave his battalion no instructions during the attack. One of his captains said Norris ordered a withdrawal but did not intend his men to go back as far as they did; that he made no attempt to straighten his lines and never left the command post during the entire day. Norris, in testifying at the later court-martial of one of his black officers, said his men had fled from the front, but at various points in his testimony he estimated the number who had fled as 300, 200, and between 30 and 50. At another court-martial he was equally confused as to whether he had or had not ordered a halt pending an artillery barrage. One black officer of the battalion, testifying at his own court-martial, said that none of his messages to battalion headquarters had been answered.[61]

Had the men received instructions from white officers or had they not, and had they fled or had they been ordered back—these were the central questions. Before courts-martial or efficiency boards had examined the evidence, Ballou was ready to blame the black officers, and he recommended the removal from command of about twenty of them without further delay. He wrote in his recommendation for removal that examination by courts or boards would gain nothing anyway, "due to the fact that nearly all of the colored officers of the battalions concerned are tarred with the same brush and unblushingly testify to the bravery and efficiency of officers that they *know* turned tail and led their men in flight." [62] In time a number of the officers were tried by courts-martial. Five were found guilty of cowardice and sentenced to death, but they were later exonerated by a War Department investigation, led by Secretary Baker, which attributed the failure of the regiment to lack of experience and equipment and added, tellingly, that there was "strongly supported evidence that withdrawal orders were carried to the front by runners," [63] just as the black officers had claimed.

Withdrawal on orders or terrified rout? The answer would clear or cloud the reputation of all black soldiers and officers. In the story of the 2d Battalion, which led the attack, and its commander Maj. Max Elser, there is some pretty dramatic evidence which seems to clear them. Major Elser in his own report on the battle wrote: "In attempting to advance my Battalion P.C. on the morning of the 26th to a position in rear of Companies 'G' and 'F' I was unable to get liaison with my advanced post, or Company 'H' laterally on account of wire and other obstacles." [64] So far as lack of liaison goes, all participants were in agreement. But Major Elser might have added one more fact, that he got lost and could not contact regimental headquarters either. With Elser missing, Major Norris of the 3d Battalion appointed Maj. Junius W. Jones to temporary command of the 2d Battalion. That happened just after noon on the first day of the battle. At eight that evening regimental commander Colonel Brown (from whose report this information is drawn), noted that Elser had withdrawn two companies but did not know where the others were. The colonel added in his report that Elser had meant to withdraw only part-way back, but that the men "did not remain at the point stated but continued withdrawal until within our own lines." [65] In Elser's own statement there is an element of contradiction about what he had meant to do: "As it was almost dark by this time, and having no liaison with any other units, I decided to withdraw until I could get in touch with the Commanding Officer, 368th Infantry. . . . There was much confusion owing to the masses of wire we had to contend with in the dark, before companies reached the French trenches. . . ." [66] Noncoms of the battalion fully agreed about the confusion. But as to the damning and often repeated charge that the men fled in panic, Elser refutes it by his own "*I decided to withdraw.*" He would surely have sent runners to try to convey this order to the units with which he had lost contact, unless he himself was fleeing in panic.

Major Elser's testimony reveals other flaws in his leadership, but nothing could shake the general assumption that it was the black officers who had failed. Elser admitted, for instance, that he had moved his command post without informing his company commanders. [67] And it is clear from the messages sent from and received at his battalion headquarters that Elser never knew what happened to his men once they moved forward. Elser charged the men with faking and being "yellow and afraid of death" [68] when more than forty of them were reported as gas casualties; but the indications are that he himself did not move toward the front until he thought that advance units had cleared away many of the obstructions, and that then he got lost and finally withdrew. Not exactly courting death, one would judge.

Colonel Brown noted that Elser had withdrawn with his men the night of 26 September and that this "was not in accordance with orders." [69] Elser admitted this and, at the time, took full responsibility for the failure of the attack. Messages from the 2d Battalion liaison officer show that Elser was absent from his post at least four hours on the 26th. [70] Such strange conduct increases the credibility of the statement of one black officer that Elser became hysterical, that he "placed his hands to his face and cried out to his personal runners to take him out of there, that he could not stand it. As a result he was in a hospital for a period of three weeks and would have been court-martialled but for the intercession of his influential friends. . . ." [71] Colonel

Brown could not have been aware of Elser's condition during the first days of battle because on 28 September he ordered the major to make a reconnaissance of the front. Elser said he could not remember ever having received such an order.[72] But something—perhaps the way he received the order—must then and there have alerted the colonel to Elser's breakdown because on the same day Brown relieved Elser from command of the battalion. Colonel Brown said he was motivated to do this by Elser's "physical exhaustion"; black officers said it was a clear case of battle fatigue.[73] A black doctor reported that Elser was treated at the 365th Infantry hospital for psychoneurosis, and that the white commander of the hospital then sent him elsewhere for further treatment.[74] Finally, there is Elser's own statement that he was a mental and physical wreck, although he attributed it to his efforts to reorganize and push his men forward.[75] There is no evidence that he made such efforts.

Of all the ironies that pepper the history of black troops in the First World War, this is the sharpest: that because of the weakness of a white officer, a weakness which for the sake of white supremacy had to be covered up, black soldiers and officers were made scapegoats, their reputation for character and ability so injured in the cover-up process that it has not yet completely healed.

The war went on for the 92d, but after the Argonne they could do no right. In the Marbache sector where they arrived on 8 October, they spent a month in patrol activity. By 8 November, 462 men had been killed or wounded, 383 in the 365th Regiment alone—but none of the higher-ranking officers was satisfied. Colonel Greer said patrol officers were "unreliable and worthless," [76] and that they returned from unfulfilled missions with whatever trumped-up stories suited their purposes. Black officers were frequently charged with not carrying out their patrols aggressively, on the ground that they did not bring back enough prisoners.[77]

Capt. Napoleon Marshall gives us some clues to why patrols may have been less than satisfactory. A recent transfer from the 369th, Marshall had had no training for patrol missions, he was not supplied with needed grenades and wire cutters, he was given only fifteen minutes to prepare to lead a raid, and he was given no clear briefing as to objectives. But Marshall took his men out, and after they had penetrated the enemy lines they were hit by a barrage. Lacking wire cutters, they had great difficulty making their way back to their own lines, but Marshall managed to get them back although he was wounded. Such a patrol would have been called—indeed was—a failure. But it does not appear that all the fault lay with Marshall and his men.[78]

Patrols and the prisoners they brought in were so important that Ballou in early November announced that patrols would be accepted as demonstrations of fitness in black officers brought up before efficiency boards.[79] On application, black officers would be given a chance of carrying out these missions—to prove courage and efficiency that had really never been reliably impugned.

Meanwhile stories were circulating among the black troops about discrimination against their comrades who had been wounded in the Argonne, which could not have inspired the patrols with an aggressive spirit. Reports came from both white and black officers that wounded black officers were not permitted to sit or lie on stretchers; that a soldier wounded in both legs had his shoes forced back on and was made to walk to an ambulance; that another soldier with hip wounds was told by the surgeon: "If I catch you lying down, I will throw you in the mud."[80]

One of the worst misfortunes black soldiers suffered was that General Bullard, newly promoted commander of the 2d Army (split off from Pershing's 1st Army) acquired the 92d Division as part of his command. On 1 November the general wrote in his diary: "The Negro Division seems in a fair way to be a failure. It is in a quiet sector, yet can hardly take care of itself, while to take any offensive action seems wholly beyond its powers. I have been here now with it three weeks and have been unable to have it make a single raid upon the enemy. Their Negro officers have an inadequate idea of what is expected of soldiers, and their white officers are too few to leaven the lump."[81] He must have missed the leavening influence of Major Elser, who a little over a month before had been relieved of his command and was presumably under treatment for battle fatigue.

It seems, from less hostile reports, that in early November the division was carrying out its patrols with smoothness, aggressiveness, and efficiency, and was repulsing enemy patrols. Men of the 365th Infantry and the 350th Machine Gun Battalion were decorated for bravery in a patrol action. The 366th beat back a German attack on a strategic bridge. At last the division won some sort of recognition from Colonel Greer, who noted that the 92d had taken control of the sector from the Germans, and that with efficient artillery support from the 349th F.A., which had just been returned to the division, "there will be no let up in the hammering of the enemy wherever found." [82] It is interesting to recall that the draftees who formed the 366th Infantry Regiment, when they had arrived at training camp fresh from the mines of Alabama, had been described as "the worst looking lot that ever reported to any of the camps."

Patrol actions had given the division a breather between the Argonne and what was to be the last Allied push, scheduled for 10 November, with the American army to advance as far as possible toward Metz. The units of the 92d Division straddled the Moselle River, the 365th and 366th on the east bank, and the 367th on the west. The disgraced 368th was held in reserve, the battle plan calling for it to be thrown in on whichever side of the river it was needed. But the trouble was that the Moselle bridges in the immediate area had all been destroyed, and it would have been necessary to station the 368th at a bridge so far behind the fighting that it could be of little use. The command posts also were too far behind the front for the liaison necessary in battle. Major Ross, who commanded a battalion of the 365th, said: "Prospective casualties for us seemed not to concern those of my superiors and their assistants who laid down the general outline for this affair and for several previous affairs." [83]

The attack began on schedule. Again the wire was impervious to any but the heaviest cutters; Ross reported that at Bois Fréhaut, which his black troops managed to take, the wire had one-and-one-half-inch barbs spaced less than an inch apart. The black troops fought their way forward that night despite heavy German counterattacks and artillery fire. Major Ross was more than satisfied with the behavior of his men and officers. The 366th advanced but was pushed back by heavy fire. In the

367th, Maj. Charles Appleton's 1st Battalion was sent in to help the 7th Division (white), whose attack had failed, and the French 56th Infantry, which was pinned down by heavy fire. Through the force of an assault by the black troops on the enemy flank, the French were able to withdraw and reform; for this, Major Appleton's battalion was awarded a unit croix de guerre. The Buffaloes had made good.[84]

News of the Armistice found the 367th and the 366th more than a kilometer in advance of their position of the day before, when the attack had begun; the 365th had pushed ahead about three kilometers. All had reached their objectives, but at the heavy cost of about 500 casualties. That brought the casualty figures of the division for the whole war to 1,700, which represented 1.5 percent of all American casualties.[85] The division represented roughly 2 percent of the combat troops of the AEF.

General Bullard never stopped berating the black division. On the day of the Armistice he wrote in his diary: "The poor 92d Negroes wasted time and dawdled where they did attack, and in some places where they should have attacked, never budged at all." The following day he added: "Two days ago and again yesterday the 92d Division would not fight; couldn't be made to attack in any effective sense. The general who commands them couldn't make them fight." [86] On objective appraisal, the 92d achieved more in the last two days of the war than any of the other divisions under Bullard's command. But the general was apparently blinded by his two hatreds, of blacks and of Ballou. Unable to deny the amount of ground taken by the division in the final assault, he found a way to denigrate it: "The 33rd Division—General George Bell—on the west, did well; the 28th Division, next, under General Hay, had some but no great success in the advance; the 7th Division, under General Wittenmeyer, had hard fighting but advanced some, perhaps half a kilometer; the 92d Division Negroes, under General Ballou, gained a good deal of ground but did the enemy little harm." [87]

Almost no one held a balanced opinion of the achievements of the 92d Division—everyone was partisan, for or against. Colonel Greer wrote to McKellar: "They have in fact been dangerous to no one except themselves and women." [88] He told the War

College that "it is an undoubted fact, shown by our experience in the war, and well known to all people familiar with negroes, that the average negro is naturally cowardly. . . ." [89] Black officers, as usual, came in for special abuse. Major Merrill told Ballou that black officers were worthless even as platoon commanders.[90] Lt. Col. R. P. Harbold reported to Pershing that a majority of the 368th's officers were cowards.[91] Greer said black officers did not care for the interests of the nation, but only for the advancement of their own race.[92] Col. George McMaster said that "the colored officer shows little capacity for leadership, aggression, or originality," and that therefore colored troops preferred to be led by whites.[93]

But there were white officers who respected and admired blacks, both troops and officers, and in general these were company and battalion commanders whose contacts with black soldiers were much closer than Greer's or Harbold's or McMaster's. Major Ross said of his battalion in the fight for Bois Fréhaut: "The officers and men showed great dash and spirit. Discipline was excellent and the battalion commanding officer was able to report that the officers and men not only destroyed, killed and ran out the occupants of M.G. emplacements on the ground and in the trees, but they advanced and held firmly under the most severe shelling of shrapnel, gas and high explosive shells of all caliber." [94] Ross boasted that in sixteen months' service not one officer of his battalion was put under arrest or called before an efficiency board; two who were court-martialed were acquitted.[95] Ross took every opportunity to express his admiration and respect for the black men he commanded: "I have heard of officers and of men and of units—large and small ones, white and also colored, that became panic stricken and useless under fire that was feeble and light both in intensity and duration compared to this, but I am ready to testify that twelve hundred fifty officers and men (colored) *did* advance and that the command did hold *without showing the faintest symptoms of panic or retreat.*" [96] Ross was embittered because, although he had recommended many of the battalion for decorations, not one was approved. "It is my opinion," he said, "that certain regular Army officers saw fit to head them off." [97]

Major Appleton was similarly proud of his battalion for the

work that earned it a unit croix de guerre. The black officers and noncoms of the field artillery won special praise. No general courts-martial were held and no efficiency boards sat in the artillery or ammunition train of the division, under command of General Sherburne. There, black lieutenants were promoted and noncoms elevated to fill the resulting vacancies. Even Pershing praised the artillery saying, "You men acted like veterans. . . ." [98] Praise in that service is particularly significant because of the initial opposition to black artillerymen, the often-expressed military opinion that black officers could never achieve competence in such a technical field, and the unpromising circumstances of the artillery when it landed in France without any of the necessary equipment.

As for the disgraced officers of the 368th, this statement by a contemporaneous historian of the unit is perhaps the most measured summing up of its disaster: "When the public realizes how meagre these men's training was—regulars, guardsmen, and national army—the cause for wonder will not be that there were so many officers relieved but that there were enough fit for this kind of combat to make the thing a success. If some troops retreated three kilometers in the face of a Prussian guard counter attack, if other troops got so disorganized in a rapid advance that they had to be taken to the rear to reform, the wonder is not that this happened but that it did not happen more. . . ." [99] A later historian, speaking of the performance of the 368th in the Argonne, expressed his findings with convincing moderation: "This action [the 368th in the Argonne] is the origin of the notorious reputation which the 92d Division soon acquired. Its later performance was not outstanding, but the evidence seems to confirm the impression that its poor reputation was largely based upon hearsay generalizations with but this one incident as a basis. . . ." [100]

General Ballou was reasonably fair in his overall assessment of the work of the 92d Division. He held the War Department responsible for assigning to it some incompetent officers, white as well as black. Also, he criticized the policy of restricting certain positions to whites, thus limiting black promotions; he thought his black officers had done fairly well, although, he said, their men had not at first trusted them, the men themselves being infected with the American belief in black inferiority. And obviously, Ballou put a great share of blame for what was wrong with the 92d on his superior, General Bullard, who, Ballou claimed, knew nothing of the facts about the black division "or else preferred to ignore them." [101]

Perhaps nothing the 92d did or did not do on the field of battle contributed so importantly to its reputation as did the lack of harmony between its commander and General Bullard. There is little doubt that Bullard was among those referred to in Ballou's statement that mistakes in the Argonne could have been corrected "had there not been too much eagerness to get the negroes out while the credit was *bad*, as many preferred it should remain." [102] If the Negroes' credit was bad, so was Ballou's as their commander; and there seems no doubt that Bullard meant to shred Ballou's credit to tatters, and get him S.O.S.'d.

Bullard chose to ignore certain statistics that did not fit his picture of the "poor negroes." Twenty-one members of the division had won the DSC, a greater number than in the 35th, 6th, 81st, or 88th divisions, and 1,700 had given their lives or their blood. But General Bullard chose to record only failure: "On their left, as liaison with the French, a battalion of the 92d, negro, division. Alas, it ran away twice; was removed on demand of the French, and later was sent home; but this fact was not generally known and as the 92d was the first division to land it was 'given a big hand' when it reached New York." [103] Bullard made mistakes even in this brief statement. First, no documentation was found of his claim that the French demanded the removal of the black troops. Furthermore, the 92d was not the first division to get home, nor even the first black division; it had been preceded by the 93d. Bullard's desire to tarnish Ballou and his black division taints the entire history of the 92d in France.

9. After the Armistice

Since time immemorial the Negro has never received treatment or consideration equal to that received by the white man, and *he never will, so there is no need to expect it.* You are unable to fight for yourself. You have never been victorious, but as long as you do right and *stay in your place,* I will fight for you.

Col. James F. Bell, commander of the 806th Pioneer Infantry, to his men, 19 February 1919.

THE Armistice of 11 November 1918 ended the fighting, but it was many months before the troops were sent home. After the cease-fire the 369th moved on through German territory, establishing military government in the towns it occupied; at last, on 10 December, it left the Rhine region to rejoin the American army in France. There AEF instructors gave the 369th a training program, which might at one time have been useful but which seemed superfluous to veterans of 191 days at the front. A musketry course had little appeal to men fresh from nine months of shooting at live targets, and: "What made it particularly galling was that this young officer had never been in combat, and the men resented being lectured by a desk jockey." [1] The reason for the training courses was not that they were useful, but simply to keep the black troops busy and out of trouble until they could be put aboard ship for home.

The 371st also moved into Germany, along with French occupation troops, but it was almost at once recalled to France. Its hurried recall was probably due in part to German propaganda, which, seeking to split the Allies over methods of occupation, aimed a blow at the American weak spot with stories of atrocities committed by black troops—especially with a film called *Honte Noire* ("Black Shame"), which showed faked scenes in which black soldiers were represented as bestial rapists.

West of the Moselle River, the 92d Division was assembled as a unit for the first time in its history. Labor, hikes, drill, and short marches filled the days, leaving no time for idle hands or feet to get into mischief. Colonel Greer saw to it that even on Sundays "the men will not be permitted to wander aimlessly around the country, but efforts will be made to have games, sports or other amusements." [2] Labor to which the combat veterans were assigned while they waited to go home included policing the camps and docks, doing construction work, serving as cooks and kitchen police, and coaling ships for their return to the States. It was during this waiting time that black soldiers and units were given the French decorations which they had merited. [3]

Black laborers in uniform—the S.O.S.—did not have as easy a time as the combat soldiers after the Armistice. There remained a massive amount of work to be done. Some was relatively light, such as feeding transients at St. Nazaire, or handling horses and mules at that port. But there were also heavy construction jobs, such as the huge Pershing Stadium near Paris, and the work of supplying wood to fuel the cookstoves and heating stoves of the camps as the winter set in. [4] Equipment and materials had to be salvaged from the battlefields, and an enormous amount of barbed wire, put up over a period of years, had to be cleared away in the French woods and fields. Trenches had to be filled in. Demolition crews were sent to remove unexploded shells, a dangerous job in which several men were injured. All the detritus of war had to be cleaned up in time for the French farmers to plant their fields again in the spring of 1919. [5]

It was all too literally true that those fields were fertilized with human blood; they contained the bodies and parts of bodies of many men killed in battle and buried where they fell. American cemeteries were to be constructed to hold the reclaimed American war dead. The largest of them was to be at Romagne, and would be called the Argonne National Cemetery. Over 6,000 black soldiers—pioneer infantrymen of the 813th, 815th, and 816th regiments—were sent to Romagne and detailed to Graves Registration for the worst job of all S.O.S. assignments: collecting all the bodies within a radius of fifty kilometers. Many of the bodies were in advanced stages of decomposition. Added to the gruesomeness of the reburial work and the desolation of the region, the troops assigned to Romagne had only the most primitive housing, totally without conveniences. Somehow, despite all the dreadfulness, these troops found and reburied at least 23,000 bodies.[6]

Military authorities and even some black leaders tried to reconcile the men of the pioneer infantry to their intolerable work by calling their assignment honored and their labor glorious. A spokesman said:

> What a wonderful sight to see those boys march up the hillsides bearing the crosses to the resting-places of the sacred dead! It reminds us of that other sacred scene in history when an African bore the cross of Christ up the little green hill far away.
> It was a privilege for me to shake the hands of these boys laden with the aroma of the dead. I said to them: "Boys, I am proud of you. You have done the most sacred task of the war. What others refused to do, you have done willingly and beautifully. I promise you that when I go back home I will speak to no audience that I do not tell them of what you have done. . . ."[7]

The black troops would gladly have exchanged their work for some less sacred job. They were not fooled. They knew they were ordered to do the dirtiest labor of the entire war, and they knew this was because they were black men. They were additionally bitter because the taboos attached to their work made them more than ever objects of segregation, discrimination, and humiliation. White soldiers, for instance, told French civilians near the post that the 813th P.I. had been assigned to reburial work because all the men were diseased. The black troops at Romagne grew so bitter and restless that the YMCA finally sent black women workers to the area, hoping that they would be able to improve the men's morale.[8]

The rewards for all the blood and sweat black troops left in France were few. They were not permitted to march in the great Allied victory parade in Paris, although the parade included black troops of both England and France. And in the huge war mural, *Le Panthéon de la Guerre*, in which were pictured those who had contributed to the final victory, black troops of all the Allies were represented, excepting only black Americans.[9] Yet these black soldiers had given not only labor and blood to the French cause, but compassion also. Moved by the plight of the many French children bereft by war, black servicemen before they went home had contributed 300,000 francs to the war-orphans' fund.[10] This was a large amount of money considering that black troops frequently had their pay withheld, for disciplinary reasons or for no reason at all. Pay for the entire 92d Division for the month of January 1919 was held back as punishment. The commander of the S.O.S. was authorized to hold up the pay of units sailing for home. The 371st Infantry got no pay after October 1918; two companies of the 372d got none after November. The pay of the 369th Infantry was stopped at the end of May 1918 except for Company C, which unaccountably received an extra month's pay.[11] Perhaps the height of pettiness in discrimination against black troops of the 369th was their exclusion from the special holiday rations issued to all other American soldiers on Thanksgiving and Christmas. Unit commanders in the division who wished to supply anything special for the holidays were obliged to buy it with company funds.[12]

At the heart of most of the post-Armistice restrictions put upon black soldiers was the fear of their mingling with French people, especially French women. M.P.'s were ruthless, on orders. When a member of the 369th at Brest had his head split open by an M.P.'s club, his protesting commander, Major Little, was told by a captain of the security forces that M.P.'s had been told "our 'Niggers' were feeling their oats a bit and that instructions had been given to 'take it out of them' quickly, just as soon as they arrived [at ports of embarkation] so as not to have any trouble later on." [13] Little also learned that enlisted M.P.'s had been told they need not treat the black commissioned personnel of the regiment as officers. Every black unit felt the tightening of the reins. The 806th P.I. was restricted to the main street of town; even the Y hut and the post office were off-limits. Almost endless examples of this sort could be cited.[14]

Another reason for restrictions on blacks, besides fear that they might have contact with French women, was uneasiness lest they become infected with a foreign, radical ideology which might lead them to demand equality when they got home. The United States Department of Justice had been busy gathering data on organizations and individuals suspected of disloyalty or subversion.[15] On the last day of January 1919, secret instructions were sent from AEF Headquarters to all American counterespionage agents and intelligence officers, warning them to watch for evidence that a secret radical organization existed among black officers: "Among the alleged avowed purposes of the organization, is protection of negro interests, collective combatting of any white effort, especially in the South, to reestablish white ascendency, the securing of equal intellectual and economic opportunity for negroes and the maintenance of the social equality between the races as established in France."[16] In addition, intelligence officers of the 92d Division were taking steps to uncover and counteract any "seditious influences" that might be lurking.[17] There was a flurry of excitement when it was learned, in January 1919, that the "radical" black leader DuBois was going to visit the 92d Division. Maj. F. P. Schoonmaker issued special instructions to all individual intelligence officers:

1. A man by name of *DuBois*, with visitor's pass, reported on his way to visit this Division. His presence at stations of any unit will be immediately reported in secret enclosures to Assistant Chief of Staff, G-2 [Major Schoonmaker], of these headquarters. Likewise prompt report will be made to G-2 of all his moves and actions while at stations of any unit.
2. The fact of this inquiry as to *DuBois* and his moves will not be disclosed to any person outside the Intelligence Service.[18]

A number of black soldiers and, by mistake, a French colonial soldier, were killed by M.P.'s. There were many rumors that others had died in illegal executions that were no better than lynchings. Sen. Tom Watson of Georgia presented to a Senate investigating committee the names of sixty-two men, many of them black, who had been executed without trial by order of military officials.[19] The army denied almost all charges. The former advocate general of the Expeditionary Forces insisted that American soldiers would not carry out execution orders "unless the victim had committed some heinous offense justifying the punishment of death in the minds of the soldiers composing the firing squad, for American soldiers are too humane and too intelligent to be made the tools for the wanton murder of their comrades."[20] The absurdities of this argument are shockingly apparent. No firing squad was authorized to determine whether or not the offense charged had been committed, or committed by the victim facing their guns; or whether the offense merited the death penalty. In the case of black soldiers, many a firing squad would have felt justified in shooting on the mere allegation that a black man had sat at a cafe table with a white woman. Finally, the advocate general's clinching absurdity was that these illegal executions could not have occurred because there was no record of them.[21]

When Senator Watson produced a photograph of a hanging at Gièvres, the advocate general had to admit that it had occurred, but he insisted this was the only hanging that had taken place there; it had occurred in June 1919, he said.[22] What was never explained or even questioned during the investigation was why, if the only execution at Gièvres had taken place in the month of June, and if the photograph in evidence showed that hanging, all the soldiers in the picture were wearing overcoats.

There was, in fact, convincing testimony that other hangings had taken place, even if they were not in the records. The Graves Registration Service, staffed by white personnel, testified that among the dead who had been reburied were men who bore the marks of hanging.[23] Sometimes the records showed executions that were denied by witnesses. Two army doctors said they knew of no hangings at the base where they were stationed from November 1918 to March 1919; the base was small enough, one of them said, that if anything of the sort had occurred they would have heard of it.[24] But there is a record of a hanging at that base on a date in January 1919, when both doctors were stationed there; furthermore, an officer testified that he had been in charge of the executions of two black soldiers at that base, and he added the convincing detail that one of them had been drugged before he mounted the gallows, to keep him quiet.[25]

From the superficiality of the Senate's investigation, and its decision on conflicting and inconclusive evidence that Senator Watson's charges were without foundation, one is inclined to suspect that the investigation was either so weak an exercise as to be pointless, or that it was perhaps run off as a convenient way to still complaints and whitewash the army. During the hearings, Senator Watson was instructed to summarize, rather than read, letters supporting his allegations; the letters would appear later in the printed report, he was told—but they did not. Furthermore, the summing up of the army's case, which aimed chiefly at discrediting the testimony of hostile witnesses, was inserted at the beginning of the report rather than, chronologically, at the end; so in the record, hostile testimony had doubt cast on it before it was presented.

At no time during their service was there a relaxation of discrimination against black soldiers. The historian of the 371st Infantry recalls the waiting time at Brest as a nightmare of anxiety. Would the regiment sail on schedule? Sailing priorities could be changed as punishment or at the whim of port authorities. Major Little of the 369th wrote that during the regiment's three weeks at Brest in January 1919, security officers found fault with the unit daily and threatened that it would be put at the bottom of the embarkation list. Rumors circulated about troops whose sailing was canceled after they were actually lined up on the docks, because of some trivial infraction of regulations. And, considering their experience in the army, black troops had good reason to fear their departure might be delayed simply because they were black. In fact, sailing priorities for the 92d Division were canceled in January 1919, and the outfit was dropped farther down on the list. The 1st Battalion of the 367th Infantry was supposed to sail for home on the U.S.S. *Virginia*, and Company D was assigned to coal it; but when the coal was aboard, the black troops were told to get their luggage off the vessel because the captain said no colored troops had ever traveled on his ship and none ever would. White soldiers took their places. The 808th P.I. had its orders revoked at the last minute and was kept on duty at Brest for two months. The 369th, although it had the outstanding band in the service, marched silently through Brest to the docks because Colonel Hayward feared that music might violate some obscure regulation and lose the regiment its sailing priority; the instruments were broken out at last, but only at the express request of the base's chief of staff.[26]

The press commented on the scant attention paid most black troops on their return home. In large Northern cities they were welcomed with respect, if not enthusiasm, but in rural areas, especially in the South, they more often met hostility.

New York was outstanding for the fine treatment of its black veterans. The 369th returned to the city on 12 February 1919 and held a victory parade up Fifth Avenue a few days later. The first New York soldiers to come home, Colonel Hayward's troops marched in the impressively solid French phalanx formation to the music of Jim Europe's band, which on its own brought out many spectators who hoped for some good jazz. But Europe played only French marches, and "on the part of the men, there was no prancing, no showing of teeth, no swank; they marched with a steady stride; and from under their battered tin hats eyes that had looked straight at death were kept to the front." [27] After the parade, city officials entertained the troops with a dinner in the armory of the 71st New York Infantry. It was the first and only time in its service that the whole regiment was assembled under one roof.[28] A month later the 367th Infantry also paraded through the city and returned its regimental standard to the Union League Club, which had presented it before the men went overseas.

But things were different in the South. There were reports of black soldiers stopped at Southern railroad stations and stripped of their uniforms.[29] In St. Joseph, Missouri, black soldiers refused to take part in the victory parade because they were to form the tail of the march, behind even the civic organizations. In Washington, D.C., the outspoken Reverend Francis Grimke, at a reception for black soldiers, listed the humiliations they had suffered, adding: "That shameful record is going to be written up, and published, so that the whole world may read it, and learn how these black men, who went out from these shores to die at their country's call, were treated simply because of the color of their skin. . . ." [30]

Most of the black troops and officers were eager to be demobilized and to pick up their civilian lives again, but there were some who would have liked to remain in the nation's peacetime army. This was a matter of great concern to the army brass. Colonel Greer, again writing to Senator McKellar, said: "Now that a reorganization of the army is in prospect, and as all officers of the temporary forces have been asked if they desire to remain in the regular army, I think I ought to bring a matter to your attention that is of vital importance not only from a military point of view but from that which all Southerners have. I refer to the question of negro officers and negro troops." [31] To his sympathetic correspondent, the senator from Tennessee, Greer could bare the heart of the matter—the "point of view . . . which all Southerners have." It explains why, in this account of injustices to black soldiers, there are so many references to Southern detractors. Greer expressed their convictions.

Greer went on to say that the 92d Division had failed in all its missions because the officers and men were cowards. [32] When a black lieutenant formerly with the 92d, Osceola McKaine, complained to the War Department about the libelous charges in Greer's letter, the colonel admitted having written it, but it was McKaine who came under attack. Could he prove that Greer had written the document? Could he prove that Greer was responsible for the publicity given his charges against the 92d? An investigation as to the truth of these charges was suggested by the General Staff, but it does not seem to have been made. [33] So the story of the "cowardly" black division—note that Greer, who knew only one battalion was involved, impugned the entire organization—that story of the black division which had failed because of "cowardice," proceeded on its long career, unimpeded by facts, constantly growing by the accretion of racist myth and uninformed rumor.

Although never officially admitted, the policy of the postwar army was to exclude black officers as far as possible. Many methods were used. In one case, when a black officer requested a hearing to defend his request to retain his commission, an examining board was extraordinarily frank: "The Board recommends that he be *not* examined. Reason: unqualified by reason of the qualities inherent in the Negro race; an opinion of the Board, based on the testimony of five white officers serving with the 368th Infantry. Negroes are deficient in moral fiber, rendering them unfit as officers and leaders of men." [34] Major Elser's unquestionable crack-up and the confusion or inefficiency of other white officers of the 368th got a coat of whitewash with the other side of the brush that tarred the Negro race.

In this particular case, the War Department overruled the examining board, but such action did not speak for the army. Much more typical was the statement of Col. I. C. Jenks: "If the time has come for Negroes and dagoes to be officers in the regular army, it is time for the white man to step out." Jenks refused to endorse the retention of Maj. Milton Dean, a black officer with twenty-two years' experience in the army, saying: "Major Dean is a very efficient officer, but for reasons which I care not to state but which are well known, I cannot recommend him." [35] Since Dean wasn't a "dago," presumably the "well known" reason was that he was black.

Those black officers who were retained were again restricted to infantry and cavalry—the four Regular black regiments—although black officers had performed well in the artillery and engineers. Reenlistment of experienced black personnel was permitted only until the four black regiments reached full strength.

But the overwhelming majority of black soldiers had had a bellyful of the army. They took their two-months' discharge bonuses and made their way back into civilian life. One of the first things they learned was that $60, the enlisted man's bonus, vanished quickly. Then quite soon they found that the American Legion, newly formed to help veterans of the war, practically barred blacks, especially in the South. In some Southern states the black vets were allowed to form their own segregated posts, but these were not permitted to send representatives to state or national conventions and their members were not eligible for office above the local post level; which is to say, black posts would not share in the power of the Legion for getting legislation, jobs, benefits, or favors for their members. The Legion's national convention in 1919 set no nationwide standards for the admission of blacks but permitted each state organization to make its own rules. State rules were generally exclusive or discouraging. As one black newspaper said, "For valor displayed in the recent war, it seems that the Negro's particular decoration is to be the 'double-cross.' " [36]

10. Home?

> You niggers are wondering how you are going to be treated after the war. Well, I'll tell you, you are going to be treated exactly like you were before the war; this is a white man's country and we expect to rule it.
>
> Remarks of a white speaker to blacks in New Orleans [1918], quoted in Blanton, "Men in the Making," *Southern Workman*, p. 20.

TO MEET the "peril" of returning colored veterans who might have been infected with foreign ideas of liberty, equality, and fraternity, the Ku Klux Klan, which had been revived in 1915, now became very visible. Klansmen paraded by night in their Halloween outfits through the streets of Georgia and Alabama towns. The attorney general of Georgia allowed the Klan to incorporate in that state, although, as one citizen pointed out, its sole purpose was subversive of the Constitution.[1] Carter Woodson wrote: "To the reactionary the uniform on a Negro man was like a red flag thrown in the face of a bull."[2] Demagogues played on the old familiar theme of black "unbridled lust" to raise prurient fears of what the returning "French-women-ruined negro soldiers" (Vardaman's phrase) would do to Southern womanhood.[3] The Mississippi legislature enacted a law which made it a crime to print, publish, or circulate materials advocating social equality or interracial marriage.[4] Seligmann acutely analyzed the focusing of attention on the black veteran: "The penalty for the social and political disabilities imposed upon the Negro is that he is constantly in the minds of white people." White contempt, he said, gave rise to white hostility; ultimately the result was "the quick resort to the rope, the pistol, the torch. . . ."[5]

There was, in fact, a great increase in violence against blacks in 1919. Discharged soldiers, still in uniform, were beaten and driven out of town in many parts of the South—the NAACP reported such incidents in Texas, Mississippi, Alabama, South Carolina, Kentucky, and also in Wyoming.[6]

After a few years in which the number of lynchings had declined, the curve had started upward again in 1917. In 1918, sixty-two Americans were lynched, fifty-eight of them black.[7] The lynchings were of incredible ferocity, taking up where the Ell Persons mob had left off. A pregnant woman was slashed open, shot, and burned, her unborn baby crushed under the feet of the mob; a man was chained, tortured, and burned to death before the eyes of a large audience, some of whom had come from as far as fifty miles away; two girls and two boys were tied and thrown off a bridge to drown. After one horrible lynching, picture postcards showing the atrocity were sold. There were eighteen lynchings in top-scoring Georgia, nine each in Louisiana and Texas, and six in Mississippi. In only two cases did the authorities attempt to prevent the mob from having its way. In one of the cases, in North Carolina, fifteen of the lynch mob were given jail sentences; the reason for this unusual action was that they had injured members of the Home Guard who had been guarding the jail.[8]

Again in 1919, the first year of peace, lynchings increased; the popular method was burning alive. Of the eighty-three killed by mobs that year, seventy-seven were black. Eleven were burned alive, and three were set on fire after they were dead. One burning was thus reported in a Dallas newspaper: "While a great many persons gathered around the burning negro, business was not suspended and there was very little excitement."[9] After a Mississippi lynching, the NAACP received a note and a newspaper account of the affair from an anonymous correspondent. The clipping said the victim "was 'advanced' all right from the end of a rope, and in order to save burial expenses his body was thrown into the Yazoo River," and the note added, "If this information does not suffice we can give you the size of the rope and the exact location of where the coon was hung."[10]

There seemed no bottom to the depravity of the lynchings; it strains belief that Americans or any other modern people could enjoy perversion rivaling the circuses of decadent Rome. But there were obviously many who enjoyed every minute of it. The

Vicksburg Evening Post said of one lynch-burning, during which the mob fired some careless shots of jubilation, that the "wounding of the bystanders did not distract interest from the central figure in the ghastly episode." [11]

Some Southern politicians encouraged mob sadism. Senator Vardaman's newsletter, *Vardaman's Weekly*, said of that lynching that although it was horrible it was justified by the victim's crime of rape—although the rape was never proved, and the victim was unable to identify the alleged rapist until after the mob seized a man and said he had committed the crime. Vardaman added: "Every community in Mississippi ought to organize and the organization should be led by the bravest and best white men in the community. And they should pick out these suspicious characters—those military, French-women-ruined negro soldiers and let them understand that they are under surveillance and that when crimes similar to this are committed, take care of the individual who commits the crime." [12]

Gov. Theodore Bilbo of Mississippi [13] made the following disingenuous statement about a case in his state where a planned, preannounced burning was permitted to occur without any attempt at official interference: "I am utterly powerless. The State has no troops, and if the civil authorities at Ellisville are helpless, the State is equally so. Furthermore, excitement is at such a high pitch throughout South Mississippi that any armed attempt to interfere with the mob would doubtless result in the death of hundreds of persons. The negro has confessed, says he is ready to die, and nobody can keep the inevitable from happening." [14]

At least ten of 1919's mob victims were black veterans, some of them still in uniform. Most of them were "lynched for the usual," just as before the war, but there were some cases that could not have occurred until after the war. In Sylvester, Georgia, Daniel Mack allegedly told a white that he had fought in France and did not intend to take mistreatment from white people. He was sentenced to jail for thirty days but was snatched from his cell by a mob and beaten to death—still in his uniform. In Pine Bluff, Arkansas, a black veteran who was told by a white woman to get off the sidewalk replied that it was a free country and he would not move. A mob took him from town, lashed him to a tree with tire chains, and shot him forty or fifty times.[15] So while Colonel Greer was berating black soldiers for being cowards, Southern mobs were killing them for not being.

There is in these stories a suggestion of change in black attitudes toward themselves and whites, a change that would take many years to develop but that would end in total upheaval of the old back-white relations. But it was only a beginning of change; and in the year 1919 when the soldiers came home, that breath of change brought blacks more rather than less suffering.

The summer of 1919 has been called the Red Summer because of the quantity of blood spilled in race riots all through the country. At least thirty-eight clashes which could be classified as race riots took place that year, the worst of them during the summer. Whites mostly believed that blacks created the tensions, that led to this extraordinary violence; that blacks had returned from the war armed and defiant, and that whites organized only in self-defense. Seligmann did not express the popular opinion in saying that blacks were justified in insisting on their rights as citizens, and, concerning the troubles of 1919, that the black man was not the problem, "but the attitude of the white man toward him." [16]

The worst riots took place in Washington, D.C.; Chicago; Omaha, Nebraska; and Elaine, Arkansas. Among the other particularly bloody clashes were riots at Charleston, South Carolina; New York City; Norfolk, Virginia; Knoxville, Tennessee; and Longview, Texas. Also, in July, fighting broke out at Bisbee, Arizona, with the people and police of the town harassing troopers of the 10th Cavalry.[17]

Although the underlying causes of the riots were profoundly economic, social, and psychological, it was the return of black veterans that seemed to trigger riots everywhere in the country. Returning black veterans were smarting from the abuse to which they had been subjected while fighting their country's war against tyranny. They were thoroughly disgusted, most of them, with the counsel of such moderate black leaders—traitors, many thought them—as Emmett Scott and Robert Moton. Scott conceived of his duty to the War Department as oiling troubled waters, even if that meant concealing the truth. He told Ralph Tyler to tone down his dispatches from France on such censorable subjects as discrimination by the YMCA or the association of black soldiers with French women. His stand is well summed up in this letter to Tyler: "I very much hope that you will preserve as much equanimity of spirit as possible. There is so much for all of us to do that you cannot for one minute permit yourself to be overcome by the injustices which surround us. In other words, it is possible, I sometimes fear, for most, or all of us to permit our indignation to eat into our vitals." [18] But the returned combat soldiers and laborers in uniform, who had been deprived and humiliated and beaten and slave-driven because they were black, were not inclined to accept a plea for equanimity of spirit.

Moton, Booker T. Washington's successor as guru of the philosophy of accommodation, was particularly galling to the black man who had gone through the miseries of war in France. After the Armistice, President Wilson had sent Moton to France to quiet unrest and to forestall trouble when the black soldiers should come home. Moton told the troops that they had made a splendid record, but that they must exercise self-control while still overseas and look for jobs—better yet, settle down as farmers—as soon as they got back to the States. "I hope," Moton said, "no one will do anything in peace to spoil the magnificent record you have made in war." [19] But the black troops were not taken in by the flattery and were not in a mood to suit their actions to the white warnings which they knew Moton was conveying—particularly not while charges against them of inefficiency, laziness, bestiality, and cowardice were being circulated.

They were much more attuned to such publications as the *Challenge*, the *Messenger*, and the *Crisis*, which minced no words about the grievances of blacks and which recommended direct action to redress them. The *Challenge* said in October 1919, as the race riots were winding down out of sheer satiation with blood and the smoke of burning flesh: "We are fully ignored by the President and lawmakers. When we ask for a full-man's share they cry 'insolent.' When we shoot down the mobist that would burn our properties and destroy our lives, they shout

'Bolshevist.' When a white man comes to our side armed with the sword of righteousness and square dealing, they howl 'Nigger-lover and bastard.' If we take our grievances to Congress they are pigeon-holed, turned over to moths. We are abandoned, cast off, maligned, shackled, shoved down the hills toward Golgotha in 'The Land of the Free and the Home of the Brave.' " [20] The *Messenger* spoke to their anger with reminders that they had been better treated by all Europeans (including Germans, the article said, ignoring or ignorant of the scurrilous German film *Honte Noire*) than by their own people at home, that they had learned how to fight, and that "the transition from shooting a white German is not very far from shooting a white American." [21] DuBois, who in his editorials of 1918 in the *Crisis* had urged blacks to "Close Ranks" and put aside their grievances in their country's time of need, in the spring of 1919 wrote: "Make Way for Democracy! We saved it in France, and by the Great Jehovah, we will save it in the United States of America, or know the reason why." [22] Marcus Garvey's "Back to Africa" movement seemed to thousands of blacks in 1919 to offer a more viable future than life in the dubious democracy of the United States.

The white racist's response to the postwar black defiance and black anger was a determination to beat the Negro down, once and for all, into his place at the bottom of American society. This was the rationale behind the many unspeakable lynchings and the riots of 1919, whatever the precipitating incident.

In Washington, D.C., the *Post* had been giving headlines almost daily in July 1919, to an alleged black crime wave. Other papers followed. The *New York Times* reported that in Washington since the beginning of the month at least six white women had been assaulted by blacks. As a matter of fact, there had been four assaults in Washington, and it was believed that one man was responsible for three of them. Three other assaults had taken place in nearby parts of Maryland. In three of the assaults, the motive seems to have been robbery rather than sexual molestation. [23]

The *Post* suggested that white military personnel stationed in Washington might "clean up" a problem—the alleged black crime wave—which seemed beyond the capability of the local police. White servicemen obliged on 19 July, a hot Saturday night, by invading a black neighborhood and indiscriminately beating up any blacks they found. White civilians joined in the Negro-hunt on Sunday. By then at least fifteen blacks were in hospitals, and eight were in jail. Of the white aggressors, only two had been jailed.

On Monday black resistance stiffened; since the police were evidently not protecting blacks they determined to protect themselves and their property. That night two blacks and four whites were killed, and more whites than blacks were injured.[24] The *Times* reported this more militant response of Washington black men as "Armed and Defiant Negroes Roam about Shooting at Whites." Groups of blacks instigated by a secret organization, the *Times* said, were driving through the city shooting from cars at any white; and "bands of negroes, hundreds of them carrying revolvers, razors and blackjacks, are gathering in various parts of the city and are making vicious attacks upon soldiers, sailors and civilians." [25] The attacks were particularly violent, the *Times* added, in the 2d, 6th, and 8th police precincts. These were, in fact, the black neighborhoods, from which it seems that blacks were fighting a defensive, not an offensive, battle; but the *Times* did not locate the precincts until the next day. The *New York World* also took up the cry that "Blacks Renew Riots in Capital." [26] Still, whether the black Washingtonians were on the offensive or the defensive, there is no question that they were armed and that they fought as they had never fought before—in the United States, that is. Many had fought that desperately in France. Finally 1,100 troops and sixty officers were sent in to quell the riot. On Wednesday, after four days of violence, quiet returned to the federal city.

The *Times* continued to view blacks as responsible for the riots. Although terrorization of Negroes was deplorable, the paper editorialized, so was black retaliation; there had been no trouble with Negroes before the war, when "most . . . admitted the superiority of the white race." [27] In *Current Opinion*, an article pointed out that although blacks had not armed until it was necessary to defend their lives and property, they had shown a new militancy born of their war experiences and training; and that there was now a surge of racial pride such as few could remember in the past. The most moving comment on the riots was that of a black woman, who said:

> The Washington riots gave me the thrill that comes once in a lifetime. I was alone when I read between the lines of the morning paper that at last our men had stood like men, struck back, were no longer dumb, driven cattle. When I could no longer read for my streaming tears, I stood up, alone in my room, held both hands high over my head and exclaimed, "Oh, I thank God, thank God!" When I remember anything after this, I was prone on my bed, beating the pillow with both fists, laughing and crying, whimpering like a whipped child, for sheer gladness and madness. The pent-up humiliation, grief and horror of a lifetime—half a century—was being stripped from me.[28]

The black men might stand like men, but the white man was far from admitting that he was of the same species. Washington lit the match of trouble; a week later, Chicago erupted. Wartime migration from the South had jammed the black belt of Chicago intolerably, so blacks began to spill over into the fringe areas where white workers lived. When the blacks reached out for living space into the white areas, their homes were bombed—twenty-four such bombings in Chicago between 1917 and 1919. More general violence began during the spring of 1919, when groups of young white toughs calling themselves "athletic clubs" raided black neighborhoods, undeterred and even supported by local police. Late in June the toughs killed two blacks. In some sections blacks retaliated by shooting at all cars carrying whites.[29] The *Chicago Tribune* cautioned black citizens that social differences would continue to exist, and that "thinking negroes must use their influence with their race. They must realize the facts and conditions. The race problem will not be settled by these outbursts. . . ."[30] Nor were the outbursts likely to be settled as long as the press headlined every racial incident in the country, as it continued to do.

The explosion occurred on Sunday, 27 July. At a crowded lakefront beach, there were segregated (by custom) black and white areas separated by an invisible line. White bathers were amusing themselves by throwing stones at black swimmers who had crossed the boundary. Some stones hit a young black boy who was drifting along, holding to some floating debris; he lost his hold and was drowned. When angry blacks demanded of a policeman that he arrest the whites, he instead arrested a black. That was when the fighting began. On Wednesday the militia was called in. Things quieted at last on Friday.[31]

White casualties in the six days were 15 dead, 193 injured, and 75 arrested; black casualties were 23 dead, 365 injured, and 154 arrested.[32] As in Washington, the violence was restricted almost entirely to the black neighborhoods, and most whites hurt or killed were those who had gone into the ghetto areas or who were wandering, by accident or design, on its fringes.

Still, as in the Washington riots, blacks were called the aggressors. The Associated Press explained that blacks got hurt because whites were defending themselves against black attacks; it stressed the depredations of "maddened blacks."[33] Again, as in Washington, the police did nothing to help frightened blacks, and they were slow to arrest marauding whites; the state's attorney himself said that some policemen "shut their eyes to offenses committed by white men while they were vigorous in getting all the colored men they could get."[34] Again, it was officially charged that a "secret organization" had supplied weapons for a scheduled outbreak of violence.[35] Again, a change in black attitudes was held responsible for the trouble. According to the *Literary Digest:* ". . . now, as if convinced that neither education nor material prosperity could advance their cause, they appear to be putting their trust in brute strength. They will fight. In Washington's 'race war' negroes were frequently the aggressors. So also in Chicago. This 'changed attitude,' as a Chicago negro puts it, would seem to have been an underlying cause of the Chicago riots. . . ."[36]

So Chicago was Washington all over again in most respects, but one distinctive and cheering feature was the stand taken by the Chicago grand jury on the imbalance between black and white arrests: "This jury has no apology to offer for its attitude with reference to requesting the state's attorney to supply it with information of crimes perpetrated by whites against blacks before considering further evidence against blacks. This attitude

gave rise to the reports in the press that this grand jury 'had
gone on strike!' . . . The reason for this attitude arose from a
sense of justice on the part of this jury. It is the opinion of this
jury that the colored people suffered more at the hands of white
hoodlums than the white people suffered at the hands of the
black hoodlums. . . ." [37]

Other riots followed the pattern set by Washington and Chicago. In Omaha the violence was precipitated by an attempt to
lynch a black man charged with rape. In Elaine, a meeting of
exploited black sharecroppers in a church was fired on by a deputy sheriff. [38] When blacks returned the fire, they were accused
of plotting a white massacre and were hunted down. In Omaha,
five whites and twenty-five blacks were officially listed as dead,
although according to many estimates the black mortality was
much higher. [39] How many died in Elaine will never be known;
twenty-five were listed as killed, but many more simply fled and
perhaps perished in the swamps; and hundreds were penned in
an unsanitary, makeshift stockade merely on grounds of belong-
ing to the farmers' union. In both Omaha and Elaine the troops
were sent in. At the request of the governor of Arkansas, 500
men arrived from Camp Pike "to repel the attack of the black
army." [40] As usual in that period of witch hunting, it was suspected that some secret subversive organization was behind the
riots. The offices and homes of farmers'-union lawyers, it was
reported in the *New York Times*, contained socialistic literature,
and the union itself was a secret society—this, although it was a
state-chartered organization. [41] General Wood, who took the
troops in at Omaha, said he saw the sinister shadow of the IWW
behind the riot; he advocated, as a way of preventing the influx
of dangerous foreign ideologies, the elimination of instruction in
foreign languages in American schools. [42] The *Times* was posi-
tive that the IWW was behind the "plot" at Elaine for blacks to
rise and massacre whites. [43]

Clearly there was a new attitude among black people, born of
the military experiences of the recent war. The *New York World*
asked bluntly: "Who is foolish enough to assume that with
239,000 colored men in uniform from the southern states alone,

as against 370,000 white men, the blacks whose manhood and patriotism were thus recognized and tested are forever to be flogged, lynched, burned at the stake or chased into concealment whenever Caucasian desperadoes are moved to engage in this infamous pastime?" [44] Couple this new black defiance with the prevailing white determination to crack it, and it is obvious that violence would become a permanent fact of American life. The white threat is expressed with racist crudity, but perfect plainness, in this letter to the *Chicago Defender* commenting on its counsel to the black farmers in Elaine to resist:

> You are agitating a proposition through your paper which is causing some of your good Bur heads to be killed and the end is not in sight yet, but you have not got sense enough to see it, go on.
> You could be of assistance to your people if you would advise them to be real niggers instead of fools. . . . We are still in the saddle and some of your good niggers are paying the price of your ignorance go on nigger and keep this up. [45]

Clearly, the precipitating factor in the race riots of the Red Summer was a head-on clash between a new black self-respect, conceived in battle and inured to violence, and the old, now threatened, white insistence on respect for white superiority. "Omaha is not ashamed," said the *New York Times*, "but Omaha is frightened." [46] Not all white Americans were racists, but a frightened white American was an easy convert.

The President of the United States, well aware of the political sensitivity of the postwar racial situation, did not use the power of his office to prevent riots or lynchings. At the time of the Washington violence the NAACP appealed to Wilson to intervene, but he did not then or at any time condemn mob violence. A black journal voiced the feelings of the black community, especially black veterans: "The relatives of returned Negro soldiers were beaten and killed on the streets of Washington, right in front of the White House, under the dome of the capitol of the greatest Republic on earth—a Republic that went to war to beat down injustice, and make the world safe for democracy. Has the head of the nation uttered one word of condemnation of the mob? If so, we have failed to see it." [47]

Many appeals to the federal government for protection against lynching brought the response that the government could do nothing. Lynching was not in violation of any federal law, administration officials explained, because that whole area of legislation had been left to the states by the Tenth Amendment. Yet, had those officials wished to exert any pressure, the government could have taken a stand against racial violence. Federal investigations, such as the one following the East St. Louis riot of 1917, were possible. Congressman Leonidas Dyer of Missouri tried several times during the Wilson years to get an antilynch law through the House, but he failed.

In the absence of legislation, a strong statement from the President might have had some deterrent influence. After one particularly brutal burning of a black man in Tennessee, the NAACP sent a delegation to protest to the President. He said he had not heard of the case and asked for a review of the facts. When the atrocity had been described, his only comment was that he could not believe such a thing had happened.[48] Only once did Wilson make a public statement against lynching. During the war there was a case in which a black man, allegedly a German sympathizer, was killed by a mob. A federal investigation was held, the only official investigation of a lynching under Wilson. And the President remarked that it was difficult to recommend democracy to other nations if American actions demonstrated that democracy offered no real protection to the weak.[49] This soft impeachment was greeted with scorn by black leaders. One of them said: "I predicted, after reading Mr. Wilson's statement published July 26, that a Negro would be lynched before the rising and setting of two suns. Did it come true? Yes, right on the minute. And I further predict more lynchings until something is done actively and not passively said. A man vested with the power, clothed with the authority, and backed by the Constitution, could have such strenuous legislation enforced that it would make the pleasurable pastime of Dixie almost impossible. . . ."[50]

But President Wilson did not care to, or perhaps dare to, offend the powerful Southerners in his administration and in Congress to protect the lives of some politically insignificant black people. The successful prosecution of the war and of his economic-reform program depended on the support of politically significant white Southerners who would not like a heavy hand laid on the "pleasurable pastime" of their constituents.

There was among both blacks and whites a good deal of post-war talk about the "New Negro," and it was true that black Americans—veterans and civilians—were not the same in 1919 as they had been in 1917. Alain Locke, one of the most expressive black leaders, said: ". . . the anticipated rewards of the Negro's patriotic response to the idealism of the 'War to Save Democracy' were not measurably realized and, spurred by the bitter disillusionments of post-war indifference there came that desperate intensification of the Negro's race consciousness and attempt at recovery of group morale. . . ." [51] To this explanation of the change, James Weldon Johnson added: "There developed also a spirit of defiance born of desperation." [52] The defiant attitude was a natural product of the discrimination and humiliation black soldiers had suffered, Johnson said, and white people ought to realize that.

Like defiance, race consciousness was intensified by white injustice to blacks, and, in 1919, by white violence, although white people generally refused to realize it. After the war, all blacks, of whatever class, were threatened. Middle-class blacks, many of whom had believed themselves safe, now joined slum dwellers in buying weapons to defend their homes and families and began to stand shoulder to shoulder with black people of lower social levels, people with whom they had nothing in common but their blackness. Black solidarity spread even beyond the national boundaries. American black leaders had hoped for a voice at the conference table at Versailles in order to press for guarantees of the rights of black people throughout the world. But no blacks were included in the American delegation to the peace conference, and a few who traveled there on their own, despite many obstacles, failed in their mission. The black Africans also failed. Thus a bond of ignored need was forged among black people who lived far apart. Pan-Africanism, in which DuBois was a leader, grew strong. [53]

The New Negro in the United States was a bewildering—and to many, a frightening—phenomenon because of the dignity of his demands and his determination to have them fulfilled *now*, not sometime in the vague future: ". . . that 'darky'—the Uncle, the Auntie—has passed to appear never again. Another type of colored man has come upon the stage: the Negro who is struggling for manhood rights, for political, economic and social freedom, for all that democracy means to the most favored. This Negro has not yet found in the white race an interpreter. He is too recent, too alarming. We are baffled by his attitude and his ambitions. We have made no provision in our social system for this new man in the old color. . . ." [54] Black American ambitions were really not so baffling; they were simply white American ambitions. "What does the Negro want? He wants to be let alone and permitted to work out his own salvation as any other race in America. He wants every right and privilege guaranteed to every American citizen by the Declaration of Independence and the Constitution of the United States." [55]

President Wilson, whose high ideals had recommended him to so many blacks and had won their votes, was a particularly bitter disappointment. Grimke said: "Then in the fulness of time came Woodrow Wilson, the ripe, consummate fruit of all this national contradiction between profession and practice, promise and performance." [56]

Without pressure from Wilson, Congress continued after the war to do nothing for the New Negro. For a time the House Judiciary Committee considered creating a "Commission on the Racial Question," authorized to investigate the causes of racial unrest and friction, but the commission was not established. Instead, Congress pressed for further legal discrimination. In what had once been a refuge for black people, the federal city itself, Congress now discouraged black newcomers; introduced bills to segregate Washington street cars; and threatened to cut off appropriations for the most prestigious black institution of higher learning, Howard University, which turned out most of the black teachers, doctors, lawyers, and other professional people. [57]

The New Negro was, in a way, much like the New White of the postwar generation. Like F. Scott Fitzgerald's characters, the New Negro had lost his innocence and his illusions. But where the white child of the war, of the "Lost Generation," substituted for faith and hope an excess of pleasure, the black child of the war substituted for faith in the white man faith in himself only; and for hope, nothing. War had taught him self-reliance; peace taught him that was all there was to believe in. The rest was pie-in-the-sky.

Once during the Red Summer Wilson complimented a group of blacks on the remarkable loyalty and patriotism of black Americans despite the unjust and illegal treatment they had suffered in the past. Out of the war, he said, would come all the rights of citizenship. He warned, however, against impatience, saying that "great principles of righteousness are won by hard fighting and they are attained by slow degrees." One of the group responded: "I fear, Mr. President, before the negroes of this country again will submit to many of the injustices which we have suffered in this country, the white man will have to kill more of them than the combined number of soldiers that were slain in the great world war." [58]

At the peak of the violence, DuBois, in the *Crisis* of August 1919, put the same declaration of a war for equal rights in his ringing prose, a trumpet call welcome to the ears of the former black soldiers:

Behold the day, O Fellow Black Men! They cheat us and mock us; they kill and slay us; they deride our misery. When we plead for the naked protection of the law, there where a million of our fellows dwell, they tell us to "GO TO HELL!" TO YOUR TENTS, O ISRAEL! And FIGHT, FIGHT, FIGHT for Freedom. [59]

Appendix: Disposal of the Colored Drafted Men

May 16, 1918.

Colored men and white men are on the same draft list irrespective of race and the colored men will be called in approximately the proportion of $1/7$th the total number drafted. There should be called in June, 56,000 colored men in order that the proportionate number of colored men be called to keep abreast of the white men called up to May 31, 1918. At the present contemplated rate of calling the draft from June 1, 1918 to December 31, 1918, 114,000 more colored draft should be called, making 170,000 colored drafted men.

From January 1, 1919 to June 30, 1919, we can count approximately on 100,000 more colored drafted men. Only a small part of these 270,000 men can be used for combatant troops. It is the policy to select those colored men of the best physical stamina, highest education and mental development for combatant troops and there is every reason to believe that these specially selected men, the cream of the colored draft, will make first class fighting troops. After this cream has been skimmed off, there remains a large percentage of colored men of the ignorant illiterate day laborer class. These men have not, in a large percent of cases, the physical stamina to withstand the hardships and exposure of hard field service, especially the damp cold winters of France. The poorer class of backwoods negro has not the mental stamina and moral sturdiness to put him in the line against opposing German troops who consist of men of high average education and thoroughly trained. The enemy is constantly looking for a weak place in the line and if he can find a part of the line held by troops composed of culls of the colored race, all he has to do is to concentrate on that, break through and then he will be in

National Archives, R.G. 165, item 8142-150 (Col. E. D. Anderson, chairman of the Operations Branch, General Staff).

rear of high class troops who will be at a terrible disadvantage. An illustration of this is the way the Germans concentrated on the Portuguese at Ypres, broke through the Portuguese and the whole line had to fall back at heavy loss, losing valuable positions and enormous stores because the enemy had found second rate troops at one spot.

The French had to remove their colored Senegalese troops and the British their Hindu troops from France because colored troops could not stand the nervous strain of trench warfare. The following is quoted from the letter of Major C. K. Lyell, assistant Military Attaché, British Embassy, Washington:

"The main disadvantage that was found in regard to them (Hindus) was their inability to stand the long shell fire in the trenches, when all that could be done was to sit tight and wait for it to stop. This seemed more than their nervous organization was able to stand." It is further stated in the above letter "The Indian troops whom we made use of in France, were drawn from many different races, each of which has its own marked characteristics, but I think it would be found in nearly every case they were of rather higher intellectual development than negro troops." It is believed that our United States troops formed from the pick of the colored drafted men will be fully equal to the requirements and make first class combatant troops who can be relied on to give a creditable account of themselves, but the mass of the colored drafted men can not be used for combatant troops and the problem is to use them in such way as to most effectively aid in the prosecution of the war. Authority has been granted for the organization of 50 quartermaster labor battalions and 46 Engineer service battalions who will be taken from the day laborer class of colored drafted men, not high grade enough to assign to combatant troops. These are assigned to the different phases and part of them have been organized and sent abroad. The remainder can be organized and sent over as needed. It is not desirable that they be organized too far ahead of time because they must be picked physically shortly before sailing for foreign service and there is no great amount of training required and the Government loses their services at useful constructive labor if they are organized months ahead of the time that they will be actually sent abroad. The physical condition of these negroes is very poor. The Surgeon General reports that approximately 50 per cent are infected with venerial [*sic*] disease. The Surgeon General stated (Col. Noble, Colonel Howard) that the present selective service regulations are being revised and new regulations being prepared which have for their object the putting of men unfit for service under a delayed classification so that they can be taken later, but men with venerial cases will be drafted in their regular order. These men are not available to be sent over seas either as combatant troops or labor or Engineer Service Battalions.

It is recommended that these colored drafted men be organized in reserve labor battalions, put to work at useful constructive labor that furthers the prosecution of the war and that when the time comes for sending Quartermaster labor or Engineer Service Battalions overseas, that the men physically qualified be selected from the Reserve labor Battalions and the required number of labor or Engineer Battalions be formed just as needed for overseas service. In this way, the colored drafted men would be performing useful work that furthers our interest in prosecuting the War from the date they are drafted. White men released by them from day labor work, would be free to spend their entire time being instructed for combatant service. Also the colored men instead of laying around camps accomplishing nothing of value, getting sicker and sicker and in trouble generally, are kept out of trouble by being kept busy at useful work and there is a chance for recommendation of the colored men as the Medical Department can be working on them in the meanwhile, curing them of venerial and other diseases and putting them in shape. This will be the first time in their lives that 9 out of 10 negroes ever had any discipline, instruction, or medical treatment, or lived under sanitary conditions and they should improve greatly and at the same time, they will be doing useful work and releasing men for training in combatant service. The following will illustrate how unfit colored drafted men are in the average for overseas service when first drafted. The following instructions were sent to the Commanding General, Camp Pike, Arkansas, as well as to other divisions and Department Commanders:

"1. Colored stevedore troops arriving with tuberculosis, old fractures, extreme flat foot, hernia, venerial diseases, all existing prior to enlistment, not able to stand hardship of climate and travel, larger proportion of sick than among white troops. Recommend elimination of unfit by rigid physical examination before embarking" Pershing.

2. The same conditions probably exists [*sic*] among colored troops, other than stevedore troops, to a certain extent. You will therefore take the necessary steps to eliminate all such unfit before departure for a port of Embarkation, by order of the Secretary of War. The Commanding General, Camp Pike, transferred 3604 colored drafted men to Port of Embarkation, Newport News, under the above instructions except he was given authority to send men suffering from venerial disease who were not receiving daily treatment. A medical examination at the Port of Embarkation showed

Total number of colored drafted men received	3604
Number of men sent directly to hospital	193
Number of men with Gonorrhoea (in camp)	955
Number of men with syphilis	52
Number of men with tuberculosis	216
Number of men with Hernia	10
Number of men with Heart trouble	112
Number of men with Rheumatism	10
Number of men with other ailments	11
Total ineffectives	1599
Total fit for duty	2045
Percentage ineffectives (who could not be sent overseas)	43.25

A further examination into this case shows that the Commanding General, Camp Pike, was not trying to unload undesirables on the Port of Embarkation. He realized they were for oversea service and he sent the pick of what he had but that is the class of men the colored drafted men were. Other examples could be given, but it would be cumulative testimony along the same lines.

It would be no use to exempt such men from the draft. Such exempted men would be replaced by others of a similar kind and the draft boards could run through the colored race in the United States and exempt a large part of them. In these days of conservation, when every rag and bone and tin can is saved, human beings cannot be wasted. These colored men have to be inducted into the service by draft in their turn and it is believed that they ought to be put right to work at useful work which will be of real assistance to the United States in prosecuting the war, and will release men available for other service.

It is recommended that authority be granted to organize 50 Reserve labor Battalions. This does not mean that 50 labor Battalions are to be immediately organized. It will give authority for the operations Division of the General Staff to organize the colored drafted men who are not high class enough to be assigned to combatant troops into reserve labor Battalions and to put these battalions to work.

It is recommended that one reserve labor Battalion be placed in each division cantonment or cantonment of similar size and one or more labor companies or labor battalions be placed in each smaller camp as may be necessary. There is in every camp, constant calls for fatigue. A rain comes and washes out the ditches, the roads get cut up and must be repaired, a lot of railway cars with supplies get accumulated and must be unloaded, etc. In every case white troops from combatant units are detailed for fatigue and the combatant instruction is delayed by that much. This work has to be done, it is always coming up, so let it be done by ignorant day laborers while they are being cured up of venerial disease, etc. and being reconstructed and let white men in combatant units have all day, every day for combat instruction. A soldier in a combat organization who is free for drill and instruction every day is bound to be ready for service oversea [*sic*] a long time before men who drill a couple of days, then work unloading cars, repairing roads, etc. for a couple of days and then go back to instruction for a day or so until something else interrupts. It may be said that fatigue details are not necessary, that if division commanders, etc. appreciated how much more important it was to hurry with their tactical instruction than to keep their division cantonments neatly policed, fatigue details would not be necessary. But Division and other commanders do want to shove ahead with their instruction, there are combatant necessities arising for fatigue men detailed from combatant units which cannot be avoided. If we had a labor battalion for each Division camp and companies, etc. for smaller camps, the ignorant and diseased negroes not suited for service overseas could do this work and the white combatant troops would be released for constant intensive training.

It may be said that while the division camps need on the average several hundred laborers a day, they do not need on the average as many as a battalion and in these days when it is not desired to waste a single man, it would seem, at first glance, a waste of men to put more labor troops in a camp than are actually needed. But men assigned to labor battalions should not be sentenced to labor for the duration of the war if they later show or develop to the point that they deserve something better. It is recommended that each one of these labor battalions have one training company. It is understood that many white men commissioned officers will not be physically fitted to stand hard service overseas. These will supply the non-commissioned officers for the reserve labor battalions and those in the training company of each labor battalion can do excellent work in developing men to the point where they can be sent to the combatant units. Thus there will always be a chance for those who deserve it, to be transferred to combatant units with the resulting opportunity for becoming non-commissioned officers. If a colored drafted man has not the physical soundness, intelligence, and education to be selected at first to go to the combatant troops and he does not develop so that he can be promoted out of the reserve labor battalion to combatant units, then of course, he can serve best as a day laborer and he should be kept where he renders the greatest use in prosecuting the war. It will not be attempted to go into the minute details of just how the men are to be transferred from the three straight labor companies of the reserve labor battalion to the training company and from the training company to combatant troops. These are details easy to arrange if the general policy is approved. Possibly it will be found advisable to have the corporals of the training companies colored and the sergeants white.

Colonel Marshall, head of the cantonment division, states in his opinion that there are ample quarters for a labor battalion in every division camp in the country and that if Division Commanders were told that they could have a labor battalion for their divisions, that they would be so anxious to get a labor battalion thereby allowing the entire time of their divisions for military training that they would arrange to make room and assign quarters for the labor battalion without further constructions. In case it is absolutely necessary to construct quarters at any camp for the labor battalions, it can be done. It is understood that no money is to be wasted. But if spending money materially assists in the prosecution of the war, that is what money is for. If barracks are necessary to shelter labor battalions and labor battalions help divisions to become trained for oversea service in shorter time, and to be more thoroughly trained, then such expense is entirely justified. Temporary arrangements can be made or men put in tent camp for the summer. Quarters can be built in three months, or at the outside in four months, from the date of authorization, so ample shelter can be arranged in the cases necessary before cold weather next winter.

The use of the reserve labor battalions in camps are not the only place where they can perform useful work and further the prosecution of the war. Colonel J. H. Alexander, in charge of the labor section, Construction Branch, Cantonment Division, Q. M. Department, states that he can use at least 25,000 and possibly to 50,000 of men in these labor battalions to great advantage in such work as preparing aviation fields, proving grounds and similar work of unskilled labor nature that does not enter into competition with union labor and where the opposition of union labor cannot be brought up. This need for labor will continue during the course of the war. Colonel Alexander is getting together a statement of where and how he can use colored labor organizations but it is not desired to enumerate the small items of where each small detachment of colored drafted men unsuited for service abroad can be used to best advantage.

The fuel and forage division has now one colored labor battalion in government forest reservation at Pisgah, North Carolina, getting out wood, to be used in the Government cantonments. General Fair believes that several battalions can be used profitably at the work of getting out wood for the use of the United States. In addition to the use of colored labor battalions composed of men not fitted for oversea service, there are various uses to which colored drafted men can be put in the military service that will release men capable of doing combatant service abroad to go abroad. The colored drafted men of higher education and technical trades, mechanics physically fit, etc. are to be sorted out and assigned to combatant divisions and units. There are a large number of mechanics and men of mechanical trades and training needed in a combatant division for combatant service and it will take every physically sound colored drafted man for the combatant troops.

Every colored drafted man with mechanical training not fitted for oversea service, can be used in the utilities companies. The utilities companies take care of the heating, water supply, lighting, sewers, drains, repairs, painting, and in general all activities in each camp or cantonment that correspond to Municipal activities in a town. Recent estimates call for a total personnel of 16,500 in the camps. General Fair states that he can use up to 7000 colored drafted men in the remount service thereby replacing an equal amount of men who have been vaccinated and innoculated against typhoid, who have been disciplined and who are available for service with combatant troops abroad. General Fair further states that the reclamation company in each camp could be colored. This will provide work for 3000 to 5000 further colored drafted men.

It is not intended to go into the details of just what numbers and in what manner colored drafted men not fitted for oversea service can perform useful work in this country, aiding in the prosecution of the war. It is merely intended to show in a general way that those colored drafted men not fitted for service overseas, who were inducted into the service up to June 30, 1918, can be profitably employed in useful constructive work in this country. The disposition of those drafted after July 1st, 1918 is a problem which can best be solved as that time approaches. In general it would seem that activities must be taken over and partially worked by labor battalions which are now handled exclusively by labor unions such as for instance the mining of part of the coal actually used by the United States Government.

Separate memorandum will be written taking up the question of each line of operations in which it is proposed to put colored drafted men not selected for combatant troops or service in labor and Engineer service battalions overseas.

It is recommended that the question of race prejudice be not considered at all in the assigning of labor battalions to camps. These camps are mainly situated in the southern states. The negroes mainly come from the southern states. It would be a saving of transportation to assemble the drafted negroes in camps nearest their homes and organize them into labor battalions and put them to work. Each southern state had negroes in blue overalls working throughout the state with a pick and shovel. When these colored men are drafted they are put in blue overalls (fatigue clothes) and continue to do work with a pick and shovel in the same state where they were previously working. If it is assumed that trouble will occur between whites and colored, that encourages it to occur, but if negroes are sent where they are needed and the possibility of trouble ignored there is not much probability of trouble occurring.

The War Plans Division in attached memorandum, subject: "Authorization of labor units for Camp Custer, Michigan, and Camp Jackson, S.C." recommends that the remainder of the fifty labor battalions previously authorized, be organized as soon as possible and assigned to the various camps where their services may be most needed. This would serve a two-fold purpose, viz.:

(a) Improve the organization and discipline of these battalions and afford sufficient time for the elimination and replacement of the unfit.

(b) Provide men to perform labor at the various camps, thereby releasing combatant troops for their proper training and instruction.

The War Plans Division suggested that these papers be referred to the Operations Branch for necessary action. The reason the letters of the Commanding Generals, Camp Custer, Mich. and Camp Jackson, S.C. were referred to the War Plans Division was that they asked for the creation of labor units outside of the fifty labor battalions originally authorized for oversea service. The Operations Division does not concur in organizing the labor battalions for oversea service as labor battalions for labor in the various camps. The labor battalions for oversea service have to be carefully selected from those physically sound and if they be organized now they will have to be completely changed just prior to sending them abroad, and it is better to take the colored men just as they come after the best are picked out for combatant units, and organize them into reserve labor battalions for camp service and to select those physically fit for overseas service just as labor battalions are needed for oversea service. Colonel John E. Stephens, Chairman Organization Branch, War Plans Division has been consulted and concurs in the policy recommended in this memorandum, that selection should be made of these men of higher intelligence, education, and sounder men physically from the colored drafted men for combatant troops and that the remainder should be kept busy at useful constructive work that furthers the prosecution of the War.

The Organization Branch, War Plans Division, has recently submitted a memorandum recommending organization of 8 additional colored Infantry Regiments and contemplates recommending the organization of 17 colored Pioneer regiments. These will take care of those colored men suited for combatant service for some time to come. The proposition of authorizing Reserve labor battalions was taken up with Colonel Stephens and he concurred, and it is requested that this memorandum be sent the War Plans Division for approval. Colonel McCammon of the Organization Branch, who has been making a study of the organization of new combatant units from the colored draft has also been consulted with reference to organization of reserve labor battalions and concurs.

The officers for these battalions should be officers unfitted for service overseas or men over draft age to be appointed as officers of the reserve labor battalions. The non-commissioned officers (white) should be selected as far as possible from white non-commissioned officers not fitted for service overseas.

It is not proposed to have these labor Battalions, which are assigned to camps, do any interior fatigue for the combatant organizations. They do work that has to be done for the camp as a whole. Colonel Noble and Colonel Howard (for the Surgeon General) have been consulted and concur. They state that the Medical Department is prepared to do the reconstructive medical work necessary on the labor battalions without interfering with their functions as labor Battalions. Major Lentz, Operations Division, who has been working out a scheme for development battalions, has been consulted and concurs. Major Lentz states that the development and reserve labor battalions will not conflict in their functions.

Final recommendation: It is recommended that authority be granted to organize, as the men become available, not to exceed 50 reserve labor Battalions to be organized in accordance with Table 316, Series D, January 28, 1918, and that the Operations Divisions, General Staff, be authorized to assign them to the various camps where they may be most needed, for service as indicated in this memorandum.

E. D. Anderson, Colonel
General Staff, Chairman,
Operations Branch.

Notes

CHAPTER 1

1. Edward Reuter, *The American Race Problem*, 3d ed. (New York, 1970), p. 67 (figures are from Census Bureau enumerations).

2. Seldon P. Spencer, *The Racial Question* (Washington, D.C., 1920), p. 6 (publication of U.S. Department of Education).

3. Reuter, *American Race Problem*, p. 242.

4. Winfield Collins, *The Truth about Lynching and the Negro in the South* (New York, 1918), p. 151; Francis T. Long, *The Negroes of Clarke County, Georgia, during the Great War* (Athens, Ga., 1919), p. 28.

5. Papers of Emmett J. Scott, Morgan State College, Baltimore, Md., box 114, file 2 (Charles Williams's report on Camps Stuart and Hill). The Scott materials will be cited hereafter as Scott Papers, with box and file numbers appended; thus: 114-2.

6. W. E. B. DuBois, "The Problem of Problems," *Intercollegiate Socialist*, December 1917–January 1918, p. 8.

7. George Brown Tindall, *South Carolina Negroes: 1877–1900* (Baton Rouge, La., 1966), p. 245.

8. "Last Year's Lynching Record," *Outlook* 115 (17 January 1917):97.

9. Ray Stannard Baker, *Following the Color Line* (New York, 1964), p. 113.

10. Henry Blumenthal, "Woodrow Wilson and the Race Question," *Journal of Negro History* 28 (January 1963):20.

11. Henry L. Johnson, *The Negro under Wilson* (n.p., ca. 1917), p. 5. Johnson was removed from his $4,000 per year post as recorder of deeds by the Democratic administration; his pamphlet was published by the Republican National Committee.

12. *Chicago Defender*, 30 June 1917, p. 12. See also W. S. Scarborough, "Race Riots and Their Remedy," *Independent* 99 (16 August 1919):223.

13. Oswald G. Villard, "The Race Problem," *Nation* 99 (24 December 1914):738. The word "Negro" appearing uncapitalized in a quotation is the usage of the source rather than that of the present writers. Most white sources customarily left this racial designation uncapitalized in the 1910s and 1920s.

14. Scott Papers, 115-2 (Scott to Benedict Crowell, assistant secre-

tary of war, 25 January 1919); ibid., 112-3 (A. L. Manly to Scott, 8 April 1918). See also National Association for the Advancement of Colored People, *Annual Report for 1918* (New York, 1919), pp. 62–63.

15. *Chicago Defender*, 7 April 1917, p. 4.

16. Kelly Miller, *The Everlasting Stain* (Washington, D.C., 1924), p. 10.

17. James Weldon Johnson, *Black Manhattan* (New York, 1930), pp. 232–33. Similar sentiments were expressed by a black draftee about to leave Saint Helena Island, S.C., for the training camp (see Grace B. House, *Soldiers of Freedom* [n.p., n.d.], p. 4).

18. H. H. Proctor, *Between Black and White* (New York, 1925), pp. 167–68.

19. A. Clayton Powell, *Patriotism and the Negro* (New York, n.d.), p. 9.

20. Editorial, *Crisis* 16 (June 1918):60.

21. House, *Soldiers of Freedom*, p. 8.

22. Robert R. Moton, *Finding a Way Out: An Autobiography* (Garden City, N.J., 1921), pp. 236–37; Napoleon B. Marshall, *The Providential Armistice: A Volunteer's Story* (Washington, D.C., 1930), p. 12. Marshall was a graduate of Harvard.

23. Walter White, *A Man Called White* (New York, 1948), pp. 35–36.

24. James Weldon Johnson, *Along This Way* (New York, 1933), pp. 232–33.

25. Spencer, *Racial Question*, p. 3.

26. Long, *Negroes of Clarke County*, p. 49.

27. Lewis B. Moore, *How the Colored Race Can Help in the Problems Issuing from the War* (New York, 1918), pp. 20–21.

28. Oswald Henderson, *The Negro Migration of 1916–1918* (Washington, D.C., 1921), p. 22. Most estimates were based loosely on the Census Bureau's figures, which were released at ten-year intervals. Herbert Aptheker (*Toward Negro Freedom* [New York, 1956], p. 112) estimated that some three-quarters of a million moved north between 1903 and 1919. Reuter, in *The American Race Problem* (p. 231), uses the figure 330,000 for the decade 1910–20. This migration was promoted by the *Chicago Defender*, which resulted in a great increase in Chicago's black population (see some of the letters to that paper in Richard Resh's *Black America* [Lexington, Mass., 1969], pp. 41–48). Other comments are found in John W. Gregory, *The Menace of Colour* (London, 1925), p. 65; and Elliott Rudwick, *Race Riot at East St. Louis* (Cleveland, Ohio, 1966), chap. 3.

29. Lorenzo J. Greene and Carter G. Woodson, *The Negro Wage Earner* (Washington, D.C., 1930), p. 247.

30. *New York Times*, 2 July 1917, p. 9. One assumes that the lower-case "n" in "negro" was the work of the *Times's* staff, rather than Powell's choice.

31. "Southern Negroes Moving North," *World's Work* 34 (June 1917):135.

32. "How the War Brings Unprophesied Opportunities to the Negro Race," *Current Opinion* 61 (December 1916):405. The statement was originally made by Wilson Jefferson in the *New York Post*. See also George E. Haynes, *The Trend of the Races* (New York, 1922), p. 116; U.S. Department of Labor, Division of Negro Economics, *The Negro at Work during the World War and Reconstruction* (Washington, D.C., 1921), p. 2.

33. Editorial, *New York Times*, 21 January 1918, p. 10.

34. The briefest list would include: in business and real estate, C. J. Walker, H. C. Haynes, William Mack Felton, Henry C. Parker, Lillian Harris, and James C. Thomas; in banking, J. Franklin Smallwood, Henry White, and J. S. Montague; in civil rights organizations, William Lewis Buckley and James Weldon Johnson; in journalism, T. Thomas Fortune and Robert Abbott; in scholarship, Carter G. Woodson; W. C. Handy, and innumerable other composers and musicians; and practically every important black athlete, topped by Jack Johnson.

35. Johnson, *Black Manhattan*, p. 233.

36. Marshall, *Providential Armistice*, p. 12. He made this statement before the conscription act was passed and while many Americans were still mentally neutral.

37. *Crisis*, May 1917, p. 23; cited from the *Louisville* (Ky.) *Courier-Journal*.

38. Ibid. 16 (July 1918):111.

39. Ibid., June 1917, p. 59.

40. J. Henry Hewlett, *Race Riots in America: Judge Lynch's Record, 1917–1924* (Washington, D.C., n.d.), pp. 9–10, 14. Another writer said that he knew of many intelligent Negroes who "hesitate to salute the flag," because "its protection is for white men only" (Algernon Jackson, *The Man Next Door* [Philadelphia, 1919], p. 33).

41. Carter G. Woodson, ed., *The Works of Francis J. Grimke* (Washington, D.C., 1942), 1:563–64.

42. Editorial, *Washington Bee*, 7 April 1917, p. 4; editorial, 14 April 1917, p. 4. Kelly Miller and George W. Cook, both professors at Howard University, were mentioned by name.

43. U.S., Congress, Senate, *Investigation Activities of the Department of Justice*, 66th Cong., 1st sess., vol. 12, Senate Document no. 153 (Washington, D.C., 1919), p. 172.

44. *Messenger*, November 1917, p. 31.

45. "Negro Conscription," *New Republic* 12 (20 October 1917):318.

46. Moton, *Finding a Way Out*, pp. 234–35.

47. *Congressional Record*, 65th Cong., 2d sess., p. 7237.

48. Collins, *Truth about Lynching*, p. 143; Moton, *Finding a Way Out*, pp. 248–49.

49. Robert R. Moton, "Fifty Thousand and Fifty Million," *Outlook* 120 (20 November 1918):452; *Crisis*, January 1918, p. 141.

50. Kate M. Herring, "How the Southern Negro Is Supporting the Government," *Outlook* 120 (20 November 1918):452–53. South Carolina lowered the black quota to $2 per person and raised the white quota to make up the difference. David Raines, of Louisiana, contributed $100,000 (NAACP, *Report for 1918*, pp. 46–48).

51. U.S. Senate, *Investigation Activities*, p. 178.

52. NAACP, *Report for 1918*, pp. 46–48.

53. Spencer, *Racial Question*, p. 4; J. W. S. Nordholt, *People Who Walk in Darkness* (London, 1960), p. 213.

54. Hewlett, *Race Riots in America*, pp. 12–13; *Crisis*, March 1918, p. 249.

55. *Crisis*, November 1918, p. 27; December 1918, p. 90; *Chicago Defender*, 6 October 1917, p. 1.

56. U.S. Army, War College, *Colored Soldiers in the U.S. Army* (Washington, D.C., 1942), pp. 6–7.

57. Ibid., pp. 11–12.

58. Ibid., p. 15.

59. Ibid., p. 17.

60. Ibid., pp. 19–20 (report of Col. Robert C. Humber, September 1942).

61. George E. Mowry, *The Era of Theodore Roosevelt* (New York, 1958), p. 213.

62. U.S. Army, War College, *Colored Soldiers*, pp. 19–20 (Humber's report).

63. U.S., Congress, House, "A Bill to Direct the Secretary of Defense to Rectify Certain Official Action Taken as a Result of the 'Brownsville Raid,' 1906," 92d Cong., 1st sess., H.R. 6866. The bill was introduced by Congressman Augustus F. Hawkins (Calif.) on 29 March 1971. As a result of Hawkins's bill, the army (on 28 September 1972) cleared the records of the men involved; but the action specifically prohibited the payment of back pay or allowances to the men involved or to their descendants. Congressman Hawkins felt that such a prohibition continued the injustice and introduced additional legislation to insure justice to those soldiers and their survivors (*New York Times*,

29 September 1972, p. 1; Hawkins to A. Barbeau, December 1972, and 20 February 1973).

64. Letter, *Literary Digest* 55 (June 1917):342–43; W. E. B. DuBois Papers, Amistad Research Center, Fisk University, Nashville, Tenn., chap. 4, Black France, pp. 2–3 (hereafter cited as Fisk Manuscripts, with a file number or title designation); Hewlett, *Race Riots in America*, pp. 12–13.

65. Fisk Manuscripts, chap. 4, Black France, pp. 13, 17–18, 21–22.

66. Ibid., pp. 6, 7–8, 10–11, 14–16. Some of these troops held against six separate German assaults on the Arras front early in the war. See also Norvel P. Barksdale, "France and the Negro," *Lincoln University Record*, October 1924, p. 13.

67. Fisk Manuscripts, chap. 4, Black France, pp. 13, 17–18, 21–22.

68. Ibid., p. 9.

69. Ibid., chap. 5, Black England, pp. 1–2, 23, 25.

70. C. Wood-Hill, *History of the British West Indies Regiment* (n.p., n.d.), p. 22.

71. Fisk Manuscripts, chap. 5, Black England, pp. 57–58 ff. Among the other cities specifically mentioned by the *West Indian* (Trinidad) were Glamorgan, Cardiff, and Berry.

72. Monroe Mason and Arthur Furr, *The American Negro with the Red Hand of France* (Boston, 1920), p. 16; W. Allison Sweeney, *History of the American Negro in the Great World War* (Chicago, 1919), p. 138 (Sweeney was a correspondent for the *Chicago Defender*); Howard W. Odum, *Wings on My Feet* (Indianapolis, Ind., 1929), pp. 58–59. Though technically fiction, the last-named work is heavily infused with authentic material. It holds up well in comparison with verifiable sources and so is considered here as a primary source of considerable historical value.

73. Army War College Records, National Archives, Washington, D.C., Record Group 165, item no. 8142-150 (Col. E. D. Anderson, chairman of Operations Branch, General Staff, to Chief of Staff, 16 May 1918, p. 2). Hereafter, records in the National Archives will be designated by *NA*, followed by the Record Group (R.G.) number and file or item number.

74. Fisk Manuscripts, chaps. 10–14, 92d Division (paper by Gen. C. C. Ballou, "Sidelights on Negro Soldiers," p. 33). Ballou had been second in command of the 24th Infantry, headed the black-officers' training school at Des Moines, and then commanded the 92d Division during its military service.

75. Charles H. Williams, *Sidelights on Negro Soldiers* (Boston, 1923), p. 230. Readers are cautioned not to confuse this extremely valuable

source with the Ballou paper in the preceding footnote. Both have the same title.

CHAPTER 2

1. NAACP, *Report for 1918*, pp. 89–90; "Last Year's Lynching Record," *Outlook*, p. 97.

2. NAACP, *Thirty Years of Lynching in the United States* (New York, 1919), pp. 25–26 (citation from the *Memphis* [Tenn.] *Press*, 21 May 1917).

3. *Crisis*, February 1918, p. 181; NAACP, *Report for 1918*, pp. 89–90. The latter source refers to the victim as Ligon Scott. This was the second lynching within a year in Dyersburg. William Thomas had been hanged in March for shooting a police officer.

4. *New York Times*, 9 July 1917, p. 7; Preston Slosson, *The Great Crusade and After* (New York, 1930), p. 259; *Congressional Record*, 65th Cong., 1st sess., p. 4698 (Thomas's remarks of 5 July 1917). See also *Independent* 89 (25 February 1917):347–48.

5. Kelly Miller, *The Disgrace of Democracy* (Washington, D.C., 1917), p. 6; *Crisis*, July 1918, p. 124.

6. Miller, *Disgrace of Democracy*, p. 6.

7. Jerome Dowd (*The Negro in American Life* [New York, 1926], pp. 57–58) gives a figure of 18,000. The exact number of black migrants to East St. Louis is uncertain; older accounts are high, perhaps too high. The most careful recent study, Rudwick's *Race Riot at East St. Louis*, states that the black population of the city tripled to about 6,000 between 1900 and 1910 (p. 5), and that the migration of 1915–17 resulted in some 5,000 additional residents (p. 166). He does not say if his figures are for East St. Louis alone or included the neighboring municipalities of Brooklyn, National City, and Monsanto. An increase in the black population of those communities would swell the statistics of what was commonly called "East St. Louis."

8. *New York Times*, 8 July 1917, sec. 2, p. 3; sec. 8, p. 5. The *Times* felt that an increase in the black "criminal element" was the major factor.

9. Abraham Epstein, *The Negro Migrant in Pittsburgh* (Pittsburgh, 1918; New York, 1969), p. 34.

10. *Congressional Record*, 65th Cong., 2d sess., House Document no. 1231, pp. 8827, 8831; U.S., Congress, House, *East St. Louis Riots* (Washington, D.C., 1918), pp. 2–3, 5–6.

11. Worth mentioning for its singular obtuseness was a finding of the congressional committee that "the Negroes gravitated to the unsani-

tary sections, existed in the squalor of filthy cabins, and made no complaint; but the white worker had a higher outlook, and the failure to provide them with better homes added to their bitter dissatisfaction with the burdens placed upon them by having to compete with black labor. . . ." (U.S. House, *East St. Louis Riots*, pp. 2–3).

12. Dowd, *Negro in American Life*, pp. 58–59; *New York Times*, 29 May 1917, p. 3. On the 30th, these troops were erroneously reported to be eight companies of the 8th Illinois, a black regiment (30 May 1917, p. 6).

13. Dowd, *Negro in American Life*, pp. 58–59; *New York Times*, 2 July 1917, p. 7; 8 July 1917, sec. 2, p. 3; *Congressional Record*, 65th Cong., 2d sess., p. 4698 (remarks of 9 July 1917); U.S. House, *East St. Louis Riots*, pp. 3–4.

14. Dowd, *Negro in American Life*, pp. 58–59; *Congressional Record*, 65th Cong., 2d sess., House Document no. 1231, pp. 8823, 8834; *New York Times*, 7 July 1917, p. 6; 4 August 1917, p. 4.

15. Dowd, *Negro in American Life*, pp. 58–59; *Congressional Record*, 65th Cong., 2d sess., p. 638 (report of Attorney General Brundage of Illinois); U.S. House, *East St. Louis Riots*, pp. 5–6; *Crisis*, September 1917, pp. 228, 231–32.

16. *Congressional Record*, 65th Cong., 2d sess., p. 637 (Sherman's remarks, 7 January 1918). See also Tillman's remarks in 1st sess., 5 July 1917, p. 5152.

17. *New York Times*, 3 July 1917, p. 1; 5 July 1917, p. 9; 8 July 1917, sec. 1, p. 1; *Congressional Record*, 65th Cong., 2d sess., p. 638; *Crisis*, September 1917, pp. 228, 231–32; Johnson, *Along This Way*, p. 319.

18. *Congressional Record*, 65th Cong., 2d sess., p. 638.

19. Ibid., pp. 8829.

20. Ibid., p. 8834; see also ibid., appendix, pp. 378–79. This material was read into the *Record* by Senator Sherman, 17 December 1917. See also *New York Times*, 10 April 1918, p. 11.

21. "What Some Americans Think of East St. Louis," *Outlook* 116 (18 July 1917):435–36. The article cites similar views from the *Houston Post* and the *Savannah Morning News*.

22. Ibid.; *Congressional Record*, 65th Cong., 1st sess., p. 5085; *New York Times*, 17 July 1917, p. 7; James K. Vardaman, *The Great American Race Problem and Its Relation to the Present War* (n.p., 1917), pp. 1–2 (speech delivered in the Senate, 16 August 1917). Franz Boas (*The Real Race Problem* [New York, 1910]) said that the "gradual process of elimination of the full-blooded Negro may be retarded by legislation, but it cannot possibly be eliminated" (p. 7).

23. Miller, *Disgrace of Democracy*, pp. 4, 14; *New York Times*, 29 July

1917, p. 1; "A Negro's March with Muffled Drums," *Survey* 38 (4 August 1917):405; *Washington Bee*, 14 July 1917, p. 1.

24. *New York Times*, 25 August 1917, p. 1; *Chicago Defender*, 15 September 1917, p. 12.

25. U.S. Army, War College, *Colored Soldiers*, pp. 19–20; U.S. Army, War College, *The Order of Battle of the United States Land Forces in the World War* (Washington, D.C., 1949), vol. 3, pt. 1, p. 384; *Crisis*, June 1918, pp. 82–83; ibid., October 1918, pp. 291–93; Edward L. N. Glass, *The History of the Tenth Cavalry* (Tucson, Ariz., 1921), pp. 82, 83–84, 86; *NA*, R.G. 94, file 141-11.4 (Hadsell to Adjutant General, 23 January 1919).

26. U.S. Army, War College, *Colored Soldiers*, pt. 2, p. 1.

27. Ibid., pt. 3, pp. 1–2; *New York Times*, 25 August 1917, p. 2 (report of Captain Snow [white] of the 24th Infantry).

28. U.S. Army, War College, *Colored Soldiers*, pt. 3, p. 2.

29. Ibid., p. 3. Accounts of the fray are extremely confused. Adding to white fears, of course, was the remembrance that Negro Regulars, of the 25th Infantry, had been involved in a similar incident at Brownsville, Texas, in 1906. See also Benjamin Brawley, *Short History of the Negro* (New York, 1918), pp. 354–55.

30. U.S. Army, War College, *Colored Soldiers*, pt. 3, pp. 2–3. In this crisis, the president of the Columbus, New Mexico, Chamber of Commerce took an entirely different view of the troopers of the 24th. He telegraphed the War Department that this regiment was one of the best-disciplined units in the army; his city would be happy to have those soldiers returned there, together with any other black soldiers the government wished to send (*NA*, R.G. 165, item 8142-19).

31. *New York Times*, 9 October 1917, p. 22; 12 December 1917, p. 7.

32. See also Johnson, *Along This Way*, pp. 322–23.

33. *Crisis*, October 1917, pp. 284–85; January 1918, p. 114.

34. *Congressional Record*, 65th Cong., 3d sess., p. 5032 (remarks of Representative Johnson of South Dakota, 4 March 1919); see also p. 3810, par. K (General Ansell to Congressman Burnett, 19 February 1919).

35. Johnson, *Along This Way*, pp. 322–23; *New York Times*, 20 February 1918, p. 4; 5 September 1918, p. 10; 25 September 1918, p. 9; NAACP, *Report for 1918*, pp. 37–38. Finally, in 1921, President Warren Harding, on the petition of some 50,000 persons, reduced the sentences of those still in prison; eventually, they were all released.

36. *New York Times*, 25 August 1917, p. 1; 26 August 1917, sec. 1, p. 3.

37. Collins, *The Truth about Lynching*, p. 87 (cited from the *Baltimore*

Sun, 12 September 1917). See also *New York Times,* 25 August 1917, p. 2; 28 August 1917, p. 18.

38. U.S. Army, War College, *Colored Soldiers,* p. 4. No evidence was produced to support the assertion that the soldiers were responsible for "restlessness" among the black population of Houston.

39. Newton D. Baker Papers, Library of Congress, Manuscript Division, Washington, D.C. (Baker to Wilson, 22 August 1918). Hereafter cited as Baker Papers.

40. "The Houston Mutiny," *Outlook* 118 (5 September 1917):10–11.

41. Anonymous letter to the *Crisis* from Memphis, published in that magazine in the January 1918 issue, p. 127.

CHAPTER 3

1. *Crisis,* June 1917, p. 62; May 1918, p. 7; Walter S. Buchanan, *The Negro's War Aims* (Birmingham, Ala., 1918), p. 4.

2. Enoch Crowder, *Second Report of the Provost Marshal General* (Washington, D.C., 1919), pp. 193–94.

3. White, *Man Called White,* pp. 35–36.

4. Williams, *Sidelights,* pp. 17–18; *Crisis,* May 1917, p. 23 (reported by George W. Cook in the *Washington Post*); Vardaman, *Great American Race Problem,* pp. 7–8.

5. Herbert Seligmann, *The Negro Faces America* (New York, 1920, 1969), p. 39. This volume stands out as the most illuminating and unbiased (though sympathetic) of contemporaneous accounts. Seligmann's magazine articles were equally perceptive.

6. *Crisis,* July 1917, p. 112; cited from the *New York Evening Post.* It is hard to conceive of a more pointed use of the uncapitalized "n" than in this series of racial appellations. As a further indication of race, some black registrants were required to tear a corner off their cards (Brawley, *Short History,* pp. 353–54). See also the report of Larry Jordan in the New York City Writers' Project, "History of the Negro in New York." This is a typescript in the Schomburg Collection and was the result of a W.P.A. project under the editorial supervision of Roi Ottley.

7. *Crisis,* May 1918, p. 8. The instructions read: "It has been called to the attention of this department that many of your white registrants have been examined by colored doctors. This matter has been taken up with the Adjutant General and he desires that this practice be discontinued" (Fisk Manuscripts, chaps. 1–9 [chap. 8]; undated letter from Clarence F. Hohnisp [?]). The *Crisis* received the letter on 25 February 1918. See also Aptheker, *Toward Negro Freedom,* p. 117; Ira DeA. Reid, "A Critical Summary: The Negro on the Home Front in World Wars I

and II," *Journal of Negro Education* 12 (1943):515; Emmett J. Scott, *The American Negro in the World War* (Chicago, 1919), p. 65.

8. Archives of the Federal Council of Churches, Press Releases, 1917–19, file 2 (report of John R. Hawkins to the annual meeting of the executive counctil of the Federal Council of Churches). These archives, in the possession of the National Council of Churches of Christ, New York City, will hereafter be designated as Federal Council, with the appropriate box and item title. See also Crowder, *Second Report*, p. 192. When Negroes tried to enlist, they were told that blacks were not wanted at that time. As a result, only about 4,000 were able to enlist (Williams, *Sidelights*, p. 22). The black enlistments were stopped for the same reasons that delayed the calling up of the black draft—lack of facilities to receive them.

9. Crowder, *Second Report*, pp. 458–59; appendix, tables 71A, 73A.

10. Long, *Negroes of Clarke County*, p. 4.

11. Sweeney, *American Negro*, p. 111.

12. Crowder, *Second Report*, p. 459; U.S. Army, War College, *Order of Battle*, vol. 3, pt. 1, p. 384.

13. Crowder, *Second Report*, pp. 194–95; Sweeney, *American Negro*, p. 113 (report of Crowder to Secretary Baker, 20 December 1918).

14. Sweeney, *American Negro*, p. 116; Williams, *Sidelights*, p. 21.

15. *Chicago Defender*, 22 February 1919, p. 1; Aptheker, *Toward Negro Freedom*, p. 117; Scott Papers, 115-4 (Frances Birthwell to W. E. B. DuBois, 1 April 1918).

16. NAACP, *Report for 1918*, p. 41. The letter from Miller was dated 3 October 1918. Even this policy, though discriminatory in itself, was not applied in the 92d Division when that unit was organized; there were black line officers, but the divisional medical staff was white.

17. Federal Council, General War-Time Committee, file 1 (minutes of conference with Keppel and Maj. Gen. Frank McIntyre, 25 September 1918). This material will be cited hereafter as Federal Council, GWC-1.

18. U.S., Congress, House, *Selective Service Act* (Washington, D.C., 1918), pp. 29–30 (answer to query of Mr. Quin of Mississippi).

19. Seligmann, *Negro Faces America*, pp. 86–87.

20. "Negro Conscription," *New Republic*, p. 317. The article implied that blacks were more sensual than white men, a well-worn cliché.

21. "Where to Encamp the Negro Troops," *Literary Digest* 55 (29 September 1917):14–15; *New York Times*, 25 August 1917, p. 1; *Chicago Defender* 15 (September 1917):12.

22. Scott, *American Negro*, p. 72. The committee was composed of: George F. Peabody, philanthropist; Oswald G. Villard, editor; T. H.

Harris, Louisiana educator; Thomas J. Jones, Phelps-Stokes Foundation; Robert R. Moton, Tuskegee Institute; John Hope, Morehouse College; Bishop George W. Clinton, A.M.E. Zion Church; and a number of others, including Scott. The first four were white; the remainder were Negroes of the moderate Southern type. Moton felt that Baker's later actions implemented the requests of the committee (see Moton, *Finding a Way Out*, pp. 243–45).

23. The original suggestion that ratios be established in all cantonments is found in a memo signed by Col. E. D. Anderson and Maj. U.S. Grant, of the General Staff, 22 September 1917 (*NA*, R.G. 165, item 8142-26).

24. Scott, *American Negro*, p. 72. As an example of the shifting involved, some of Alabama's black draftees were sent to camp in Iowa.

25. This situation prevailed throughout the war; as late as May 1918, Baker delayed calling black inductees because there were no facilities available for them.

26. *New York Times*, 1 September 1917, p. 4. The War Department eventually worked out the problem by establishing a separate cantonment for each division of the National Army, with a small black unit, usually a regiment, attached for training purposes. The black units were not intended to function overseas as part of the white divisions to which they were attached for training. This explains why, when the 92d Division was organized entirely of black soldiers, it was never assembled as a division until after it arrived in France.

27. Scott Papers, 114-2 (Williams's reports on Camp Meade, p. 3; Camp Sevier, pp. 3–4; and Camp Wadsworth, pp. 3–4). Charles Williams served as Emmett Scott's most active and reliable observer. He visited every camp where there were black soldiers and sent a brief, though comprehensive, report to Scott. Copies of all these reports are in the Scott Papers. See ibid. (letter from a black sergeant, Co. C, 304th Stevedores, to W. E. B. DuBois, 18 December 1918); ibid., 114-3 (Williams's special report on conditions at Camp Pike, pp. 8–9; and his report on Camp Beauregard, p. 4). YMCA programs sent into Camp Pike were given in every hut except the one reserved for the black troops; the only exceptions were two speakers who specifically requested permission to address the black soldiers (Pike report, p. 5). See also Young Men's Christian Association, *Service with the Fighting Man* (New York, 1922), 1:402; Williams, *Sidelights*, pp. 96, 110; Fisk Manuscripts, War Material Miscellaneous, file 2 (statement of Sgt. Maj. Charles E. Conick, 369th Infantry, on YMCA, n.d.). War Material Miscellaneous papers will be designated hereafter as WMM-2.

28. Scott Papers, 113-5, dispatch from Ralph Tyler, n.d. Scott in-

formed Tyler that this particular dispatch would not be cleared by the War Department (hence, was unpublishable) and urged him to be more circumspect in the future (ibid., Scott to Tyler, n.d.).

29. Jane Olcott, comp., *The Work of Colored Women* (New York, 1919), p. 38; Addie W. Hunton and Katherine M. Johnson, *Two Colored Women with the American Expeditionary Forces* (New York, 1920), pp. 35–37.

30. Ridgley Torrence, *The Story of John Hope* (New York, 1948), pp. 222–23; YMCA, *Service with the Fighting Man*, 2:177–78. In this area, where there were some 30,000 black soldiers, sixty men at a time were detailed to help in the YMCA facility.

31. Williams, *Sidelights*, pp. 112–13.

32. James E. Sadler, *The Negro from Jamestown to the Rhine* (n.p., n.d.), p. 29; J. A. Jamieson et al., *Complete History of the Colored Soldiers in the World War* (New York, 1919), pp. 69–70. The *Buffalo* (N.Y.) *Express* estimated that at least 300 black nurses served in France, but only because they "passed" and military authorities were unaware of their "race" (*Crisis*, April 1919, p. 295; quotes a Nettie Jackson).

33. "Democracy and the Colored Soldier," *Playground* 13 (September 1919):260–61; Hunton and Johnson, *Two Colored Women*, p. 21.

34. Federal Council, "Religious Publication Service Clip Sheet," for release on 18 March 1918.

35. Williams, *Sidelights*, pp. 88–89; Olcott, *Colored Women*, pp. 13, 15, 17, 32; Mason and Furr, *American Negro*, pp. 154–55; Fisk Manuscripts, chaps. 10–14 (chap. 13, 93d Division).

36. Glenn Frank, "Clash of Color," *Century* 99 (November 1919):94–95.

37. U.S. Army, War College, *Colored Soldiers*, p. 113 (report of Maj. Gen. W. H. Hay to Col. Allen J. Greer, 13 April 1919); p. 128 (Gen. W. P. Jackson to Greer, 14 April 1919); p. 110 (report of Greer to Assistant Commandant, General Staff College, 13 April 1920). Greer was probably the most consistently bigoted opponent of the Negro among military men; he was almost as vitriolic as Vardaman.

38. *NA*, R.G. 165, item 8142-46 (T. W. Hammond to Chief of Staff, 13 November 1917).

39. Ibid., item 8142-150, p. 2. See app. below for the full text of Colonel Anderson's report.

40. Ibid., item 8142-17.

41. Ibid. See also Scott Papers, 115-4 (DuBois to Baker, 6 December 1917).

42. George O. Ferguson, "The Intelligence of Negroes at Camp Lee, Virginia," *School and Society* 9 (14 June 1919):726. Psychologist Carl C. Brigham arrived at slightly different IQ figures in *A Study of Ameri-*

can Intelligence (Princeton, N.J., 1923), p. 124; graph, p. 198. See also James G. Harbord, *The American Army in France* (Boston, 1936), p. 27. Harbord ranks among those officers who were consistently antiblack.

43. George O. Ferguson, "The Mental Status of the American Negro," *Scientific Monthly* 12 (June 1921):533–34.

44. George O. Ferguson, "The Psychology of the Negro: An Experimental Study," *Archives of Psychology*, 1916, pp. 127–28.

45. Ferguson, "Intelligence of Negroes," p. 723.

46. Ibid. See also Ferguson, "Mental Status," pp. 540–41.

47. William McDougall, *Is America Safe for Democracy?* (New York, 1921), pp. 47–48.

48. Ibid.

49. Ferguson, "Intelligence of Negroes," pp. 724–25.

50. Ibid., pp. 725–26.

51. Carl C. Brigham, *A Study of American Intelligence* (Princeton, N.J., 1923), pp. xvii, 191–92. Later studies showed that the Beta test also required a degree of literacy. For Brigham's change of mind, see his "Intelligence Tests of Immigrant Groups," *Psychological Review* 37 (March 1930):165.

52. Scott, *American Negro*, p. 74; U.S. War Department, *The Official Record of the United States' Part in the Great War* (Washington, D.C., 1923), p. 18.

53. A. G. Love and C. B. Davenport, "A Comparison of White and Colored Troops in Respect to the Incidence of Disease," *Proceedings of the National Academy of Sciences* 5 (March 1919):58.

54. Ibid., pp. 58–60. Their report was summarized in "The Health of Colored Troops," *Literary Digest* 61·(14 June 1919):23.

55. Arthur B. Spingarn, "The Health and Morals of Colored Troops," *Crisis*, August 1918, p. 166.

56. *NA*, R.G. 94, file 148-50.4; ibid., box 453 (report of 1st Lt. L. P. Close, 313th Labor Battalion, 11 March 1919); Scott Papers, 114-2 (Williams on Sevier and Eustis; Williams on Lee; Williams on Hill); ibid., 115-4 (Brigadier General Hutchinson, commanding Camp Pike, to Scott, 30 May 1918); Williams, *Sidelights*, pp. 140–41.

57. Scott Papers, 114-2 (Williams's report on Camps Bowie and Meade, 8 February 1919).

58. *NA*, R.G. 165, item 8142-123 (Lutz Wahl to Chief of Staff, 8 April 1918).

59. Scott Papers, 114-2 (Williams's reports on Holabird, 30 January 1919, and Eustis, 14 February 1919); ibid., 114-3 (Williams's reports on McClellan, 7 November 1918, and Sheridan, 14 November 1918; Williams to Scott, 16 November 1918); Williams, *Sidelights*, pp. 26–27.

60. Scott Papers, 114, files 2 and 3 (see Williams's reports on the

various camps); ibid., 115-1 (Pvt. Willie Bell to Scott, 2 January 1919); *NA*, R.G. 94, file 168-11.4 (Col. P. M. Goodrich's report on the 164th Depot Brigade, Funston, 14 November 1918); ibid., file 134-11.4 (Capt. John B. G. Babcock's report, January 1919).

61. Scott Papers, 114-2 (Williams on Holabird, Travis, Sevier, and Eustis; complaint to NAACP from Homer Butler, 442d Reserve Labor Battalion); ibid., 114-3 (Williams on Camp Lee); ibid., 115-1 and 115-2 (complaints from Columbus, Ohio, Reserve Depot; from Camps Travis, Meade, etc.); *NA*, R.G. 94, file 148-50.4; ibid., file 168-11.4 (report of Col. Ivers W. Leonard, 24 September 1918).

62. Scott Papers, 114-2 (Williams's reports on Camps Lee, Humphreys, and Hill); Williams, *Sidelights*, pp. 140–41; *NA*, R.G. 94, file 168-11.4 (undated, unsigned, penciled report from Camp Lee); ibid., box 453 (report of 1st Lt. Close of the 313th Labor Battalion).

63. Scott Papers, 114-2 (Williams, "Résumé on Conditions Surrounding Negro Troops," 5 August 1918, p. 2).

64. Arthur B. Spingarn, "The War and Venereal Disease among Negroes," *Social Hygiene* 4 (July 1918):334–35.

65. H. L. McNeil, "Syphilis in the Southern Negro," *Journal of the American Medical Association* 67 (30 September 1916):1001–4; S. C. Jamison, "Certain Phases of Syphilis in the Negro Female from the Standpoint of Medical Diagnosis," *New Orleans Medical and Surgical Journal* 69 (1916–17):96–97; F. P. Boas, "The Relative Prevalence of Syphilis among Negroes and Whites," *Social Hygiene* 1 (1914–15):616; H. H. Hazen, "Syphilis in the American Negro," *Journal of the American Medical Association* 65 (8 August 1914):463; Love and Davenport, "White and Colored Troops," p. 59.

66. U.S. War Department, *Annual Report, 1918* (Washington, D.C., 1919), pp. 508–9.

67. Ibid., p. 516. W. Levin, in a note in the *Journal of Laboratory and Clinical Medicine* (November 1919), said that Wassermann tests at Camp Funston showed a rate of syphilis of 13.8 percent in whites, 24.1 percent in blacks.

68. Arthur B. Spingarn, *Address to the Fifteenth Annual Session of the National Association of Teachers in Colored Schools* (Washington, D.C., 1918), p. 2. Tuberculosis, pulmonary disorders, organic heart disease, and infant mortality were listed as the primary causes for this higher black mortality.

69. George Walker, *Venereal Disease in the American Expeditionary Forces* (Baltimore, 1922), pp. 122–23.

70. Ibid., p. 1.

71. Ibid., p. 101.

72. Ibid.

73. *NA*, R.G. 165, item 8142-150. See also app. below.

CHAPTER 4

1. Scott, *American Negro*, pp. 82, 84; Gunnar Myrdal, *The American Dilemma* (New York, 1944), 2:1308 n; Seymour J. Schoenfeld, *The Negro in the Armed Forces* (Washington, D.C., 1945), pp. 17–18. The efforts of Secretary Baker were frequently circumvented by other civilian and military officials. Edward M. Coffman, (*War to End All Wars* [New York, 1968], pp. 158–86) discusses a number of conflicts between the War Department and the AEF; Coffman points out (pp. 69–70) that Baker's concern about race matters led him, in the 1930s, to suggest the Gunnar Myrdal study of the American race problem.

2. Scott, *American Negro*, pp. 84–86; *Congressional Record*, 65th Cong., 1st sess., p. 1896; White, *Man Called White*, pp. 35–36.

3. Williams, *Sidelights*, pp. 37–38.

4. Scott, *American Negro*, p. 90.

5. Edgar H. Webster, *Chums and Brothers* (Boston, 1920), p. 144.

6. Scott, *American Negro*, pp. 87–88.

7. Dowd, *Negro in American Life*, pp. 233–34.

8. *NA*, R.G. 165, item 8142-181 (Gen. Frank McIntyre to Adjutant General, 1 August 1918); ibid., item 8142-61 (Henry Jervey to Adjutant General, 29 December 1917); Eugene Varlin, *The Negro and the U.S. Army* (New York, n.d.), p. 11. Varlin, a Socialist, was opposed to the entire military structure, and this bias should be borne in mind in using his observations.

9. Williams, *Sidelights*, p. 42.

10. Lucy France Pierce, "Training Colored Officers," *Review of Reviews* 56 (December 1917):640; Scott Papers, 112-2 (unsigned typescript by the "Official Historian" of the camp, submitted in accordance with Special Order no. 245, 6 November 1918, p. 10); *Congressional Record*, 65th Cong., 1st sess., appendix, p. 246 (from the remarks of Murray Hulburt to the House, 26 May 1917). Eighty-four men were detailed from each of the infantry regiments (24th and 25th); fifty-seven men from the 10th Cavalry and twenty-five from the 9th Cavalry. The presence of these Regulars meant that the camp started with a nucleus of candidates who were already familiar with army life and the "army way" of conducting its business. The civilian candidates came from the military districts into which the country had been divided: Northeastern (40), Eastern (240), Southeastern (430), Southern (75), Central (195), and Western (20) (John L. Thompson, *History and Views of the Colored Officers Training Camp* [Des Moines, Iowa, 1917], pp. 6–8).

11. Williams, *Sidelights*, pp. 41–42.

12. Ibid., p. 43. A clergyman who attended one of their concerts said: "It is not enough to say that by their demeanor while among us, their conduct on the streets, in the theaters and business houses, they

have brought honor to their race. They are, rather, an honor to the race of men."

13. "Democracy and the Colored Soldier," pp. 260–61; *Crisis*, June 1918, p. 62.

14. *NA*, R.G. 165, item 8142-20 (Adjutant General to Secretary of War, 5 September 1917).

15. Highly qualified experts, high scorers on tests, and some who rose from the ranks were exceptions.

16. U.S. Army, War College, *Colored Soldiers*, p. 103 (C.C. Ballou to Assistant Commandant, General Staff College, 14 March 1920). Ballou is also quoted as saying that only a high-school education was required of black officer candidates (Ulysses G. Lee, comp., *Employment of Negro Troops* [Washington, D.C.: Office of the Chief Military Historian, 1966], pp. 17–18.

17. William N. Colson and A. B. Nutt, "The Failure of the Ninety-second Division," *Messenger*, September 1919, pp. 22–23. For the wide range of age and education among black officers, see Coffman, *War to End All Wars*, pp. 318–19.

18. U.S. Army, War College, *Colored Soldiers*, p. 106 (Ballou's report).

19. Williams (*Sidelights*, p. 46) reported the number as 625; Sweeney (*American Negro*, p. 79) reported that 638 graduated. Kelly Miller, in *World War for Human Rights* (Washington, 1919), erroneously, but dramatically, stated that the commissioning took place at 11:00 A.M. of 11 November 1917, exactly one year before the Armistice.

20. U.S. Army, War College, *Colored Soldiers*, p. 127.

21. Col. James Moss, of the 367th Infantry, stated that his ninety-five black officers compared quite favorably with whites (*New York Times*, 23 January 1918, p. 18); W. P. Jackson found particular fault with the captains in organizing the 368th Infantry (U.S. Army, War College, *Colored Soldiers*, pp. 127–28). Jackson had commanded black troops in Cuba and the Philippines; his officers, though, were white. While respecting the black man as a soldier, Jackson did not respect him as a man; he said that the Negro was "really a grown up child."

22. *NA*, R.G. 94, file 16-11.4 (report of Col. Dan Moore, commanding the 349th Field Artillery); *NA*, R.G. 165, item 8142-125 (D. W. Ketcham to Chief of Staff, 20 April 1918); Williams, *Sidelights*, pp. 48–49, 174–75.

23. U.S. Army, War College, *Colored Soldiers*, p. 103 (Ballou's report); Scott Papers, 115-4 (Scott to DuBois, 8 January 1918); *NA*, R.G. 165, item 8142-74 (Biddle to Adjutant General, 21 January 1918).

24. Williams, *Sidelights*, pp. 51–52.

25. Ibid., pp. 48–49, 53, 56–57.

26. Ibid., p. 54; *Crisis*, September 1918, p. 237; Hunton and Johnson, *Two Colored Women*, p. 212; Scott, *American Negro*, pp. 334–35.

27. *NA*, R.G. 165, item 6292-95 (Col. W. F. Clark, General Staff, to Chief of Staff, 6 May 1919).

28. Comment by Emmett Scott, *New York Times*, 6 January 1918, sec. 4, p. 4.

29. Williams, *Sidelights*, p. 50.

30. *NA*, R.G. 165, item 8142-166 (Frank McIntyre to Chief of Staff, 16 July 1918).

31. W. E. B. DuBois, "An Essay toward a History of the Black Man in the Great War," *Crisis* 18 (June 1919):80. This was the 372d Infantry.

32. *NA*, R.G. 165, item 9750-24 (Graves to Adjutant General, 24 April 1918); *NA*, R.G. 120, file 16-11.4 (typescript History of the 317th Engineers, pp. 1–2).

33. Williams, *Sidelights*, pp. 50, 58–59; Webster, *Chums and Brothers*, pp. 168–69; Colson and Nutt, "Failure of the Ninety-second Division," pp. 23–24; Scott Papers, 113-5 (petition from men at Camp Jackson to Ralph Tyler [a black journalist], 26 September 1918); ibid., 114-2 (Charles Williams's special report on Camp Dodge, p. 1). *NA*, R.G. 120, file 16-11.4 (History of the 317th Engineers, pp. 1–2).

34. John Richards, "Some Experiences with Colored Soldiers," *Atlantic Monthly* 124 (August 1919):190.

35. U.S. Army, War College, *Colored Soldiers*, p. 128 (Jackson's report to Greer, 14 April 1919).

36. Ibid., p. 102 (Ballou's report).

37. Ibid., p. 99. He added, "I cannot escape the conviction that, although not possessed of complete information, we nevertheless had enough, derived from previous experience, to have done better."

38. Williams, *Sidelights*, pp. 48–49; *NA*, R.G. 165, item 8142-152 (Snow to Chief of Staff, 16 May 1918). Snow quotes liberally from the inspection report of Brig. Gen. Eli A. Melmick, 1 May 1918.

39. U.S. Army, War College, *Order of Battle*, p. 914.

40. After the war, however, when there was no longer a chance of promotion to general rank, Young was reactivated and again sent to Liberia; he suffered a recurrence of "blackwater fever" and died in 1922.

41. Hunton and Johnson, *Two Colored Women*, pp. 43–44; *Chicago Defender*, 16 June 1917, p. 1; 30 June 1917, p. 8; Trevor Bowen, *Divine White Right* (New York, 1934), p. 66; *Crisis*, February 1918, p. 165.

42. Baker Papers, item 216 (Wilson to Baker, 25 June 1917).

43. Ibid., item 7 (Baker to Gen. Tasker Bliss, n.d., handwritten memorandum).

44. Ibid., item 219 (Baker to Wilson, 26 June 1917, unsigned carbon copy).

45. Ibid., item 7-2 (Wilson to John Sharp Williams, 29 June 1917).

46. Young was assigned for duty to the adjutant general of Ohio and there raised a regiment of dismounted cavalry, but the War Department later decided the regiment was not needed and disbanded it.

47. John J. Pershing, *My Experiences in the World War* (New York, 1931) 2:228–29. That Pershing was imbued with the army tradition that black soldiers must have white officers is also evident from General Ballou's report of the test that Pershing gave Ballou for the colonelcy (see U.S. Army, War College, *Colored Soldiers*, pp. 99–100). This statement should also refute Kelly Miller's contention that Pershing was the moving force behind the Des Moines school (Miller, *World War*, pp. 530–31).

CHAPTER 5

1. The number of men in black National Guard units is frequently stated as between 10,000 and 14,000, about double the actual strength.

2. Scott, *American Negro*, pp. 32–34. Scott used an overall figure of 10,000. At the same time, he gave a breakdown by units (though he omitted the Separate Company of Tennessee). The U.S. War Department, Militia Bureau (*Report of the Acting Chief of the Militia Bureau, 1918* [Washington, D.C., 1918], pp. 112–20) gives numbers for all units except the separate companies of Massachusetts and Connecticut. See also Sweeney, *American Negro*, p. 75; and Dowd, *Negro in American Life*, pp. 215–16.

3. Scott, *American Negro*, p. 197. Hayward, who was white, had been a star athlete at the University of Nebraska. In the Spanish-American War, he rose to the rank of colonel of militia. Rejecting President Taft's offer of appointment as assistant postmaster general, he undertook the practice of law in New York, rising to assistant district attorney and public service commissioner. He was a personal friend of New York's Governor Charles S. Whitman (see "Col. Bill Hayward and His 'Black Watch,' " *Literary Digest* 60 [8 March 1919]: 59). See also Johnson, *Black Manhattan*, pp. 233–34; Sweeney, *American Negro*, p. 135; Arthur Little, *From Harlem to the Rhine* (New York, 1936), pp. 3, 31, 102; Marshall, *Providential Armistice*, p. 12. Besides Hayward, the other five original officers were all Negroes: Capts. Charles W. Fillmore (who originated the idea of a black guard regiment) and Napoleon B. Marshall, 1st Lts. George W. Lacey and James Reese Europe, and 2d Lt. D. Lincoln Reid. Hunton and Johnson (*Two Colored Women*, p. 69)

insisted that the unit was supposed to have a full complement of black officers, but unfavorable conditions led to few attempts by blacks to qualify.

4. Sweeney, *American Negro*, p. 135; Little, *Harlem to the Rhine*, pp. 115–19; Jamieson et al., *Complete History*, p. 68 (Hayward to his former law partner, William Pitzer of Kansas City).

5. Little, *Harlem to the Rhine*, pp. 7, 9–11.

6. Ibid., pp. 42–43, 45–46; *NA*, R.G. 120, file 16-11.4 (Hayward's report to Colonel l'Esperance, pp. 2–3); Sweeney, *American Negro*, p. 136; *New York Times*, 5 July 1917, p. 9; 6 July 1917, p. 9.

7. Little, *Harlem to the Rhine*, pp. 46–47.

8. *New York Times*, 31 August 1917, p. 4.

9. Little, *Harlem to the Rhine*, pp. 50–51.

10. Ibid., pp. 54–58.

11. Ibid., pp. 59–62, 64–66. Emmett Scott, who went to Spartanburg to look at conditions there, does not mention the incident, although he does speak of the haste with which the regiment was sent to France (Scott, *American Negro*, pp. 79–80).

12. This received wide coverage, as both Europe and Sissle were well known in the world of entertainment (Scott, *American Negro*, pp. 79–80; Little, *Harlem to the Rhine*, p. 67; Nordholt, *People Who Walk*, p. 214).

13. Scott, *American Negro*, pp. 80–81.

14. Little, *Harlem to the Rhine*, p. 71.

15. *A Pictorial History of the Negro in the Great World War, 1917–1919* (New York, 1919), p. 22 (report of Sgt. H. Matthews of Co. C).

16. Ibid.; *Chicago Defender*, 3 November 1917, p. 8.

17. *New York Times*, 7 June 1918, p. 8.

18. Scott, *American Negro*, p. 76; Mason and Furr, *American Negro*, p. 19; Sweeney, *American Negro*, p. 165; U.S. War Department, Militia Bureau, *Report of the Acting Chief*, p. 124; *Chicago Defender*, 26 May 1917, p. 1; Miles V. Lynk, *Negro Pictorial Review of the Great War* (Memphis, Tenn., 1919), p. 12. Dennison was a Texan who went to Chicago to practice law. After serving as assistant city prosecuting attorney, he became assistant corporation counsel for Chicago and held that position when America entered the war. He went to France with his regiment but was later replaced on grounds of ill health.

19. Jamieson et al., *Complete History*, pp. 100–101; cited from the *Tribune*, 13 February 1919.

20. William S. Bradden, *Under Fire with the 370th Infantry, A.E.F.* (Chicago, n.d.), p. 19.

21. Ibid., p. 26; *NA*, R.G. 165, item 8142-39 (Bliss to commanding officer, 33d Division, 15 October 1917); ibid., item 8142-40 (Maj. Gen.

John Biddle, acting chief of staff, to General Bell, commanding the 33d Division, 6 November 1917); ibid., item 8142-46 (Maj. T. W. Hammond to Chief of Staff, 13 November 1917).

22. William L. Judy, *A Soldier's Diary* (Chicago, 1930), pp. 36–37 (entry of 5 November 1917).

23. Bradden, *Under Fire*, pp. 28–30 (Bradden to his Chicago parish, 19 October 1917).

24. Sweeney, *American Negro*, pp. 165–66; *NA*, R.G. 165, item 8142-55 (Graves to Adjutant General, 7 December 1917); Williams, *Sidelights*, p. 211; *Crisis*, March 1918, pp. 242–43.

25. Bradden, *Under Fire*, pp. 43–44 (letter, 15 March 1917). The date obviously should read 1918.

26. Ibid.; Williams, *Sidelights*, p. 211; U.S. Army, War College, *Colored Soldiers*, p. 130 (Col. George H. McMaster, commanding the 365th Infantry, to Greer, 28 April 1919).

27. *New York Times*, 13 October 1917, p. 8. The workman was later reported to have been hard of hearing. Seven hundred workmen struck the project until the black soldiers were removed from duty as guards.

28. *NA*, R.G. 165, item 9397-13 (Thomas to Joseph Tumulty, 6 July 1917).

29. *New York Times*, 9 November 1918, p. 13; *Crisis*, January 1918, p. 142.

30. *NA*, R.G. 94, file 16-11.4 (Secretary of War to Adjutant General, 23 November 1917).

31. *NA*, R.G. 165, item 8142-61 (Henry Jervey to Adjutant General, 29 December 1917).

32. In agreeing to the training of black officers, the army had stated its position against having any of field rank (see p. 58 and chap. 4, n. 8, p. 217).

33. See n. 18 above on Colonel Dennison.

34. *NA*, R.G. 120, file 293-11.4 (report of Col. Brooke Payne, 7 August 1919); Dowd, *Negro in American Life*, pp. 215–16; Scott, *American Negro*, p. 239; Mason and Furr, *American Negro*, pp. 19–21, 26. In the last-mentioned work, the regimental historians described Col. Glendie Young as "well-meaning" but with some Southern prejudices; this opinion was not unanimous. The white officers were mostly young lawyers; though they had some experience with the National Guard, they had been left behind—or were declared unneeded—by their original regiments.

35. *NA*, R.G. 120, file 148-11.4 (report of 2d Lt. R. A. Page, 340th Labor Battalion, 10 March 1919); Chester D. Heywood, *Negro Combat Troops in the World War* (Worcester, Mass., 1928), p. 1; Scott, *American Negro*, p. 231.

36. DuBois, "History of the Black Man," p. 73.

37. Heywood, *Negro Combat Troops*, p. 2.

38. Mason and Furr, *American Negro*, p. 19. For the addresses of the regimental officers, see Percy E. Deckard, *List of Officers of the 371st Regiment* (Allegany, N.Y., 1929), pp. 49–127.

39. Mason and Furr, *American Negro*, p. 19.

40. Scott, *American Negro*, p. 78.

41. Heywood, *Negro Combat Troops*, p. 10.

42. Ibid., pp. 5–7; Laurence Stallings, *The Doughboys* (New York, 1963), p. 361 (Stallings was coauthor with Maxwell Anderson of the noted play about World War I, *What Price Glory*); *NA*, R.G. 120, file 293-11.4 (typescript History of the 371st Infantry). On 14 October, 1,000 men were sent to the 301st Stevedores at Newport News; on 15 October, 680 were transferred to the 156th Depot Brigade at Camp Jackson; and on 20 November, 500 went to Camp Upton for service with a combat unit (presumably the 367th Infantry). In addition, 200 were washed out by medical examinations, and, on 8 December, 168 unfit men were transferred to the 156th Depot Brigade.

43. Stallings, *Doughboys*, p. 313.

44. *NA*, R.G. 165, item 8142-141 (Lytle Brown to Chief of Staff, 14 May 1918).

45. *New York Times*, 10 October 1917, p. 4; *NA*, R.G. 120, file 292-13.6 (Col. J. D. Leitch to Chief of Staff, 9 October 1917); *NA*, R.G. 165, item 9796-298 (Henry Jervey to Adjutant General, 14 May 1918); ibid., item 9210-95 (E. D. Anderson to Chief of Staff, 15 May 1918); Shipley Thomas, *The History of the AEF* (New York, 1920), pp. 110, 479; Scott, *American Negro*, pp. 130–31; Maurice de Castlebled, *History of the AEF* (New York, 1937), p. 154; Arthur W. Page, *Our 110 Days Fighting* (Garden City, N.J., 1920), pp. 259–60. By the end of October, units were established in the following camps: Camp Grant, Illinois, the 365th Infantry, 350th Machine Gun Battalion, and headquarters of the 183d Infantry Brigade; Camp Upton, New York, the 367th Infantry, 351st Machine Gun Battalion, and headquarters of the 184th Infantry Brigade; Camp Dix, New Jersey, 349th and 350th Field Artillery regiments, 317th Trench Mortar Battery, and headquarters of the 167th Field Artillery Brigade; Camp Meade, Maryland, the 368th Infantry and the 351st Field Artillery; Camp Dodge, Iowa, the 366th Infantry; Camp Sherman, Ohio, 317th Engineers and the 325th Signal Battalion; Camp Funston, Kansas, the 349th Machine Gun Battalion, Headquarters' Troop, Divisional Headquarters, and the divisional trains. Page gives 26 October as the date of organization; De Castlebled gives 24 October.

46. This is not too different from Secretary Baker's projection of 30,000 black draftees trained for combat.

47. *New York Times*, 23 March 1918, p. 9; 3 June 1918, p. 7; *NA*,

R.G. 165, item 9796-282 (Henry Jervey to Adjutant General, 11 May 1918); ibid., item 8142-50 (Biddle to Adjutant General, 15 November 1917).

48. Charles C. Lynde, "Mobilizing Rastus," *Outlook* 118 (13 March 1918): 417; *NA*, R.G. 120, file 28–12.6 (Maj. N. C. Shinerich to Inspector General, 31 January 1918).

49. *NA*, R.G. 165, item 8142-29 (Chief of Staff to Adjutant General, 7 October 1917).

50. *NA*, R.G. 120, file 292-65.1 (complete list of officers of the division). The list of field and staff officers can be found in Scott, *American Negro*, pp. 131–34.

51. DuBois, "History of the Black Man," p. 70.

52. *Crisis*, June 1918, p. 62 (letter from Ballou).

53. A comparative study of the 35th and 92nd divisions was made for the Army War College by the Inspector General's Office. It will be referred to in greater detail in a later chapter.

54. U.S. Army, War College, *Colored Soldiers*, p. 52. Col. A. A. Starbird, Inspector General's Office, inspected the 35th Division on 27 November 1917, and the 92nd Division on 25 January 1918.

55. Fisk Manuscripts, chaps. 14–16 (2d Lt. James B. Morris to DuBois, 24 June 1919).

56. Scott, *American Negro*, pp. 131–32; *Pullman Porters' Review, Military Supplement* (n.p., n.d.), p. 5.

57. James A. Moss, "The Negro as a Soldier," *Southern Workman* 47 (June 1918):313; Hunton and Johnson, *Two Colored Women*, p. 52; Union League Club, *The Presentation of Colors to the 367th Regiment of Infantry* (New York 1918), no pagination.

58. Osceola McKaine, "The Buffaloes," *Outlook* 119 (22 May 1918):146.

59. *New York American;* cited in Union League, *Presentation of Colors*.

60. Sweeney, *American Negro*, pp. 206–7; *NA*, R.G. 120, file 292-11.4 (report of 31 December 1917).

61. Williams, *Sidelights*, p. 159.

62. *NA*, R.G. 165, item 8142-125 (D. W. Ketcham to Chief of Staff, 20 April 1918). The inspection was made by Col. W. E. Cole, commander of the 167th Field Artillery Brigade, 30 March 1918. Cole had ordered his black officers (when he commanded the 351st Field Artillery) to remove all insignia of rank and to supply themselves with enlisted men's clothing. Although white officers had better facilities, these black commissioned personnel were provided only with mess tins. When Emmett Scott had such discriminations stopped, Cole cursed him over the phone (Fisk Manuscripts, WMM-3 [R. F. Nash to Secretary of NAACP, 15 May 1918]). General Ballou made a statement similar to that of Cole's (see above, p. 61).

63. Scott, *American Negro*, p. 134; *NA*, R.G. 165, item 9210-114 (Henry Jervey to Adjutant General).

64. Colson and Nutt, "Failure of the Ninety-second Division," pp. 22–23. At least half of the men in this battalion did come from South Carolina; the remainder were from Missouri (17%), New York (12%), Kansas (8%), Virginia and Massachusetts (4% each), and a scattering from other states (*NA*, R.G. 120, file 16-11.4 [report of 1st Lt. Oscar C. Brown, 351st Machine Gun Battalion, n.d.]).

65. Fisk Manuscripts, WMM-1 (report of Benjamin H. Mosby on machine-gun units, pp. 1–2).

66. Ibid., chaps. 10–14, 92d Division (Ballou, "Sidelights," pp. 13–14).

67. Williams, *Sidelights*, p. 48; DuBois, "History of the Black Man," p. 84.

68. War Department, *Annual Report, 1918*, p. 632 (report of Surgeon General); Fisk Manuscripts, WMM-3 (Roscoe C. Bruce, assistant superintendent of schools, Washington, D.C., to War Department, 27 November 1917; C. H. Winslow, Federal Board of Vocational Education, to Bruce, 27 November 1917; Emmett Scott to Bruce, 5 December 1917); *NA*, R.G. 165, item 8689-198 (E. D. Anderson to Chief of Staff, June 1918; Henry Jervey to Adjutant General, 4 June 1918).

69. Jamieson et al., *Complete History*, p. 7.

70. The emphasis is Ballou's. See Scott, *American Negro*, pp. 97–98; Hunton and Johnson, *Two Colored Women*, pp. 45–48.

71. Fisk Manuscripts, WMM-3 (Ballou to DuBois, 13 April 1918).

72. U.S. Army, War College, *Colored Soldiers*, pp. 58–59 (Ballou to General Chamberlain, inspector general; emphasis is Ballou's).

73. Ibid., p. 57; again Ballou's emphasis.

74. *New York Times*, 14 April 1918, sec. 1, p. 10.

75. Even Emmett Scott, who generally viewed the war experiences of blacks through rose-colored glasses, admitted that "at no time during his incumbency as the head of the Division was General Ballou able to regain the confidence of the colored masses, with whom he had been immensely popular prior to this episode. . . .." (Scott, *American Negro*, p. 97).

76. Fisk Manuscripts, chaps. 10–14; George W. Lee, *A Brave Black Division* (Memphis, Tenn., ca. 1923), pp. 8–9.

CHAPTER 6

1. Varlin, *Negro*, p. 16.

2. *NA*, R.G. 165, item 8142-18½ (S. Auley [?], Jr., assistant director of naval intelligence, to Colonel Van Devan, 21 August 1917; includes an enclosure from an aide in Florida).

3. Ibid., item 8142-46 (Maj. T. W. Hammond to Chief of Staff, 13 November 1917).

4. Ibid., item 8142-150 (E. D. Anderson to Chief of Staff, 16 May 1918, p. 1).

5. Ibid., pp. 1–2.

6. Ibid., p. 6.

7. Ibid., item 8142-149 (E. D. Anderson to Chief of Staff, 22 May 1918).

8. Ibid., item 8142-150, p. 2.

9. *New York Times*, 5 December 1917, p. 16.

10. *NA*, R. G. 165, item 8689-53 (memo for Chief of Staff, 3 October 1917; Bliss to Adjutant General, 30 October 1917).

11. Ibid., item 8142-199 (Lt. Col. J. W. Barker, General Staff, to Chief of Staff, 6 May 1919).

12. Ibid., item 8689-68. The original suggestion was made by Col. W. G. Austin, Quartermaster's Corps, to the Quartermaster General on 9 November 1917. See also ibid., item 8689-71 (P. D. Lochridge to Chief of Staff, 14 December 1917). The civilian was identified as a Stanley King.

13. Ibid., item 8689-253 (Lytle Brown to Chief of Staff, 18 July 1918). See also ibid., item 8689-282 (Brown to Chief of Staff, 29 August 1918).

14. Ibid., item 8689-28 (Bliss to Adjutant General, 7 August 1917; General Orders no. 107, 14 August 1917); ibid., item 8689-45 (Bliss to Adjutant General, 17 September 1917); *NA*, R.G. 120, file 121-12.0 (Services of Supply records from Base Section 5; typescript History of the Stevedores). The same shuffling and reshuffling continued after their arrival in France; companies were scattered about as they were needed and were quite often separated from their headquarters.

15. *NA*, R.G. 165, item 8689-42 (General H. L. Scott, chief of staff, to Adjutant General, 19 September 1917; authorized in General Orders no. 125, 22 September 1917).

16. Ibid., item 8689-201 (Henry Jervey to Director of War Plans Division, 5 June 1918; confirmed, Lytle Brown to Chief of Staff, 14 June 1918); *NA*, R.G. 120, file 148-11.4 (report of Captain Knowles for January 1919; Major Byrnes's report of 18 March 1918); Scott Papers, 114-2 (Williams's report on Holabird, 30 January 1919); *Crisis*, July 1918, p. 134.

17. *NA*, R.G. 165, item 10017-26 (Bliss to Adjutant General, 16 October 1917). This file also contains a rough draft of the orders which make War Department thinking even clearer. The original wording was: ". . . and foremen of colored laborers. Chief of Engineers bases this organization on large experience with colored laborers in the South. . . ."

18. Ibid., item 10017-33 (Grant to Chief of War College Division, General Staff, December 1917).

19. Ibid. (P. D. Lochridge to Chief of Staff, 7 December 1917). Lochridge's record, on many occasions, showed him to be no particular friend of black Americans.

20. Ibid., item 8142-150, p. 6.

21. Ibid., item 8689-185 (Lytle Brown to Chief of Staff, 31 May 1918).

22. Ibid., item 8142-146 (Brown to Chief of Staff, 4 June 1918).

23. Ibid., item 8689-266 (E. D. Anderson to Chief of Staff, 25 July 1918).

24. Ibid., item 9796-149 (Henry Jervey to Adjutant General, 13 March 1918).

25. John H. Williams, *A Negro Looks at War* (New York, 1940), p. 7.

26. Williams, *Sidelights*, pp. 28–29.

27. Federal Council, GWC-1 (minutes of the conference of 25 September 1917).

28. *NA*, R.G. 165, item 8142-284 (Lytle Brown to Chief of Staff, 19 August 1918).

29. Ibid., item 8142-114 (D. W. Ketcham to Chief of Staff, 21 April 1918).

30. Ibid.

31. *Crisis*, August 1918, pp. 187–88.

32. *NA*, R.G. 165, item 8689-329 (Lytle Brown to Chief of Staff, 10 October 1918).

33. Scott Papers, 114-2 (Williams's report on Camp Humphreys, 23 January 1918, pp. 1–2; Williams's report on the Canton [Baltimore] Warehouses, 28 January 1918, pp. 1–2). Part of the battalion was stationed at the warehouses.

34. *NA*, R.G. 120, file 168-11.4 (records for the week of 17–22 June 1918).

35. Ibid., box 375 (inspection report of Col. James G. Hannah, 23 September 1918).

36. Ibid., file 148-50.4 (note attached to report, Hannah to Goodrich, 30 October 1918; italics are Hannah's).

37. These were the training companies suggested by Colonel Anderson.

38. Ibid., file 148-11.4. This shows the questions asked, and the responses given. The number of hours per week in training averaged eleven. Only two of the battalions had rifles; though 65 percent had pistol ranges for use by the white noncoms. Only 5 percent of the units queried had their own drill areas.

39. Scott Papers, 114-2 (Williams's report on Camp Meade, 8 Feb-

ruary 1919, pp. 2–3); *NA*, R.G. 120, file 148-11.4 (report of Captain Knowles, 447th Reserve Labor Battalion, February 1919); ibid., file 148-50.4.

40. *NA*, R.G. 120, file 148-50.4; Scott Papers, 114-2 (Williams's report on Camp Bowie, 20 December 1918).

41. Scott Papers, 114-3 (Williams's report on Camp Lee).

42. Ibid., 115-1 (unsigned letter from Camp Humphreys, 31 May 1919).

43. *NA*, R.G. 120, file 148-50.4.

44. Ibid., file 134-56.2 (Hannah's report on Camp Greene, 21 October 1918); ibid., file 168-11.4 (report of Maj. H. J. Murphy, 1st Development Battalion, 155th Depot Brigade, to Adjutant General, 8 October 1918); ibid., file 168-11.4 (report of Lt. W. H. Grace, 3d Development Battalion, 160th Depot Brigade, to Adjutant General, 30 September 1918); ibid., file 168-11.4 (report of Lt. John L. Ott to Adjutant General, 1 August 1918); ibid., file 168-11.4 (report of 1st Lt. Harold W. Morse, 2d Development Battalion, 159th Depot Brigade, 2 December 1918); *Crisis*, November 1918, p. 33.

45. *NA*, R.G. 120, file 168-11.4 (report of Maj. A. McCullen, chaplain, on Camp Sevier illiterate school, 1 December 1918).

46. Ibid., file 134-11.4; also ibid., file 148-11.4 (unsigned report of 17 December 1918). A total of just thirty-five days elapsed between the initial organization (or authorization) of the 335th Labor Battalion at Camp Pike and its embarkation for France. These men were issued surplus Civil War uniforms.

47. Ibid., file 148-11.4 (report of Lt. Col. W. B. Longborough on his inspection of Camp Dix, 13–14 November 1918).

48. Ibid. (report from Camp Taylor).

49. Scott Papers, 115-1 (unsigned letter from Camp Humphreys, 31 May 1919).

50. Ibid. (letter dated 12 March 1919); see also ibid., 114-2 (NAACP complaint; Williams on the "Military Police," 31 October 1918, pp. 1–2; Williams to Scott, 1 February 1919); Fisk Manuscripts, WMM-3 (Robert F. Tinsley, "The Stone Wall," p. 18, typescript). Tinsley, a member of the 8th Illinois before the war, was assigned to Camp Grant as the YMCA secretary. See also ibid. (unsigned letter from Camp Stuart, 17 January 1919); Spingarn, "Health and Morals," p. 166; *Chicago Defender*, 2 February 1918, p. 11; 2 November 1918, p. 1.

51. Scott Papers, 115-2 (letter from the men of the battalion). Colonel Dulin informed the men that he would pay a reward of $500 for identification of the man or men who complained about their treatment. He promised that the writers would be lynched. There is in this file of

the Scott Papers a pathetic collection of letters cataloging complaints from men in a number of camps. Almost all of them deal with physical or verbal abuse of the black troops.

52. *NA*, R.G. 165, item 10871-31 (E. D. Anderson to Chief of Staff, 24 September 1918; Henry Jervey to Adjutant General, 25 September 1918).

53. Ibid., item 8689-89 (Graves to Adjutant General, 7 February 1918). See also ibid., item 8689-321 (Maj. Theodore Barnes to Chief of Staff, 21 September 1918; and E. D. Anderson to Adjutant General, same date); Fisk Manuscripts, chaps. 10–14 (chap. 10, Battalions of Labor), pp. 45–46. See also Enoch J. Dunham, Co. B, 324th Labor Battalion, to DuBois, 14 July 1919. The men arrested as ringleaders were identified as: Colbert Mitchell, Robert Brown, Thomas Thomas, George Williams, Charles Peals, Bill Brocks, and Albert Rankins. The officers in charge of Company B were 1st Lieutenant Cusemire (from Mississippi) and 2d Lieutenant Dorthman (from Georgia).

54. Jamieson et al., *Complete History*, p. 63.

55. *NA*, R.G. 120, file 11.4 (Historical Narrative of the Port of Embarkation, Hoboken, N.J.); Walter Delsarte, *The Negro, Democracy, and the War* (Detroit, 1919), p. 15; David L. Ferguson, "With This Black Man's Army," *Independent* 97 (15 March 1919):368. Ferguson, a former Kentucky preacher, served as a black YMCA secretary in France. See also Heywood Broun, *The A.E.F.* (New York, 1918), pp. 19–20; Floyd Gibbons, *And They Thought We Wouldn't Fight* (New York, 1918), pp. 70–71; W. H. Muston, *Over There* (Yoakum, Tex., ca. 1923), p. 35; Sweeney, *American Negro*, pp. 133–34; and Alban B. Butler, *Happy Days* (New York, 1929), cartoon, p. 4.

56. Benedict Crowell and R. F. Wilson, *The Road to France* (New Haven, Conn., 1921), 1:25.

57. Delsarte, *Negro*, p. 15; the contractor was identified as George Freeman.

58. U.S. Army, General Staff, Historical Branch, *Organization of the Services of Supply* (Washington, D.C., 1921), pp. 20–23. The base sections were: (1) St. Nazaire; (2) La Pallice (Bassens, St. Sulpice, Contras-en-Gironde); (3) Liverpool; (4) Le Havre; (5) Brest; (6) Marseilles; (7) La Pallice (La Rochelle, Rochefort, Aigrefeuille); (8) Italy; and (9) Antwerp, Rotterdam (for the Army of Occupation). The Intermediate Section had headquarters at Nèvres, and distribution centers at Gièvres, Montierchaume, Mehun-sur-Yèvre, St. Aignan, and Blois. The main bases of the Advance Section were at Leffol-le-Grande (Vosges) and Is-sur-Tille (Côte d'Or).

59. William J. Wilgus, *Transporting the A.E.F. in Western Europe* (New York, 1931), opposite p. 198; Crowell and Wilson, *Road to France*,

1:162–63; Isaac Marcossan, *S.O.S.: America's Miracle in France* (New York, 1919), p. 109.

60. Miller, *World War*, p. 542.

61. *NA*, R.G. 120, file 121-12 (records of the Services of Supply, Base Section 5, History of the Stevedore Troops, Brest); ibid., file 148-11.4 (report of Capt. Luther M. Meekins, 319th Labor Battalion, 1 April 1919); file 148-11.4 (report of Lt. Claude I. Freeman, 331st Labor Battalion, n.d.); Odum, *Wings on My Feet*, p. 200.

62. *NA*, R.G. 120, file 148-10.7 (reports of the 330th and 343d labor battalions); ibid., file 148-11.4 (report of Capt. Ray Elliott, 334th Labor Battalion, 1 March 1919).

63. This was the former German ship *Vaterland*, listed as 59,957 gross tons under U.S. Registration as *Leviathan*.

64. Frederick A. Pottle, *Stretchers* (New Haven, Conn., 1929), p. 260; Williams, *Sidelights*, p. 142; Odum, *Wings on My Feet*, pp. 206–8; Haynes, *Trend of the Races*, pp. 114–15. (A professor at Fisk University, Haynes was appointed head of the Bureau of Negro Economics, Department of Labor.) See also Marcossan, *S.O.S.*, p. 65; Harold Riegelman, *War Notes of a Casual* (New York, 1931), p. 38; Miller, *World War*, p. 542.

65. Marcossan, *S.O.S.*, pp. 76–77; Williams, *Sidelights*, p. 145; *NA*, R.G. 120, file 16-11.4 (History of the 328th Labor Battalion; report of Capt. Dudley C. Hull, 324th Labor Battalion); ibid., file 148-10.7 (reports of the 320th, 329th, and 332d labor battalions).

66. Marcossan, *S.O.S.*, pp. 157–58.

67. Ibid., pp. 103–4; Harbord, *American Army*, pp. 367–81; James G. Harbord, *Leaves from a War Diary* (New York, 1925), p. 351. The special train was equipped by General Hagood, who complained that, when food supplies ran out, the black porters sold sandwiches which they had brought along for just that purpose. He felt that the porters were deliberately "fouling up" the provisioning of the train (Johnson Hagood, *The Services of Supply* [Boston, 1927], pp. 126–27). See also Ernest C. Peixotto, *The American Front* (New York, 1919), pp. 19–20.

68. Little, *Harlem to the Rhine*, p. 103.

69. Marcossan, *S.O.S.*, pp. 103–4.

70. James G. Bliss, *History of the 805th Pioneer Infantry* (St. Paul, Minn., 1919), pp. 28–29; Peixotto, *American Front*, pp. 171–72.

71. Hunton and Johnson, *Two Colored Women*, p. 123.

72. *NA*, R.G. 120, file 16-11.4.

73. Ibid., file 134-11.4; Williams, *Sidelights*, pp. 152–53.

74. Williams, *Sidelights*, p. 151.

75. Carter G. Woodson, *The Negro in Our History* (Washington, D.C., 1921), pp. 516–17.

76. Williams, *Sidelights*, p. 151.

77. U.S. Army, War College, *Colored Soldiers*, p. 73 (Lt. Col. L. M. Purcell to General commanding Base Section no. 3, 7 August 1918).

78. Ibid., p. 72 (General Atterbury, director general of transportation, to A.E.F. Chief of Staff, 15 February 1918).

79. Ibid., pp. 74–76 (H. K. Taylor to Pershing, 15 September 1918).

80. Ibid.

81. Hagood, *Services of Supply*, p. 106.

82. Ibid., p. 275 (memo from General Harbord, 7 August 1918).

83. Harbord, *American Army*, pp. 391–92.

84. Harbord, *War Diary*, p. 347.

85. U.S., Congress, Senate, *Alleged Executions without Trial in France* (Washington, D.C., 1923).

86. *NA*, R.G. 120 (Organization Records of the 804th Company).

87. Ibid.

88. Williams, *Sidelights*, pp. 147–48.

89. *NA*, R.G. 165, item 8142-142 (Lytle Brown to Chief of Staff, 16 May 1918).

90. Stallings, *Doughboys*, p. 176.

91. *NA*, R.G. 165, item 8689-382 (Lytle Brown to Chief of Staff, 12 April 1919). Pershing's request was made by cable on 5 April 1919. See also *NA*, R.G. 120, file 148-11.4 (History of Service Battalion, Replacement Depot, 11 April 1919). The unit historian was Lieutenant Walter Butler, who said: "This change resulted in a more dignified organization name and tended to inform outsiders of the true purpose of the battalion. . . . Primarily to establish that the battalion was in no sense a penal institution, or a place to which its members had been sent by way of punishment, this wise change was made."

CHAPTER 7

1. U.S., American Battle Monuments Commission, *93d Division: Summary of Operations in the World War* (Washington, D.C., 1944), p. 35.

2. Irvin S. Cobb, *The Glory of the Coming* (New York, 1918), pp. 300–301.

3. *NA*, R.G. 120, file 16-11.4 (report of Colonel Hayward to Colonel l'Espérance, pp. 4–5).

4. *NA*, R.G. 120, file 7-12.5 ("Cable History of Colored Soldiers" [typescript, compiler, and date of compilation unknown], Pershing's

cable no. 454). This correspondence took place in January and February 1918.

5. Ibid. (Biddle to Pershing, no. A726).

6. Ibid. (Pershing to Biddle, no. P592, 11 February 1918; Biddle to Pershing, no. A800, 16 February 1918; Pershing to Biddle, no. P626, 21 February 1918).

7. Pershing, *My Experiences*, 1:291.

8. Harbord, *American Army*, p. 189; Deckard, *371st Regiment*, p. 41.

9. Harbord, *American Army*, p. 189; *NA*, R.G. 120, file 7-12.5 (Pershing's cable no. P720, 12 March 1918).

10. *NA*, R.G. 120, file 7-12.5 (March to Pershing, no. A932, 16 March 1918).

11. *Pictorial History*, p. 31 (George B. Compton to unidentified friend; cited from the *New York Sun*, sometime in January 1918).

12. Stallings, *Doughboys*, pp. 314–15; Sweeney, *American Negro*, pp. 166–67.

13. Heywood, *Negro Combat Troops*, p. 33; Jamieson et al., *Complete History*, p. 50; Sweeney, *American Negro*, p. 33; Deckard, *371st Regiment*, p. 22.

14. Woodson, *Negro in Our History*, p. 524; Aptheker, *Toward Negro Freedom*, p. 119; Johnson, *Black Manhattan*, pp. 244–45; France, Assemblée Nationales, *Annales*, n.s., 1919 Session Ordinaire; Chambre, *Débats*, 25 July 1919, p. 3365.

15. Assemblée Nationales, Chambre, *Débats*, p. 3366. See also the account in *New York Times*, 26 July 1919, p. 7.

16. Little, *Harlem to the Rhine*, pp. 126, 133, 136–37. The orders were signed on 10 February 1918 by Orrin Wolfe, Pershing's adjutant general. Wolfe still referred to the regiment as the 15th New York. Little said of the trip: "During the entire thirty-seven days of our absence from the regiment, not even one complaint was made by civil authority or military authority" (Ibid., p. 135).

17. Ibid., pp. 172–73; Williams, *Sidelights*, p. 197; Sweeney, *American Negro*, p. 137.

18. *New York Times*, 21 May 1918, p. 6; 22 May 1918, p. 12; Little, *Harlem to the Rhine*, pp. 192–201; "Col. Bill Hayward," p. 59; Sweeney, *American Negro*, p. 146.

19. "Bush Germans Better Watch That 'Chocolate Front,' " *Literary Digest* 57 (15 June 1918):44; citation from the *New York World*.

20. Cobb, *Glory of the Coming*, pp. 283–84.

21. Ibid., pp. 294–95.

22. *Crisis*, April 1919, p. 288; cited from the *Buffalo* (N.Y.) *Courier*.

23. Sweeney, *American Negro*, p. 139.

24. Little, *Harlem to the Rhine*, pp. 305–7.

25. Ibid., p. 227; *NA*, R.G. 120, file 16-11.4 (Hayward's report to l'Espérance, pp. 6–7); U.S. Army, General Staff, Historical Branch, *Brief Histories of Divisions, U.S. Army, 1917–1918* (Washington, D.C., 1921), p. 86; Dowd, *Negro in American Life*, pp. 199–200; Williams, *Sidelights*, p. 199.

26. Hunter Liggett, *AEF* (New York, 1928), pp. 98–99; Little, *Harlem to the Rhine*, p. 228; Hunton and Johnson, *Two Colored Women*, p. 72; Williams, *Sidelights*, p. 198; Francis W. Halsey, *The Literary Digest History of the World War* (New York, 1920), 5:218; *New York Times*, 25 February 1919, p. 5.

27. "Not One of the Famous 369th Was Ever Taken Alive," *Literary Digest* 60 (15 March 1919):94.

28. Ibid., p. 96; Little, *Harlem to the Rhine*, pp. 239–40, 242–43; Williams, *Sidelights*, pp. 200–201; *NA*, R.G. 120, file 16-11.4 (Hayward's report to l'Espérance, pp. 5–6).

29. *NA*, R.G. 120, file 293-11.4; Page, *Our 110 Days Fighting*, pp. 97–99; Thomas, *History of the AEF*, pp. 237–38. Thomas also said (p. 195): "In other words the French Fourth Army was playing at least as big a part in squeezing the enemy out of the Argonne Forest as was our own Army—a fact which is often lost sight of in studying the minutiae of the attacks of the American Army." Liggett (*AEF*, pp. 190–91) insists that the French attack in the Argonne bogged down and that they fell behind the American advance. See also Dowd, *Negro in American Life*, pp. 202–3; Mason and Furr, *American Negro*, pp. 114–18; U.S., American Battle Monuments Commission, *93d Division*, pp. 9–10. Corporal Elmer Earl of Company K saw fifty of the fifty-eight men in his unit cut down by German fire; he was awarded the DSC for bringing in the wounded men. In the same action, Pvt. Elmer McCowin (Co. K) carried messages through heavy enemy fire. Gassed, he refused to leave his post and was also awarded the DSC (Sweeney, *American Negro*, pp. 151–52).

30. *NA*, R.G. 120, file 293-11.4. In this advance they encountered a number of men from Company K, 372d U.S. Infantry. These men had remained in the outskirts of Sechault after their attack had failed on the previous day. These men joined in the attack of the 369th. See also Little, *Harlem to the Rhine*, pp. 284–85.

31. Little, *Harlem to the Rhine*, pp. 291, 294–95, 310–11 (the two French regiments were identified as the 163d and the 363d Infantry); *New York Times*, 9 February 1919, sec. 3, p. 6.

32. Stallings, *Doughboys*, p. 319.

33. *NA*, R.G. 120, file 293-11.4 (Report of Activities of the 369th Infantry, pp. 9–10).

34. DuBois, "History of the Black Man," p. 73.

35. Little, *Harlem to the Rhine*, pp. 326, 336.

36. *NA*, R.G. 120, file 16-11.4 (Hayward's report to l'Espérance, pp. 3-4, 9-10).

37. Little, *Harlem to the Rhine*, pp. xi-xii.

38. U.S. Army, War College, *Colored Soldiers*, pp. 83-84; Williams, *Sidelights*, p. 205; Schoenfeld, *Negro*, pp. 21-22; Marshall, *Providential Armistice*, p. 3; *Crisis*, January 1919, p. 133. The award was made in December 1918.

39. The story of the 370th, which follows, suggests that these officers may have been transferred because they were considered good officers.

40. Bradden, *Under Fire*, p. 84 (Bradden to his parish, 19 August 1918); Sweeney, *American Negro*, p. 135; Scott Papers, 112-2 (unsigned manuscript by "official historian" of 92d Division, p. 14). Though Captain Fillmore received the croix de guerre for his exploits with the 369th, it was not formally awarded until after his transfer to the 370th. See also Hunton and Johnson, *Two Colored Women*, p. 74.

41. Stallings, *Doughboys*, p. 315.

42. Hunton and Johnson, *Two Colored Women*, p. 78; Bradden, *Under Fire*, p. 77 (Bradden to his parish, 18 July 1918).

43. U.S. Army, War College, *Colored Soldiers*, pp. 60-61.

44. Bradden, *Under Fire*, pp. 71, 73-74. Jess Willard, the white prizefighter who took the heavyweight title from the black champion Jack Johnson in 1915, was known as the "White Hope."

45. Ibid., pp. 65-66.

46. Ibid., pp. 90-91; DuBois, "History of the Black Man," p. 78.

47. DuBois, "History of the Black Man," p. 78.

48. U.S. Army, War College, *Colored Soldiers*, pp. 62-63 (report of Roberts to Col. Fox Conner at G.H.Q., 12 August 1918).

49. Sweeney, *American Negro*, pp. 157-58.

50. U.S. Army, War College, *Colored Soldiers*, pp. 62-63.

51. *NA*, R.G. 120, file 293-11.4 (Roberts's report of 2 January 1919, p. 1); Williams, *Sidelights*, pp. 212-13; Hunton and Johnson, *Two Colored Women*, pp. 79-80; Sweeney, *American Negro*, p. 157.

52. Bradden, *Under Fire*, pp. 89-90.

53. Ibid., pp. 91-92; U.S., American Battle Monuments Commission, *American Armies and Battlefields in Europe* (Washington, D.C., 1938), p. 42; Williams, *Sidelights*, pp. 213-14; *NA*, R.G. 120, file 293-11.4 (Roberts's report).

54. U.S. Army, War College, *Colored Soldiers*, p. 126. General Rondeau added that he felt two things could be done to improve the efficiency of the regiment, but the translator of the document ("L.R.E.") did not see fit to include Rondeau's suggestions.

55. Sweeney, *American Negro*, pp. 154–55.

56. U.S. Army, War College, *Colored Soldiers*, pp. 117–18.

57. *NA*, R.G. 120, file 293-11.4 (Roberts's report, p. 2).

58. Williams, *Sidelights*, pp. 214–15; U.S., American Battle Monuments Commission, *93d Division*, p. 26 (p. 34 gives a figure of 445). The Battle Monuments Commission's *American Armies* (p. 104) gives the figure as 504 men.

59. Hunton and Johnson, *Two Colored Women*, pp. 81–82.

60. U.S. Army, War College, *Colored Soldiers*, p. 84.

61. Mason and Furr, *American Negro*, pp. 43–44.

62. U.S. Army, War College, *Colored Soldiers*, p. 64 (Tupes to Pershing, 24 August 1918).

63. Mason and Furr, *American Negro*, pp. 75–76.

64. Ibid., pp. 100–102; DuBois, "History of the Black Man," pp. 75–76.

65. Paul C. Davis, "The Negro in the Armed Forces," *Virginia Quarterly Review* 24 (1948):505.

66. Dowd, *Negro in American Life*, p. 217 (information provided by Colonel Tupes); Mason and Furr, *American Negro*, p. 114; Heywood, *Negro Combat Troops*, pp. 161–62.

67. Van Allen was from the original black company of the 6th Massachusetts. See Warren H. Miller, *The Boys of 1917* (Boston, 1939), pp. 366–67; U.S. Army, War College, *Colored Soldiers*, pp. 66–67; *NA*, R.G. 120, file 16-11.4; Williams, *Sidelights*, pp. 235–36, 239–40; Mason and Furr, *American Negro*, p. 124; Chellis V. Smith, *Americans All* (Boston, 1925), pp. 130–31; *New York Times*, 3 July 1919, p. 9; Heywood, *Negro Combat Troops*, p. 181; Sweeney, *American Negro*, p. 190. Sweeney (p. 182) quoted Goybet as saying, in his message of 8 October: "The 'Red Hand' sign of the division, has, thanks to you, become a bloody hand which took the Boche and made him cry for mercy. You have well avenged our glorious dead."

68. U.S., American Battle Monuments Commission, *American Armies*, p. 427; Williams, *Sidelights*, p. 237.

69. Mason and Furr, *American Negro*, pp. 139–40.

70. Scott Papers, 113-5 (Tyler to Scott, 19 October 1918).

71. U.S. Army, War College, *Colored Soldiers*, p. 84 (Order no. 12,921 "D", General Headquarters, French Armies of the East, 15 January 1919).

72. Heywood, *Negro Combat Troops*, p. 32; De Castlebled, *AEF*, p. 157.

73. Dowd, *Negro in American Life*, p. 208.

74. Heywood, *Negro Combat Troops*, p. 39 (Col. Carl Boyd to Col. Perry Miles, 15 May 1918).

75. Ibid., p. 290.

76. Scott, *American Negro*, p. 238 (quoting Lt. John B. Smith of Greenville, S.C.).

77. Heywood, *Negro Combat Troops*, p. 105 (Quillet's memo of 29 July 1918).

78. *NA*, R.G. 120, file 293-23.9 (order signed by Samusson and issued to the town mayors of the Meuse Department, 31 August 1918). To this is appended the following note: "This document to be regarded as Confidential until W. D. decision as to its publication. By order of Col. O. L. Spaulding." Maj. T. R. Carswell signed the note, dating it 14 May 1936. It was finally declassified in 1947.

79. Heywood, *Negro Combat Troops*, pp. 111–12 (Quillet's memo, citing report from a Lieutenant Gouin, 9 August 1918; see also, p. 125). Most of these officers, of course, were young and inexperienced. In time—if they survived—they did these things in the natural course of their duties. Had the officers been black, however, one suspects that extensive publicity would have been given to Goybet's remarks. The weaknesses would have been attributed to racial inferiorities.

80. Dowd, *Negro in American Life*, pp. 210–11 (Maj. Charles Greenough to Dowd, 20 June 1926 [Greenough was in command of the 2d Battalion]).

81. Heywood, *Negro Combat Troops*, pp. 154–55; *NA*, R.G. 120, file 293-11.4 (Miles's report); Scott, *American Negro*, pp. 232–33 (Colonel Miles's report) and 237 (report of Capt. W. R. Richey of Laurens, S.C.). Dowd (*Negro in American Life*, pp. 208–10) gives the name as Vières Farm.

82. Scott, *American Negro*, p. 238; Fisk Manuscripts, chaps. 14–16 (2d Lt. James B. Morris to DuBois, 24 June 1919).

83. *NA*, R.G. 120, file 16-11.4 (report on 371st Infantry, pp. 1–2). Scott (*American Negro*, p. 232) essentially agreed, although he listed only three 77-mm. guns. He added that they captured an ammunition dump and a number of railroad cars. They also took large quantities of lumber, hay, and other supplies. In addition, they shot down three German planes. The regimental monument near Ardeuil lists the names of nine officers and 113 men killed in action near that spot. See Deckard, *371st Regiment*, p. 23.

84. *NA*, R.G. 120, file 293-12.3.

85. Heywood, *Negro Combat Troops*, pp. 198–99.

86. Ibid., p. 227.

87. *NA*, R.G. 120, file 293-11.4 (Goybet to General Garnier-Duplesses, commanding the 9th French Army Corps). Though dated 8 August 1918, the date must be in error; the letter obviously refers to the Champagne offensive of September of 1918.

88. Mason and Furr, *American Negro*, pp. 43–44.

CHAPTER 8

1. Dowd, *Negro in American Life*, p. 102.

2. Robert L. Bullard, *Personalities and Reminiscences of the War* (New York, 1925), p. 295.

3. Ibid., pp. 291–92.

4. Pershing, *My Experiences*, 2:45 (Pershing to Marshal Haig, 5 May 1918).

5. Ibid., p. 46.

6. Scott Papers, 114–2 (Williams's report on the 92d Division); Williams, *Sidelights*, pp. 63–64. Boutte reported that the black officers of the divisional staff were provided with a special side table in the dining room (Fisk Manuscripts, WMM-3 [Confidential Diary of Divisional Interpreter]).

7. DuBois, "History of the Black Man," p. 79.

8. Fisk Manuscripts, WMM-3 (Boutte's diary, pp. 7–8).

9. *NA*, R.G. 120, file 16-11.4 (typescript History of the 349th Field Artillery); Fisk Manuscripts, chaps. 10–14, 92d Division (report of Col. Walter E. Prosser, 349th F. A., p. 3).

10. *NA*, R.G. 120, file 16-11.4.

11. Ibid. (Colonel Moore's report, 29 July 1918); Fisk Manuscripts, chaps. 10–14, 92d Division (Prosser's report, p. 3).

12. U.S. Army, War College, *Colored Soldiers*, p. 55.

13. Ibid., pp. 52–53; italics are Colonel Starbird's.

14. Ibid., pp. 54–55.

15. Pershing, *My Experiences*, 2:228–29.

16. *NA*, R.G. 120, file 16-11.4 (report on 317th Engineers); Williams, *Sidelights*, pp. 174–75.

17. William O. Ross and Duke L. Slaughter, *With the 351st in France* (Baltimore, Md., 1923), pp. 13–15.

18. Ibid., p. 19; Hunton and Johnson, *Two Colored Women*, p. 55.

19. Scott Papers, 114-2 (Williams's report on the 92d Division, p. 34); Fisk Manuscripts, WMM-3 (Ernest McKinney, 325th Signal Battalion, to DuBois, 17 May 1919).

20. Fisk Manuscripts, chaps. 10–14, 92d Division (Ballou, "Sidelights," pp. 16–17).

21. Hunton and Johnson, *Two Colored Women*, pp. 60–61.

22. Williams, *Sidelights*, p. 74.

23. Ibid., pp. 74–75.

24. Fisk Manuscripts, chaps. 10–14, 92d Division (Ballou, "Sidelights," pp. 21–22).

25. Bullard, *Personalities and Reminiscences*, pp. 296–97; Scott Papers, 114-2 (Williams on the 92d Division, p. 27).

26. Fisk Manuscripts, chaps. 17–18, Miscellaneous (Captain Pat-

terson's typescript on French preference for black rather than white Americans); Scott Papers, 114-2 (Williams on 92d Division, p. 31).

27. Scott Papers, 113-5 (Greer to McKellar, 6 December 1918).

28. U.S. Army, War College, *Colored Soldiers*, app. 14, p. 54; Dowd, *Negro in American Life*, pp. 222–23; *NA*, R.G. 120, file 16-11.4 (report on 317th Engineers).

29. Fisk Manuscripts, chaps. 14–16, 366th Infantry (Barnum to commanding officer, Co. F, 366th Infantry, 22 December 1918). These troops went into action without their medical personnel, who were left in the training area to provide temporary field hospitals for the 81st Division (mostly South Carolinians). See ibid., chaps. 17–18, Miscellaneous. (DuBois on black doctors, p. 8).

30. *NA*, R.G. 120, file 292-20.1 (intelligence summaries); ibid., file 292-11.4 (historical reports); ibid., file 292-33.1 (operations reports); ibid., file 292-32.14 (Operations Memo of A. A. Hickox, 13 September 1918).

31. *NA*, R.G. 94, file 48-46.1 (Colonel Lochridge to Chief of Staff, 20 October 1918). See also *NA*, R.G. 120, file 292-65.1 (list of officers, 1 November 1918). Of the 144 captaincies in the division, only 74 were open to black officers.

32. *NA*, R.G. 165, item 8142-184 (Gen. Frank McIntyre to Adjutant General, 15 August 1918).

33. Scott Papers, 113-5 (orders of 11 September 1918).

34. Ibid., 113-2 (Scott to Thompson, 14 March 1919).

35. *NA*, R.G. 120, file 292-13.6 (Lochridge to Chief of Staff, 20 October 1918).

36. Scott Papers, 113-5 (orders of 11 September 1918).

37. Edward M. Coffman, *War to End All Wars* (New York, 1968), p. 319.

38. Hunton and Johnson, *Two Colored Women*, pp. 53–54.

39. Warner D. Ross, *My Colored Battalion* (Chicago, 1920), pp. 114–15.

40. U.S., American Battle Monuments Commission, *92d Division: Summary of Operations in the World War* (Washington, D.C., 1944), p. 11; *NA*, R.G. 120, file 292-32.1 (Field Order no. 12, 25 September 1918).

41. Scott Papers, 112-2 (unidentified newspaper clipping on 368th Infantry, citing remarks of Captain Mehlinger and Lieutenant Coleman); Lee, *Brave Black Division*, p. 20; Dowd, *Negro in American Life*, pp. 225–26; Liggett, *AEF*, pp. 168–69; Marshall, *Providential Armistice*, p. 7.

42. DuBois, "History of the Black Man," p. 80; *NA*, R.G. 120, file 292-33.6 (Colonel Brown's report, pp. 18–19); U.S., American Battle Monuments Commission, *92d Division*, p. 11; Lee, *Brave Black Division*, pp. 23–24.

43. *NA*, R.G. 120, file 292-33.6 (Colonel Brown's report, app. D [Major Elser's report], p. 27; app. R [Capt. J. W. Jones, Co. F], pp. 40–41; app. T [Capt. Bob Thomas, Co. H], p. 42; app. X [Capt. R. A. Williams, Co. M], pp. 45–46). See also U.S., American Battle Monuments Commission, *92d Division*, p. 13.

44. Scott Papers, 111-4 (report from noncoms, 368th Infantry, pp. 5–6).

45. *NA*, R.G. 120, file 292-33.6 (Colonel Brown's report, app. D, pp. 28–29); U.S., American Battle Monuments Commission, *92d Division*, pp. 15–16; Miller, *Boys of 1917*, pp. 364–65; Lynk, *Negro Pictorial Review*, pp. 38–39.

46. *NA*, R.G. 120, file 292-33.6 (Colonel Brown's report, pp. 12, 40–41, 45–46, 55–56); DuBois, "History of the Black Man," pp. 81–82. Indicative of the nature of the difficulties are some of the remarks made in individual citations for bravery. In General Orders no. 36, 29 November 1918, the citation of Lt. Nathan O. Goodlow spoke of "a continual gunfire"; that of Wagoner Tom Brown spoke of a "shell swept road." General Orders no. 38, 8 December 1918, in citing Pvt. Charles E. Boykin, said that the "woods . . . were found to be alive with machine guns" (Fisk Manuscripts, chaps. 14–16, 92d Division).

47. *NA*, R.G. 120, file 292-33.6 (Brown's report, pp. 57–58).

48. U.S., American Battle Monuments Commission, *92d Division*, p. 25.

49. Blount, *Reminiscences*, p. 45; Williams, *Sidelights*, pp. 167–68.

50. Colonel Starbird's summary of these reasons, p. 141 above, is illuminating reading after the narrative of the 368th under fire.

51. Thomas, *History of the AEF*, pp. 257–58.

52. Ibid., p. 256.

53. Bullard, *Personalities and Reminiscences*, pp. 294–95.

54. DuBois, "History of the Black Man," p. 82.

55. Liggett, *AEF*, pp. 168–69; Bullard, *Personalities and Reminiscences*, pp. 292–93.

56. Harvey Cushing, *From a Surgeon's Journal* (Boston, 1936), p. 464 (entry of 2 October 1918). This was less than one week after the 368th failed in its attack.

57. *NA*, R.G. 120, file 16-11.4 (typescript, "The Inefficiency of Negro Officers," n.d., no signature).

58. Ibid., file 292-33.6 (Brown's report on Argonne offensive).

59. Ibid., file 16-11.4 ("Inefficiency of Negro Officers"). Yet, another source quotes Merrill as commenting on the attack of his battalion on the town of Binarville: ". . . I have never seen a finer spirit shown by soldiers of any race. They look with utter scorn upon danger" (Lee, *Brave Black Division*, p. 23).

60. Scott Papers, 113-5 (Ralph Tyler to Scott, n.d.).

61. DuBois, "History of the Black Man," pp. 81–82. Norris was a graduate of the Plattsburg Officers' Training Camp and had been a captain at regimental headquarters until his promotion just before the attack. Yet General Bullard (*Personalities and Reminiscences*, p. 294) insisted that the white officers assigned to the division were able, Regular army men. See also Scott Papers, 112-6 (Major Dean's memo); Fisk Manuscripts, WMM-1 (typescript extract from courts-martial of Capt. Daniel Smith, pp. 80, 161–68, 180–83). Because he was the ranking officer, Smith, though under arrest, took command of Company K. See ibid., WMM-2 (Crawford courts-martial, p. 51); ibid., chaps. 14–16, inserts (Vance H. Marchbanks to DuBois, 15 January 1926).

62. *NA*, R.G. 120, file 16-11.4; Ballou's report (pp. 1–2) contains a list of the officers and the charges against them. See also ibid., file 292-65.1 (Ballou to commanding officer, IV Corps, requesting the removal of twenty officers).

63. *New York Times*, 8 November 1918, p. 8.

64. *NA*, R.G. 120, file 292-33.6 (Colonel Brown's report, app. D [Major Elser's report]).

65. Ibid., app. Z, pp. 50–51.

66. Ibid., app. D.

67. Scott Papers, 112-6 (Major Dean to Scott, n.d.).

68. *NA*, R.G. 120, file 16-11.4 ("Inefficiency of Negro Officers").

69. Ibid., file 292-33.6 (Brown's report of 15 November 1918, p. 6).

70. DuBois, "History of the Black Man," p. 82; Fisk Manuscripts, chaps. 14–16 (chap. 16; messages of liaison officer, 2d Battalion, to Major Elser); ibid., WMM-3 (memo from liaison officer, 2d Battalion).

71. Fisk Manuscripts, chaps. 17–18, Miscellaneous (Patterson's report on French preference for Negroes, p. 5).

72. *NA*, R.G. 120, file 292-33.6 (Brown's report, app. Z); DuBois, "History of the Black Man," p. 82.

73. *NA*, R.G. 120, file 292-33.6 (Brown's report, p. 15); ibid., file 16-11.4 ("Inefficiency of Negro Officers"); DuBois, "History of the Black Man," p. 81.

74. Fisk Manuscripts, chaps. 17–18, Miscellaneous (Wright's report on medical services of 92d Division, p. 16).

75. *NA*, R.G. 120, file 292-33.6 (Brown's report, p. 15); ibid., file 16-11.4 ("Inefficiency of Negro Officers"); DuBois, "History of the Black Man," p. 81.

76. *NA*, R.G. 120, file 292-32.15 (Greer's memo bulletin, 16 October 1918).

77. Ibid. (Wells to Ballou, 19 October 1918); Fisk Manuscripts, chaps. 14–16, 92d Division (information on courts-martial of 1st Lt. Archie McLee).

78. Marshall, *Providential Armistice*, pp. 8–9, 10–11. He required hospitalization for his wounds.

79. Fisk Manuscripts, chaps. 14–16, 368th Infantry (Adjutant, 368th Infantry, to Capt. Richard Simmons, 3 November 1918). Though Simmons appeared before a board, it had not yet reached a decision. This file contains similar letters to other officers whose cases were pending before boards.

80. Ibid. (Capt. Louis R. Mehlinger [white] to commanding officer, 368th Infantry, 27 September 1918). This complaint was signed by nine officers and three men of the medical detachment. The two officers specifically mentioned were 1st Lt. James C. Pinckston and 1st Lt. James Banks.

81. Bullard, *Personalities and Reminiscences*, pp. 294–95. At least two of the white divisions in his command, the 35th and the 79th, had not performed creditably in the Argonne (see p. 27).

82. *NA*, R.G. 120, file 292-32.14 (Operations Order no. 41, 7 November 1918).

83. Ross, *My Colored Battalion*, p. 37.

84. Ibid., pp. 52, 57, 62; *NA*, R.G. 120, file 292-33.2 (report of Maj. A. E. Sawkins, 2d Battalion, 366th Infantry, 17 November 1918). See also ibid. (General Barnum's report); James A. Moss and Harry S. Howland, *America in Battle* (Paris, ca. 1920), pp. 435–36.

85. *NA*, R.G. 120, file 292-32.6 (Operations Map). Also ibid. (Martin's report); U.S. War Department, *Official Record*, pp. 125–28; Dowd, *Negro in American Life*, p. 230; U.S., American Battle Monuments Commission, *92d Division*, p. 34.

86. Bullard, *Personalities and Reminiscences*, p. 296.

87. Ibid., p. 303; the 7th was the division that, according to Major Appleton, needed help from his battalion.

88. Scott Papers, 113-5 (Greer to McKellar, 6 December 1918); Greer's letter, designed to keep black officers out of the postwar army, was in violation of a law forbidding military personnel from attempting to influence legislation. Scott was provided with a copy of the letter by Ralph Tyler.

89. U.S. Army, War College, *Colored Soldiers*, pp. 110–11 (Greer to Assistant Commandant, General Staff College, 13 April 1920).

90. Ibid., pp. 121–22 (J. N. Merrill to Ballou, 3 October 1918).

91. Ibid., pp. 124–25 (Harbord to Ballou, 12 October 1918).

92. Ibid., pp. 110–11 (Greer's letter).

93. Ibid., pp. 130–31 (McMaster to Greer, 28 April 1919, in reply to Greer's letter, 13 March). For a full discussion of the contempt and distrust for black officers by white officers, from General Bullard on down (except for General Ballou), see Coffman, *War to End All Wars*, pp. 317–20.

94. *NA*, R.G. 120, file 292-33.6 (report of Major Ross).
95. Ross, *My Colored Battalion*, p. 6.
96. Ibid., p. 64; italics are Ross's.
97. Ibid., pp. 9–10.
98. Sweeney, *American Negro*, p. 215; DuBois, "History of the Black Man," pp. 83–84.
99. Page, *Our 110 Days Fighting*, pp. 139–40.
100. Davis, "Negro in the Armed Forces," pp. 503–4.
101. Dowd, *Negro in American Life*, p. 102.
102. Ibid., pp. 100–101.
103. Robert L. Bullard, *American Soldiers Also Fought* (New York, 1936), pp. 97–98.

CHAPTER 9

1. Little, *Harlem to the Rhine*, pp. 348–49.
2. *NA*, R.G. 120, file 292-50.4 (Greer's orders, 6 December 1918); De Castlebled, *AEF*, p. 155.
3. Little, *Harlem to the Rhine*, pp. 339–41; Williams, *Sidelights*, pp. 237–38; Heywood, *Negro Combat Troops*, pp. 248–49.
4. *Gangplank News*, 25 June 1919, p. 49 (last issue of newspaper of Embarkation Service, Services of Supply); Bliss, *805th Pioneer Infantry*, pp. 34–36; *NA*, R.G. 120, file 134-11.4; ibid., file 148-11.4 (report of 2d Lt. Anton C. Adams, 335th Labor Battalion). The latter file contains the historical records of those units involved in the important fuelwood project. Station lists of these units are in file 148-10.7. The units involved included the 314th, 320th, 323d, 329th, and 331st labor battalions, all black units.
5. Odum, *Wings on my Feet*, pp. 259–61; Bliss, *805th Pioneer Infantry*, p. 32.
6. YMCA, *Service with the Fighting Man*, 2:177; Sadler, *Jamestown to the Rhine*, pp. 20–21.
7. Proctor, *Between Black and White*, p. 164. See also report of William G. Shepherd, *New York Evening Post* (cited from Hunton and Johnson, *Two Colored Women*, pp. 237–38).
8. YMCA, *Fighting Man*, 2:176–77; Torrence, *John Hope*, pp. 222–23 (report to Jesse Moreland); Hunton and Johnson, *Two Colored Women*, p. 125.
9. Rossa B. Cooley, "Is There an Explanation?" *Outlook* 121 (10 September 1919): 39. Robert T. Kerlin, *Voice of the Negro* (New York, 1920), pp. 38–39 (cites the *Savannah* [Ga.] *Journal*, 4 October 1919);

Hunton and Johnson, *Two Colored Women*, p. 188; Williams, *Sidelights*, pp. 246–47; Gregory, *Menace of Colour*, pp. 66–67.

10. *Stars and Stripes*, 6 December 1918, p. 1; John T. Winterich, *Squads Write* (New York, 1931), p. 121; Sadler, *Jamestown to the Rhine*, pp. 20–21.

11. *NA*, R.G. 120, file 7-12.5 (Cable History of Colored Troops, p. 10 [Harbord's dispatches no. S953, 6 February 1919, and no. S824, 16 January 1919]).

12. Heywood, *Negro Combat Troops*, pp. 231–34 (Colonel Miles's memo, 25 November 1918).

13. Little, *Harlem to the Rhine*, pp. 351–52.

14. *NA*, R.G. 120, file 292-33.5 (War Diary of 367th Infantry, 6 January 1919); Samuel E. Blount, "Reminiscences of Samuel E. Blount" (typescript in Schomburg Collection), pp. 61–62; Hunton and Johnson, *Two Colored Women*, p. 186; Fisk Manuscripts, WMM-2 (Norval P. Barksdale, History of the 806th Pioneer Infantry, typescript, pp. 5–6); ibid., Chap. 10, Battalions of Labor, p. 47 (James A. Mance, Boulder, Colo., formerly of 530th Engineers, Co. A, to Du-Bois, n.d.); ibid., p. 65 (Colonel Young's memorandum no. 7 to the troops near Is-sur-Tille, n.d.).

15. U.S., Congress, Senate, *Investigation Activities of the Department of Justice.*

16. *NA*, R.G. 120, file 205-27.7 (Records of the Fifth Division). The document bore the endorsement of Brig. Gen. D. E. Nolan, G-2 at Pershing's headquarters.

17. Ibid., file 292-36 (memo of Capt. Louis Mehlinger, 368th Infantry, 24 November 1918.

18. Scott Papers, 115-3; *Crisis*, July 1919, pp. 128–29. The message, dated 1 January 1919, was authorized by Brigadier General Erwin, 92d Division.

19. U.S. Senate, *Alleged Executions*, pp. 55–59.

20. Ibid., p. viii.

21. Ibid., p. 328.

22. Ibid., pp. 91–92; the picture was reproduced opposite p. 71.

23. Ibid., pp. 502, 505, 568 (testimony of Richard Sullivan); pp. 494–97 (testimony of Capt. Charles Wynne).

24. Ibid., p. 761 (Perkins's testimony); p. 764 (Lovelle's testimony). The latter was there from August 1918 until February 1919.

25. Ibid., pp. i–iv, 473–74.

26. Little, *Harlem to the Rhine*, pp. 353–54, 355–56; Heywood, *Negro Combat Troops*, pp. 248–49; Blount, "Reminiscences," p. 63; Scott Papers, 113-5; *NA*, R.G. 120, file 134-11.4 (report on 808th Pioneer Infantry).

27. Johnson, *Black Manhattan*, pp. 235–36; Little, *Harlem to the Rhine*, p. 361; *New York Times*, 18 February 1919, p. 1. The entire front page of the *Times's* pictorial section, 23 February 1919 (sec. 5) was devoted to pictures of the parade.

28. Sweeney, *American Negro*, p. 135.

29. Carter G. Woodson, *Negro Makers of History* (Washington, D.C., 1928), pp. 330–31; *Chicago Defender*, 9 April 1919, p. 16; *New York Times*, 19 December 1919, p. 3.

30. Woodson, *Francis J. Grimke*, 1:590.

31. Scott Papers, 113-5 (Greer to McKellar, 6 December 1918).

32. Woodson, *Negro in Our History*, pp. 521–22.

33. Gen. Lytle Brown said that Greer admitted having written the letter, although it was not on government stationery (*NA*, R.G. 165, item 6292-96 [Lytle Brown to Chief of Staff, 5 June 1919; and Frank McIntyre to Adjutant General, 10 June 1919]).

34. Scott Papers, 110-3 (press release from Scott's office, 7 May 1919).

35. Ibid., 113-5 (Ralph Tyler, from Marbache, France, to Scott, 8 December 1918). See also ibid., 114-2 (Williams on 92d Division, p. 44). On the other hand, Colonel Hayward resigned his commission with the 15th New York shortly after the war. Colored officers had proved their merit, he felt; therefore, some capable black should be selected to take over the regiment (Sweeney, *American Negro*, p. 237).

36. Cited from the *Hot Springs Echo*. See also Kerlin, *Voice of the Negro*, pp. 72–73; Fisk Manuscripts, WMM-1 (petition to the national Legion from New Orleans [C. W. Brooks and Sherman Sabon]; Alexandria, La. [P. G. Davis and John Andrews]; and Shreveport, La. [William Wallace and M. L. Wilson]).

CHAPTER 10

1. Fisk Manuscripts, WMM-1 (William H. Caston to Attorney General T. W. Gregory, 14 January 1919).

2. Woodson, *Negro in Our History*, p. 528.

3. Frank, "Clash of Color," p. 89; Myrdal, *American Dilemma*, 2:745.

4. Frederick G. Detweiler, *The Negro Press in the United States* (Chicago, 1922), pp. 154–55.

5. Seligmann, *Negro Faces America*, p. 39.

6. NAACP, *Report for 1919*, pp. 39–40. The white assailants included a local banker, a deputy sheriff, and the town marshal (*New York Times*, 1 November 1919, p. 3).

7. *New York Times*, 31 December 1918, p. 4.

8. NAACP, *Report for 1918*, pp. 30–32; Robert R. Moton, "The Lynching Record for 1918," *Outlook* 121 (22 January 1919):159.

9. Seligmann, *Negro Faces America*, pp. 260–61; NAACP, *Report for 1919*, p. 19; NAACP, *Burning at the Stake in the United States* (New York, 1919), pp. 10–11.

10. *New York Times*, 17 March 1919, p. 14.

11. NAACP, *Burning at the Stake*, pp. 4, 6–7; cites the *Evening Post*, 15 May 1919.

12. Ibid., p. 8.

13. Later senator from Mississippi; at the time of Bilbo's death in 1947, Congress was investigating charges that he had won election through anti-Negro campaigning and bribery.

14. NAACP, *Report for 1919*, p. 24; *New York Times*, 27 June 1919, p. 17.

15. Walter F. White, *Rope and Faggot* (New York, 1929), p. 112; *Chicago Defender*, 10 May 1919, p. 10; NAACP, *Burning at the Stake*, p. 15; NAACP, *Report for 1919*, p. 19; Kerlin, *Voice of the Negro*, pp. 104–5 (cites the *Boston Guardian*, 13 September 1919).

16. Herbert J. Seligmann, "What Is Behind the Negro Uprisings?" *Current Opinion* 67 (September 1919):154; YMCA, *Service with the Fighting Man*, 2:411.

17. For reports on the riot in Charleston, see NAACP, *Report for 1919*, p. 36; *New York Times*, 11 May 1919, sec. 1, p. 3; *Chicago Defender*, 17 May 1919, p. 1. For other riots: New York City, *New York Times*, 4 July 1919, p. 9, and 16 September, p. 1; Longview, Tex., ibid., 12 July, p. 20; Norfolk, Va., ibid., 22 July, p. 2, and NAACP, *Report for 1919*, p. 35. On the Knoxville trouble, see Kerlin, *Voice of the Negro*, pp. 83–84 (citing the *Kansas City* [Mo.] *Call*, 4 October, 1919); *New York Times*, 1 September, p. 1, and 2 September, p. 4. In the Bisbee, Ariz., trouble, Colonel Snyder, commanding the black troopers, says that the police demanded (and got) the soldiers' service revolvers. They then attacked the black soldiers; at least nine separate attempts were made to kill individual troopers. This was on 3 July (*New York Times*, 22 July 1919, p. 2).

18. Scott Papers, 113-5 (Scott to Tyler, 26 December 1918).

19. Moton, *Finding a Way Out*, pp. 262–63; "With the Negro Troops," *Southern Workman* 48 (January 1919):87.

20. Kerlin, *Voice of the Negro*, p. 19; cites the *Challenge*, October 1919.

21. Editorial, "Returning Soldiers," *Messenger*, March 1919, p. 6; "The Remedy for Race Riots," ibid., p. 20.

22. "Returning Soldiers," *Crisis*, May 1919, p. 14.

23. *New York Times*, 20 July 1919, sec. 2, p. 1; 21 July 1919, p. 1; Frank, "Clash of Color," p. 87; Kerlin, *Voice of the Negro*, pp. 17–18 (cites an editorial from the *Norfolk* [Va.] *Journal and Guide*, 2 August 1919, which said: "The soldiers and sailors who undertook to lynch Joseph Collins, . . . put themselves in the position of knowing more . . . than the Federal Trial Judge. For which they should be made to answer to the civil as well as to the military authorities—if not, why not?").

24. Woodson, *Negro in Our History*, p. 259. This source estimated black casualties for the first two days as about 300. The *New York Times* (22 July 1919, pp. 1–2) listed two dead of each race and about seventy hospitalized.

25. *New York Times*, 22 July 1919, pp. 1–2.

26. Ibid.; also 23 July 1919, p. 8; Seligmann, *Negro Faces America*, p. 122.

27. *New York Times*, 23 July 1919, p. 8.

28. Francis J. Grimke, *The Race Problem* (Washington, D.C., 1919), p. 8.

29. Chicago Commission on Race Relations, *The Negro in Chicago: Study of Race Relations and a Race Riot* (Chicago, 1922), pp. 2–3, 12–13, 55–56.

30. Ibid.; George E. Haynes, "Race Riots in Relation to Democracy," *Survey* 42 (8 August 1919): 697–98; "Why the Negro Appeals to Violence," *Literary Digest* 62 (9 August 1919):11; Carl Sandburg, *The Chicago Race Riots* (New York, 1919), p. 3.

31. *New York Times*, 28 July 1919, p. 1. The policeman involved was suspended later in the week (ibid., 30 July 1919, pp. 4–5) but eventually was exonerated by the Civil Service Commission (Chicago Commission, *Negro in Chicago*, p. 4).

32. *New York Times*, 30 July 1919, pp. 1, 3; 5 August 1919, p. 16. The Chicago Commission (*Negro in Chicago*, p. 21) reported 193 whites and 365 blacks injured. It pointed out that, while 65 percent of the black victims were beaten, a similar percentage of white casualties were either shot or stabbed (see also pp. 25, 34–35).

33. *New York Times*, 29 July 1919, p. 2; 30 July 1919, p. 3.

34. Chicago Commission, *Negro in Chicago*, pp. 34, 38–39.

35. *New York Times*, 31 July 1919, p. 1; "Why the Negro Appeals," p. 11.

36. "Why the Negro Appeals," p. 11.

37. Chicago Commission, *Negro in Chicago*, pp. 35–36; Kerlin, *Voice of the Negro*, pp. 82–83 (citing the *Chicago Defender*, 6 September 1919).

38. White, *Man Called White*, pp. 48–49; Brawley, *Short History*, pp. 362–63. In support of the blacks' contention that they had not initiated

the shooting, there were many women and children in the church building at the time.

39. White, *Man Called White*, p. 47.

40. Ibid., pp. 47–48; Brawley, *Short History*, pp. 362–63.

41. *New York Times*, 4 October 1919, p. 7; 5 October 1919, p. 10.

42. Ibid., 5 October 1919, sec. 2, p. 1.

43. Ibid., 8 October 1919, p. 18.

44. "The Blunder of Race Riots," *Independent* 99 (9 August 1919): 176; citing an editorial from the *New York World*.

45. Detweiler, *Negro Press*, p. 21. The letter was sent from Arkansas.

46. *New York Times*, 30 September 1919, p. 5.

47. *Charleston* (S.C.) *Messenger*, cited in Kerlin, *Voice of the Negro*, pp. 37–38.

48. Hewlett, *Race Riots in America*, pp. 12–13.

49. L. E. Elliott, "The Negro Problem in the United States," *Pan-American Magazine* 27 (August 1918):177; Robert T. Kerlin, *The Negro's Reaction to the World War* (Norfolk, Va., n.d.), pp. 7–8.

50. Hewlett, *Race Riots in America*, p. 7.

51. Alain L. Locke, *The Negro in America* (Chicago, 1933), pp. 12–13. See also Kerlin, *Voice of the Negro*, pp. 3–4; and John Hope Franklin, *Slavery to Freedom* (New York, 1956), pp. 472–73.

52. Johnson, *Black Manhattan*, p. 246.

53. Seligmann, *Negro Faces America*, pp. 58–59; Kerlin, *Negro's Reaction*, pp. 4–5.

54. Kerlin, *Negro's Reaction*, pp. 5–6.

55. M. W. Bullock, "What Does the Negro Want?" *Outlook* 123 (17 September 1919):110.

56. Archibald H. Grimke, *Shame of America*, p. 15.

57. Ray S. Baker, "Gathering Clouds along the Color Line," *World's Work* 32 (June 1916):232.

58. "Why the Negro Appeals," p. 11.

59. *Crisis*, August 1919, p. 179.

Bibliography

Voluminous materials are available to the student of black participation in World War I; before listing individual items, it may be useful to mention some of the major repositories of original and printed matter dealing with the subject.

The mass of documentary material in the National Archives (cited in footnotes as *NA*) is truly staggering; although it is fairly well catalogued, merely sifting through it to find precisely what is being sought is a major task. The New York Public Library has a wealth of printed information. The World War I collection at the main library is outstanding; especially useful were the many first-person war narratives, which unfortunately are poorly indexed or not indexed at all. At the 135th Street branch of the New York Public Library, the Schomburg Collection of Negro Literature and History contains many rare items.

The personal papers of Emmett J. Scott, which repose in the library of Morgan State College in Baltimore, are quite extensive, including copies of much of the official correspondence concerning black soldiers that came across Scott's desk in the War Department and also Scott's postwar papers when he was secretary of Howard University. Fisk University, in its Amistad Research Center, has some of the papers of W. E. B. DuBois. Most pertinent to this study are the notes for and a draft of his proposed History of the Black Man in World War I, which would be even more valuable if documented.

Among general contemporaneous accounts, *Sidelights on Negro Soldiers* by Charles Williams is one of the most important of printed sources. Scott's *American Negro in the World War* is also useful, but might have been more so if Scott had not rushed it into print, possibly to capture the market before similar books appeared, and if he had not glossed over a number of problems of black soldiers, perhaps because he felt that to expose them would reflect unfavorably on his performance in the War Department as advisor on Negro matters.

Among the many regimental histories that appeared soon after the war, several are of outstanding interest. Of those written by white officers about their black commands, special mention must be made of Arthur Little's *From Harlem to the Rhine*, about the 15th New York National Guard which became the 369th Infantry Regiment; Warner D. Ross's *My Colored Battalion*, about the 92d Division; and Chester Heywood's *Negro Combat Troops in the World War* and Percy Deckard's *List of Officers of the 371st Regiment*, both dealing with the 371st Infantry. These accounts are best read in conjunction with narratives by black participants in the war, among the most illuminating of which are *The American Negro with the Red Hand of France* by Monroe Mason and Arthur Furr, dealing with the 93d Division, and *Two Colored Women with the American Expeditionary Forces* by Addie Hunton and Katherine Johnson, which describes the war from the viewpoint of two black YMCA workers. William S. Bradden's *Under Fire with the 370th Infantry, A.E.F.* is an interesting account by the chaplain of the Illinois black National Guard regiment, although it is somewhat flawed by the author's intense personal biases.

An itemized list follows, grouped under the usual bibliographic headings. In order to make the bibliography as broadly useful as possible, some magazine articles and pamphlets, not specifically referred to in the text or notes of this volume, have been included because of their pertinence to the general subject of black soldiers in World War I.

General Works

Aptheker, Herbert. *Toward Negro Freedom*. New York: New Century, 1956.

Bowen, Trevor. *Divine White Right*. New York: Harper, 1934.

Coffman, Edward M. *War to End All Wars*. New York: Oxford University Press, 1968.

De Castlebled, Maurice. *History of the AEF*. New York: Bookcraft, 1937.

Dowd, Jerome. *The Negro in American Life*. New York: Century, 1926.

Franklin, John Hope. *From Slavery to Freedom*. New York: Knopf, 1956.

Gossett, Thomas F. *Race: The History of an Idea in America.* Dallas, Tex.: Southern Methodist University Press, 1963.

Greene, Lorenzo J., and Carter G. Woodson. *The Negro Wage Earner.* Washington, D.C.: Association for the Study of Negro Life and History, 1930.

Gregory, John W. *The Menace of Colour.* London: Seeley, Service, 1925.

Locke, Alain L. *The Negro in America.* Chicago: American Library Association, 1933.

Miller, Warren H. *The Boys of 1917.* Boston: Page, 1939.

Montagu, Ashley. *Man's Most Dangerous Myth.* New York: Praeger, 1963.

Mowry, George E. *The Era of Theodore Roosevelt.* New York: Harper, 1958.

Myrdal, Gunnar. *The American Dilemma.* 2 vols. New York: Harper, 1944.

Niles, John J. *Songs My Mother Never Taught Me.* New York: Macaulay, 1929.

Nordholt, J. W. S. *People Who Walk in Darkness.* London: Burke, 1960.

Resh, Richard, ed. *Black America.* Lexington, Mass.: Heath, 1969.

Reuter, Edward. *The American Race Problem.* 3d ed. New York: T. Y. Crowell, 1970.

Rudwick, Elliott. *Race Riot at East St. Louis.* Cleveland, Ohio: Meridian, 1966.

Schoenfeld, Seymour J. *The Negro in the Armed Forces.* Washington, D.C.: Associated Publishers, 1945.

Slosson, Preston. *The Great Crusade and After.* New York: Macmillan, 1930.

Stallings, Laurence. *The Doughboys.* New York: Harper & Row, 1963.

Tannenbaum, Frank. *Darker Phases of the South.* New York: Putnam's, 1924.

Tindall, George Brown. *South Carolina Negroes: 1877–1900.* Baton Rouge, La.: Louisiana State Press, 1966.

Torrence, Ridgley. *The Story of John Hope.* New York: Macmillan, 1948.

Woodson, Carter G. *Negro Makers of History*. Washington, D.C.: Associated Publishers, 1928.

Contemporary Accounts

Adams, James G. *Review of the American Forces in Germany*. Coblenz: Published by the author, 1921.

The Americans in the Great War. 3 vols. Clermont-Ferrand, France: Michelin, 1920.

Baker, Ray Stannard. *Following the Color Line*. New York: Harper & Row, 1964.

Bliss, James G. *History of the 805th Pioneer Infantry*. St. Paul, Minn.: Privately published, 1919.

Brawley, Benjamin. *Short History of the Negro*. New York: Macmillan, 1918.

Brigham, Carl C. *A Study of American Intelligence*. Princeton, N.J.: Princeton University Press, 1923.

Broun, Heywood. *The A.E.F.* New York: Appleton Co., 1918.

Chicago Commission on Race Relations. *The Negro in Chicago: Study of Race Relations and a Race Riot*. Chicago: Commission on Race Relations, 1922.

Collins, Winfield. *The Truth about Lynching and the Negro in the South*. New York: Neale, 1918.

Cox, Ernest. *White America*. Richmond, Va.: White America Society, 1923.

Crowell, Benedict, and R. F. Wilson. *The Road to France*. 2 vols. New Haven, Conn.: Yale University Press, 1921.

Delsarte, Walter. *The Negro, Democracy, and the War*. Detroit: Wolverine, 1919.

Detweiler, Frederick G. *The Negro Press in the United States*. Chicago: University of Chicago Press, 1922.

Epstein, Abraham. *The Negro Migrant in Pittsburgh*. Pittsburgh, Pa.: 1918; New York: Arno, 1969.

Gibbons, Floyd. *And They Thought We Wouldn't Fight*. New York: Doran, 1918.

Gibson, John W. *Progress of a Race*. Naperville, Ind.: Nichols, 1920.

Glass, Edward. *The History of the Tenth Cavalry*. Tucson, Ariz.: Acme, 1921.

Halsey, Francis W. *The Literary Digest History of the World War.* New York: Funk & Wagnalls, 1920.

History of the American Field Service in France. 3 vols. Boston: Houghton Mifflin, 1920.

Jackson, Algernon. *The Man Next Door.* Philadelphia: Neaula, 1919.

Jamieson, J. A., et al. *Complete History of the Colored Soldiers in the World War.* New York: Bennett & Churchill, 1919.

Johnsen, Julia C., comp. *Selected Articles on the Negro Problem.* New York: Wilson, 1921.

Kerlin, Robert T. *Voice of the Negro.* New York: Dutton, 1920.

Lynk, Miles V. *Negro Pictorial Review of the Great War.* Memphis, Tenn.: 20th Century Art, ca. 1919.

McDougall, William. *Is America Safe for Democracy?* New York: Scribner's, 1921.

Marcossan, Isaac. *S.O.S.: America's Miracle in France.* New York: Lane, 1919.

Mayo, Katherine. *That Damn "Y".* Boston: Houghton Mifflin, 1920.

Miller, Kelly. *Appeal to Conscience.* New York: Macmillan, 1918.

———. *The Disgrace of Democracy.* Washington, D.C.: Published by the author, 1917.

———. *The Everlasting Stain.* Washington, D.C.: Associated Publishers, 1924.

———. *World War for Human Rights.* Washington, D.C.: Jenkins & Keller, 1919.

Moss, James A., and Harry S. Howland. *America in Battle.* Paris: Clarke, ca. 1920.

Muller, William G. *The Twenty-fourth Infantry.* N.p.: Published by the author, 1923.

Nave, George F. *The New Negro's Attitude toward His Government.* Muskegee, Okla.: Published by the author, 1917.

Nearing, George. *Black America.* New York: Vanguard, 1929.

Page, Arthur W. *Our 110 Days Fighting.* Garden City, N.J.: Doubleday, Page, 1920.

Peixotto, Ernest C. *The American Front.* New York: Scribner's, 1919.

A Pictorial History of the Negro in the Great World War, 1917–1919. New York: Toissant, 1919.

Scott, Emmett J. *The American Negro in the World War*. Chicago: Homewood, 1919. Reprinted as *Scott's Official History of the American Negro in the World War*. New York: Arno Press and the *New York Times*, 1969.

———. *Negro Migration during the Great War*. New York: Oxford, 1920.

Seligmann, Herbert. *The Negro Faces America*. New York: Harper, 1920; Harper & Row, 1969.

Skillman, Willis R. *The AEF*. Philadelphia: Jacobs, 1920.

Smith, Chellis V. *Americans All*. Boston: Lothrop, Lee & Shepherd, 1925.

Southern Sociological Congress. *Democracy in Earnest*. Washington, D.C.: Southern Sociological Congress, 1918.

Stoddard, Lothrop. *The Rising Tide of Color against White World Supremacy*. New York: Scribner's, 1920.

Sweeney, W. Allison. *History of the American Negro in the Great World War*. Chicago: Cuneo-Henneberry, 1919.

Thomas, Shipley. *The History of the AEF*. New York: Doran, 1920.

Thompson, John L. *History and Views of the Colored Officers Training Camp*. Des Moines, Iowa: Bystander, 1917.

Walker, George. *Venereal Disease in the American Expeditionary Forces*. Baltimore: Medical Standard Book Co., 1922.

White, Walter F. *Rope and Faggot*. New York: Knopf, 1929.

Woodson, Carter G. *The Negro in Our History*. Washington, D.C.: Associated Publishers, 1921.

Young Mens' Christian Association. *Service with the Fighting Man*. 2 vols. New York: Association Press, 1922.

Personal Narratives

Bradden, William S. *Under Fire with the 370th Infantry, A.E.F.* Chicago: Published by the author, n.d.

Bullard, Robert L. *American Soldiers Also Fought*. New York: Longmans, Green, 1936.

———. *Personalities and Reminiscences of the War*. New York: Doubleday, Page, 1925.

Butler, Alban. *Happy Days*. New York: Coward & McCann, 1929.

Cobb, Irvin S. *The Glory of the Coming.* New York: Doran, 1918.

Coppin, Levi. *Unwritten History.* Philadelphia: A. M. E. Book Concern, 1919.

Cushing, Harvey. *From a Surgeon's Journal.* Boston: Little, Brown, 1936.

Deckard, Percy E. *List of Officers of the 371st Regiment.* Allegany, N.Y.: Allegany Citizens, 1929.

Edward, William J. *Twenty-five Years in the Black Belt.* Boston: Cornhill, 1918.

Hagood, Johnson. *The Services of Supply.* Boston: Houghton Mifflin, 1927.

Harbord, James G. *The American Army in France.* Boston: Little, Brown, 1936.

———. *Leaves from a War Diary.* New York: Dodd, Mead, 1925.

Heywood, Chester D. *Negro Combat Troops in the World War.* Worcester, Mass.: Commonwealth, 1928.

Hunton, Addie W., and Katherine M. Johnson. *Two Colored Women with the American Expeditionary Forces.* New York: Brooklyn Eagle, 1920.

Johnson, James W. *Along This Way.* New York: Viking, 1933.

———. *Black Manhattan.* New York: Knopf, 1930.

Judy, William L. *A Soldier's Diary.* Chicago: Judy Publishing, 1930.

Liggett, Hunter. *Commanding an American Army.* Boston: Houghton Mifflin, 1925.

———. *AEF.* New York: Dodd, Mead, 1928.

Little, Arthur. *From Harlem to the Rhine.* New York: Corvici, 1936.

McCarthy, C. F. *A Year at Camp Gordon.* Wilkes-Barre, Pa.: McCarthy, 1920.

MacIntyre, William. *Colored Soldiers.* Macon, Ga.: Burke, 1923.

McKay, Claude. *A Long Way From Home.* New York: Furman, 1937.

Mason, Monroe, and Arthur Furr. *The American Negro with the Red Hand of France.* Boston: Cornhill, 1920.

Moton, Robert R. *Finding a Way Out: An Autobiography.* Garden City, N.J.: Doubleday, Page, 1921.

Niles, John J. *Singing Soldiers.* New York: Scribner's, 1927.

Pershing, John J. *My Experiences in the World War.* 2 vols. New York: Stokes, 1931.

Pottle, Frederick A. *Stretchers*. New Haven, Conn.: Yale University Press, 1929.

Proctor, H. H. *Between Black and White*. New York: Pilgrim, 1925.

Riegelman, Harold. *War Notes of a Casual*. New York: Published by the author, 1931.

Ross, Warner D. *My Colored Battalion*. Chicago: Published by the author, 1920.

Ross, William O., and Duke L. Slaughter. *With the 351st in France*. Baltimore, Md.: Afro-American, 1923.

Shanks, David S. *As They Passed through the Port*. Washington, D.C.: Cory, 1927.

Snively, Harry H. *The Battle of the Non-Combatants*. New York: Business Bourse, 1933.

Tippett, Edwin J., Jr. *Who Won the War?* Toledo, Ohio: Toledo Typesetting & Printing, 1920.

Webster, Edgar H. *Chums and Brothers*. Boston: Badger, 1920.

White, Walter F. *A Man Called White*. New York: Viking, 1948.

Wilgus, William J. *Transporting the A.E.F. in Western Europe*. New York: Columbia University Press, 1931.

Williams, Charles H. *Sidelights on Negro Soldiers*. Boston: Brimmer, 1923.

Winterich, John T., ed. *Squads Write*. New York: Harper, 1931.

Woodson, Carter G., ed. *The Works of Francis J. Grimke*. 4 vols. Washington, D.C.: Associated Publishers, 1942.

Fiction

Daly, Victor. *Not Only War*. Boston: Christopher, 1932.

Dionne, Jack. *"Cullud" Fun*. Houston, Tex.: Rhein, 1932.

Hill, Leslie. *The Wings of Oppression*. Boston: Stratford, 1921.

Jamieson, Roscoe C. *"Negro Soldiers" and Other Poems*. Kansas City, Kan.: Neil, 1918.

Leonard, William. *"The Lynching Bee" and Other Poems*. New York: Huebsch, 1920.

Mack, Charles E. *Two Black Crows in the A.E.F.* Indianapolis, Ind.: Bobbs-Merrill, 1928.

Majors, C. L. *World War Jokes*. Ramer, Tenn.: Majors, 1930.

Odum, Howard. *Wings on My Feet.* Indianapolis, Ind.: Bobbs-Merrill, 1929.

Seward, Walter E. *Negroes Call to the Colors.* Athens, Ga.: Knox Institute Press, 1919.

Shackelford, Theodore H. *"My Country" and Other Poems.* Philadelphia: Klopp, 1918.

Government Publications

Crowder, Enoch. *Second Report of the Provost Marshal General.* Washington, D.C.: Government Printing Office, 1919.

France, Assemblée Nationales. *Annales,* n.s., 1919 Session Ordinaire. Paris, 1920.

Lee, Ulysses G., comp. *Employment of Negro Troops.* Washington, D.C.: Office of the Chief of Military History, Government Printing Office, 1966.

Pershing, John J. *Final Report: Commander in Chief, American Expeditionary Forces.* Washington, D.C.: Government Printing Office, 1919.

Spencer, Seldon P. *The Racial Question.* Washington, D.C.: Government Printing Office, 1920.

U.S. Adjutant General's Office. *Summary of Casualties in the AEF.* Washington, D.C.: Government Printing Office, 1919.

U.S., American Battle Monuments Commission. *American Armies and Battlefields in Europe.* Washington, D.C.: Government Printing Office, 1938.

———. *92d Division: Summary of Operations in the World War.* Washington, D.C.: Government Printing Office, 1944.

———. *93d Division: Summary of Operations in the World War.* Washington, D.C.: Government Printing Office, 1944.

U.S., American Expeditionary Forces, Engineer Corps. *Historical Report of the Chief Engineer.* Washington, D.C.: Government Printing Office, 1919.

U.S. Army, Adjutant General. *Report of the Adjutant General of the Army, 1918.* Washington, D.C.: Government Printing Office, 1918.

U.S. Army, General Staff, Historical Branch. *Brief Histories of Divisions, U.S. Army, 1917–1918.* Washington, D.C.: Government Printing Office, 1921.

———. *Organization of the Services of Supply.* Washington, D.C.: Government Printing Office, 1921.

U.S. Army, War College. *Colored Soldiers in the U.S. Army.* Washington, D.C.: Government Printing Office, 1942.

———. *The Order of Battle of the United States Land Forces in the World War.* 3 vols. Washington, D.C.: Government Printing Office, 1949.

U.S., Congress. *Congressional Record.* 65th and 66th Congresses. Washington, D.C.: Government Printing Office, 1917–20.

U.S., Congress, House. *East St. Louis Riots.* Washington, D.C.: Government Printing Office, 1918.

———. *Selective Service Act.* Washington, D.C.: Government Printing Office, 1918.

U.S., Congress, House, Committee on Foreign Affairs. *Authorizing the Erection of a Monument to the 93d Division: Hearings on H.R. 9694.* Washington, D.C.: Government Printing Office, 1926.

U.S., Congress, House, Committee on the Library. *Negro Soldiers' and Sailors' Memorial.* Washington, D.C.: Government Printing Office, 1919.

U.S., Congress, Senate. *Alleged Executions without Trial in France.* Washington, D.C.: Government Printing Office, 1923.

———. *Investigation Activities of the Department of Justice.* Washington, D.C.: Government Printing Office, 1919.

U.S. Department of Labor, Division of Negro Economics. *The Negro at Work during the World War and Reconstruction.* Washington, D.C.: Government Printing Office, 1921.

U.S. Department of State. *Colored Soldiers in the French Army.* Washington, D.C.: Government Printing Office, 1919.

U.S. War Department. *Annual Report, 1918.* Washington, D.C.: Government Printing Office, 1919.

———. *Battle Participation of Organizations of the American Expeditionary Forces in France, Belgium, and Italy.* Washington, D.C.: Government Printing Office, 1920.

———. *The Medical Department of the United States Army in the World War.* Washington, D.C.: Government Printing Office, 1925.

———. *The Official Record of the United States' Part in the Great*

War. Washington, D.C.: Government Printing Office, 1923.

U.S. War Department, Militia Bureau. *Military Protection, U.S. Guards*. Washington, D.C.: Government Printing Office, 1919.

———. *Report of the Acting Chief of the Militia Bureau, 1918*. Washington, D.C.: Government Printing Office, 1918.

Miscellaneous Pamphlets

Boas, Franz. *The Real Race Problem*. New York: National Association for the Advancement of Colored People, 1910.

Brock, George D., comp. *Within the Heart of the Colored Soldier*. N.p., n.d.

Bruce, John E. *A Tribute for the Negro Soldier*. New York: Bruce & Franklin, 1918.

Buchanan, Walter S. *The Negro's War Aims*. Birmingham, Ala., 1918.

Buell, Charles T. *The Great World War*. Newark, Ohio: Buell, ca. 1924.

Chew, Abraham. *A Biography of Col. Charles Young*. Washington, D.C.: Pendleton, 1923.

Circle for Negro War Relief. *Report of the Circle for Negro War Relief*. N.p., n.d.

Cochell, William H. W. *My Travel in France in World's War*. Memphis, Tenn., n.d.

Curtis, Mary. *The Black Soldier*. Washington, D.C.: G.D. Morris, 1915.

Diary and Experiences of Battery E. Trenton, N.J., 1919.

Donald, Henderson H. *The Negro Migration of 1916–1918*. Washington, D.C.: Association for the Study of Negro Life and History, 1921.

536th Engineers Service Battalion: Companies A and B. N.p., n.d.

Ford, James W. *The Negro and the Imperialist War of 1914–1918*. N.p., 1929.

Foster, Obadiah M. *The Modern Warfare and My Experiences in France*. [Washington]: Goines, 1919.

Gant, Lucius L. *The Destiny of the American Negro*. [Nashville, Tenn.]: S.S. Publishing Board, 1920.

Grimke, Archibald H. *The Shame of America*. Washington, D.C.: American Negro Academy, 1924.

Grimke, Francis J. *The Race Problem*. Washington, D.C., 1919.

Hampton in Wartime. Hampton, Va.: Hampton Institute, 1918.

Handbook of Camp A. A. Humphreys. N.p., n.d.

Harrison, William H. *Colored Boys' and Girls' Inspiring United States History*. N.p.: Published by the auther, 1921.

Hawkins, John R. *Fourteen Specific Articles as a Basis of Democracy at Home*. Washington, D.C., 1918.

Hayes, D. H. *The Colored Man's Part in the War*. Atlanta, Ga.: Hamilton, ca. 1919.

Haynes, George E. *The Trend of the Races*. New York: Council of Women for Home Missions and Missionary Education Movement in the United States and Canada, 1922.

Heroes of 1918. N.p.: Pullman Porters' Review, n.d.

Hewlett, J. Henry. *Race Riots in America: Judge Lynch's Record, 1917–1924*. Washington, D.C., n.d.

House, Grace B. *Soldiers of Freedom*. N.p., n.d.

Johnson, Charles B. *The World War and Democracy, as Regards the Negro (The Truth)*. N.p., n.d.

Johnson, Henry L. *The Negro under Wilson*. N.p.: Republican National Committee, ca. 1917.

Kerlin, Robert T. *The Negro's Reaction to the World War*. Norfolk, Va., n.d.

Lee, George W. *A Brave Black Division*. Memphis, Tenn., ca. 1923.

Lightfoot, G. M., et al. *Howard University in the War*. Washington, D.C.: Howard University, n.d.

Long, Francis T. *The Negroes of Clarke County, Georgia, during the Great War*. Athens, Ga., 1919.

Marshall, Napoleon B. *The Providential Armistice: A Volunteer's Story*. Washington, D.C., 1930.

Miller, Kelly. *The Negro in the New Reconstruction*. Washington, D.C.: Howard University, n.d.

Miner, Uzziah, et al., eds. *Modern Artilleryman*. Camp Dix, N.J., 1919.

Moore, Lewis B. *Patriotism through Education*. New York, 1919.

———. *How the Colored Race Can Help in the Problems Issuing from the War*. New York, 1918.

Morel, E. O. *The Horror on the Rhine*. N.p.: [England ?], 1920.

Muston, W. H. *Over There*. Yoakum, Tex.: Bankers, ca. 1923.

National Association for the Advancement of Colored People. *Annual Reports*. New York: NAACP, 1917–20.

———. *Burning at the Stake in the United States*. New York: NAACP, 1919.

———. *Thirty Years of Lynching in the United States*. New York: NAACP, 1919.

Olcott, Jane, comp. *The Work of Colored Women*. New York: YMCA, 1919.

Pickins, William. *The Negro in the Light of the Great War*. Baltimore, Md.: Daily Herald, n.d.

Powell, A. Clayton. *Patriotism and the Negro*. New York: Beehive, n.d.

Pullman Porters' Review, Military Supplement. N.p.: Pullman Porters' Review, n.d.

Refutation of the Charges Made in the Campaign against the French Colored Troops in the Rhenish Occupied Territories. N.p., n.d.

Sadler, James E. *The Negro from Jamestown to the Rhine*. N.p., n.d.

Sandburg, Carl. *The Chicago Race Riots*. New York: Harcourt, Brace, 1919.

Snyder, E. L., ed. *Colored Soldiers in France*. N.p., n.d.

Spingarn, Arthur B. *Address to the Fifteenth Annual Session of the National Association of Teachers in Colored Schools*. Washington, D.C., 1918.

Union League Club. *The Presentation of Colors to the 367th Regiment of Infantry*. [New York]: Parsons, [1918].

Vardaman, James K. *The Great American Race Problem and Its Relation to the Present War*. N.p., 1917.

Varlin, Eugene. *The Negro and the U.S. Army*. New York: Pioneer, n.d.

War Camp Community Service. *The War Camp Community Service and the Negro Soldier*. N.p., 1920.

White, Walter F. *Philadelphia Race Riots, July 26–31, 1918*. New York, 1918.

Williams, John H. *A Negro Looks at War*. New York: New Workers Library, 1940.

Williams, John R. *A Trench Letter*. N.p., 1918.

Wood-Hill, C. *History of the British West Indies Regiment.* N.p., n.d.

Periodicals

"After the War: A Symposium." *Southern Workman* 48 (March 1919):134–40.

"The American Negro as a Fighting Man." *Review of Reviews* 58 (August 1918):210–11.

"The American Negro in France." *Current History Magazine* 13 (March 1921):479–80.

"An Appeal to America Not Yet Written by Woodrow Wilson." *Nation* 109 (9 August 1919):160.

Atwell, E. T. "The Experience of the War in Organizing Recreation for Colored Soldiers and Its Application to Peace Time." *Proceedings of the National Conference of Social Work* 47 (1920):331–33.

Baker, Ray S. "Gathering Clouds along the Color Line." *World's Work* 32 (June 1916):232–36.

———. "The Negro Goes North." *World's Work* 34 (July 1917):314–19.

Barksdale, Norvel P. "France and the Negro." *Lincoln University Record,* October 1924, pp. 8–16.

"The Black Troops on the Rhine." *Nation* 112 (9 March 1921):365–66.

Blanton, Joshua E. "Men in the Making." *Southern Workman* 48 (January 1919):17–24.

Blumenthal, Henry. "Woodrow Wilson and the Race Question." *Journal of Negro History* 28 (January 1963):1–23.

"The Blunder of Race Riots." *Independent* 99 (9 August 1919):176–78.

Boas, F. P. "The Relative Prevalance of Syphilis among Negroes and Whites." *Social Hygiene* 1 (1914–15):610–16.

Brigham, Carl C. "Intelligence Tests of Immigrant Groups." *Psychological Review* 37 (March 1930): 158–65.

Bullock, M. W. "What Does the Negro Want?" *Outlook* 123 (17 September 1919):110.

"Bush Germans Better Watch That 'Chocolate Front.' " *Literary Digest* 57 (15 June 1918):43–47.

"The Cause and Remedy for Race Riots." *Messenger*, September 1919, p. 20.

Clement, Rufus E. "Problems of Demobilization and Rehabilitation of the Negro Soldier after World Wars I and II." *Journal of Negro Education* 12 (1943):533–42.

"Col. Bill Hayward and His 'Black Watch.' " *Literary Digest* 60 (8 March 1919):59.

Colson, William N. "An Analysis of Negro Patriotism." *Messenger*, August 1919, pp. 23–25.

———. "Propaganda and the American Negro Soldier." *Messenger*, July 1919, p. 25.

———. "The Social Experience of the Negro Soldier Abroad." *Messenger*, October 1919, pp. 26–27.

Colson, William N., and A. B. Nutt. "The Failure of the Ninety-second Division." *Messenger*, September 1919, pp. 22–24.

Cooley, Rossa B. "Is There an Explanation?" *Outlook* 121 (10 September 1919):39.

"Croix de Guerre and Rare Praise for American Negro Troops." *Literary Digest* 60 (18 January 1919):55–60.

Davis, Paul C. "The Negro in the Armed Forces." *Virginia Quarterly Review* 24 (1948):499–520.

"Democracy and the Colored Soldier." *Playground* 13 (September 1919):259–66.

"The Discovery of France by Jos. Williams, Colored Dough-Boy." *Literary Digest* 61 (12 April 1919):80–84.

DuBois, W. E. B. "Black Labor Moves North." *Nation* 116 (9 May 1923):539–41.

———. "The Black Man in the Revolution of 1914–1918." *Crisis* 17 (March 1919):218–23.

———. "An Essay toward a History of the Black Man in the Great War." *Crisis* 18 (June 1919):63–87.

———. "The Problem of Problems." *Intercollegiate Socialist*, December 1917–January 1918, pp. 5–9.

"East St. Louis Riots." *Literary Digest* 55 (14 July 1917):10–11.

Elliott, L. E. "The Negro Problem in the United States." *Pan-American Magazine* 27 (August 1918):173–92.

Embree, Edwin R. "With the Negro Troops." *Survey* 40 (10 August 1918):537–38.

"The End of the Houston Riots." *Outlook*, vol. 117 (19 December 1917).

Ferguson, David L. "With This Black Man's Army." *Independent* 97 (15 March 1919):368.

Ferguson, George O. "The Intelligence of Negroes at Camp Lee, Virginia." *School and Society* 9 (14 June 1919):721–26.

———. "The Mental Status of the American Negro." *Scientific Monthly* 12 (June 1921):533–43.

———. "The Psychology of the Negro: An Experimental Study." *Archives of Psychology*, 1916, pp. 123–28.

Ferris, William H. "The Colored Man and the Great War." *Favorite Magazine*, pp. 240–41 (offprint, date unknown).

Frank, Glenn. "Clash of Color." *Century* 99 (November 1919):86–98.

"A Futile Attempt at Sedition." *Outlook* 115 (18 April 1917):684.

Gannett, Lewis S. "Those Black Troops on the Rhine—and the White." *Nation* 112 (25 May 1921):733–34.

"German Plots among Negroes." *Literary Digest* 54 (21 April 1917):1153.

Giddings, Franklin H. "The Black Man's Rights." *Independent* 99 (2 August 1919):153.

Grant, Frances B. "Negro Patriotism and Negro Music." *Outlook* 121 (26 February 1919):343–47.

Hart, Irving S. "Keeping Up Morale at Camp Alexander, Virginia." *Southern Workman* 48 (May 1919):225–30.

Haynes, George E. "The Negro and National Reconstruction." *Public* 22 (8 February 1919):131–33.

———. "Race Riots in Relation to Democracy." *Survey* 42 (8 August 1919):697–99.

———. "What the Negro Thinks of Race Riots." *Public* 22 (9 August 1919):848–49.

Hazen, H. H. "Syphilis in the American Negro." *Journal of the American Medical Association*, 8 August 1914, pp. 463–66.

"The Health of Colored Troops." *Literary Digest* 61 (14 June 1919):23.

Herring, Kate M. "How the Southern Negro Is Supporting the Government." *Outlook* 120 (20 November 1918):452–53.

Hilts, Helen M. "Hampton Training and War Service." *Southern Workman* 47 (July 1918):335–44.

"La 'Honte Noire.' " *L'Illustration*, 13 August 1921, p. 145.

"The Houston Mutiny." *Outlook* 117 (5 September 1917):10–11.

"How Shall the Black Man's Burden Be Lifted." *Current Opinion* 71 (19 August 1919):111–12.

"How the War Brings Unprophesied Opportunities to the Negro Race." *Current Opinion* 61 (December 1916):404–5.

"Intelligence of Negroes as Compared with Whites." *Current Opinion* 71 (November 1921):640–41.

Jamison, S. C. "Certain Phases of Syphilis in the Negro Female from the Standpoint of Medical Diagnosis." *New Orleans Medical and Surgical Journal* 69 (1916–17):96–97.

Johnson, James W. "What the Negro Is Doing for Himself." *Liberator* 1 (June 1919):29–31.

"Last Year's Lynching Record." *Outlook* 115 (17 January 1917):97.

Laurence, H. B. "Why the Negro Fights." *Southern Workman* 47 (August 1918):400.

Lauzurne, Stephane. "The Black Troops." *Outlook* 127 (16 March 1921):423–24.

Leonard, Oscar. "The East St. Louis Pogram." *Survey* 38 (7 July 1917): 331–33.

Love, A. G., and C. B. Davenport. "A Comparison of White and Colored Troops in Respect to the Incidence of Disease." *Proceedings of the National Academy of Sciences* 5 (March 1919):58–67.

Lovewell, Reinette. "Backing the Negro Troops." *Southern Workman* 47 (November 1917):524–26.

"Lynching: An American Kultur?" *New Republic* 14 (13 April 1918):311–12.

Lynde, Charles C. "Mobilizing Rastus." *Outlook* 118 (13 March 1918):412–17.

McKaine, Osceola E. "The Buffaloes." *Outlook* 119 (22 May 1918):144–47.

———. "With the Buffaloes in France." *Independent* 97 (11 January 1919):50.

McNeil, H. L. "Syphilis in the Southern Negro." *Journal of the American Medical Association* 67 (30 September 1916):1001–4.

McNutt, William S. "Not a Negro Slacker." *Colliers Weekly* (offprint).

Moorland, Jesse E. "The Y.M.C.A. with Colored Troops." *Southern Workman* 48 (April 1919):171–75.

Moss, James A. "The Negro as a Soldier." *Southern Workman* 47 (June 1918):313.

Moton, Robert R. "The American Negro and the World War." *World's Work* 36 (May 1918):74–76.

———. "Fifty Thousand and Fifty Million." *Outlook* 120 (20 November 1918):451–52.

———. "The Lynching Record for 1918." *Outlook* 121 (22 January 1919):159.

———. "Negro Troops in France." *Southern Workman* 48 (May 1919):219–24.

"The Negro at Bay." *Nation* 108 (14 June 1919):931.

"Negro Conscription." *New Republic* 12 (20 October 1917): 317–18.

"Negro Educators and Our War Efforts." *Survey* 40 (4 May 1918):132–33.

"The Negro in the War." *Current History Magazine* 11 (December 1919):536–41.

"A Negro's Faith in American Justice." *Southern Workman* 47 (December 1918):591–92.

"A Negro's March with Muffled Drums." *Survey* 38 (4 August 1917):405–6.

"A New Color Line." *Public* 22 (8 February 1919):129.

"The Ninety-Second Division in Action." *Southern Workman* 48 (January 1919):41–43.

"Not One of the Famous 369th Was Ever Taken Alive." *Literary Digest* 60 (15 March 1919):94–96.

"Omaha." *Nation* 109 (11 October 1919):491.

"Other Hampton Men at the Front." *Southern Workman* 48 (January 1919):43–46.

"Our Own Race War." *North American Review* 210 (October 1919):436–38.

"Our Own Subject Race Rebels." *Literary Digest* 62 (2 August 1919):25.

Pierce, Lucy F. "Training Colored Officers." *Review of Reviews* 56 (December 1917):640.

"Played Leap-Frog Wid Shells All Ovah France." *Literary Digest* 60 (18 January 1919):68.

Poling, Daniel. "Physically Compentent and Morally Fit." *Outlook* 119 (10 July 1918):415–17.

"The Problem of the Negro Soldier." *Outlook* 117 (24 October 1917):279–80.

"Racial Tension and Race Riots." *Outlook* 122 (6 August 1919):532–34.

"Recreation for Colored Soldiers." *Southern Workman* 47 (December 1918):572–74.

Reid, Ira DeA. "A Critical Summary: The Negro on the Home Front in World Wars I and II." *Journal of Negro Education* 12 (1943):511–20.

"The Remedy for Race Riots." *Messenger*, March 1919, p. 20.

Richards, John. "Some Experiences with Colored Soldiers." *Atlantic Monthly* 124 (August 1919):184–90.

Satterthwaite, Thomas E. "The Recent Increase in Venereal Diseases." *New York Journal of Medicine*, 30 October 1920, pp. 678–80.

Scarborough, W. S. "Race Riots and Their Remedy." *Independent* 99 (16 August 1919):223.

Scott, Emmett J. "The Participation of Negroes in World War I: An Introductory Statement." *Journal of Negro Education* 12 (1943):288–97.

Seligmann, Herbert J. "Protecting Southern Womanhood." *Nation* 108 (14 June 1919):938–39.

———. "What Is Behind the Negro Uprisings?" *Current Opinion* 67 (September 1919):154–55.

Smith, Bolton. "The Negro in War-Time." *Public* 21 (31 August 1918):1110–13.

"Southern Negroes Moving North." *World's Work* 34 (June 1917):135.

Spingarn, Arthur. "The Health and Morals of Colored Troops." *Crisis* 16 (August 1918):166–68.

———. "The War and Venereal Disease among Negroes." *Social Hygiene* 4 (July 1918):333–46.

Stephenson, Mary L. "The Red Cross and Negro Troops." *Southern Workman* 47 (December 1918):593–94.

Tate, Merze. "The War Aims of World Wars I and II and Their Relation to the Darker Peoples of the World." *Journal of Negro Education* 12 (1943):521–32.

"These Colored Fighers Never Lost Their Sense of Humor." *Literary Digest* 61 (10 May 1919):63–64.

Thirkield, Wilbur. "No Longer 'Nigger' but American Negro." *Christian Advocate* 93 (31 October 1918):1386.

"A Thirty Years' Record in Lynching." *"World's Work* 39 (March 1920):433–34.

"To Lynch or Not to Lynch." *Outlook* 115 (24 January 1917):137–38.

"Training Negroes for Officers." *Literary Digest* 55 (21 July 1917):50.

"Us Angry-Saxums." *Atlantic Monthly* 122 (September 1918):425–27.

Villard, Oswald G. "The Race Problem." *Nation* 99 (24 December 1914):738–40.

"What Some Americans Think of East St. Louis." *Outlook* 106 (18 July 1917):435–36.

"What the Negro Is Doing to Help Win the War." *Literary Digest* 58 (27 July 1918):39–40.

"What the South Thinks of Northern Race Riots." *Literary Digest* 62 (16 August 1919):17–18.

"Where to Encamp the Negro Troops." *Literary Digest* 55 (29 September 1917):14–15.

White, Walter F. " 'Massacring Whites' in Arkansas." *Nation* 109 (6 December 1919):715–16.

"Why the Negro Appeals to Violence." *Literary Digest* 62 (9 August 1919):11.

Williams, Charles H. "Negro Y.M.C.A. Secretaries Overseas." *Southern Workman* 47 (January 1918):9–16.

Williams, W. T. B. "The World War and the Negro." *Southern Workman* 47 (January 1918):31–32.

"With the Negro Troops." *Southern Workman* 48 (January 1919):31–32.

Work, Monroe N. "The Negro and Democracy." *Southern Workman* 47 (May 1918):219–22.

Bibliographical Material

Dornbusch, C. E., comp. *Histories of American Army Units.* Washington, D.C.: Government Printing Office, 1936.

Dunlap, M. E. "Special Collections of Negro Literature in the United States." *Journal of Negro Education* 4 (1935):482–89.

Hampton Institute. *A Classified Catalog of the Negro Collection.* Hampton, Va.: Hampton Institute, 1940.

Lewinson, Paul. *A Guide to Documents in the National Archives: For Negro Studies.* Washington, D.C.: Government Printing Office, 1947.

Library of Congress, Division of Bibliography. *List of References on the Negro and the European War.* Washington, D.C.: Government Printing Office, n.d.

———. *Negro Newspapers on Microfilm.* Washington, D.C.: Government Printing Office, 1953.

Porter, Dorothy, et al. *A Catalog of Books in the Moorland Collection.* Washington, D.C.: Howard University, 1939.

Newspapers

American Embarkation News (published by and for American troops at Le Mans, France)

Baltimore Afro-American

Chicago Defender

Gangplank News (published by and for American troops at St. Nazaire, France)

New York Age

New York Amsterdam News

New York Times

Pittsburgh Courier

Stars and Stripes

Washington Bee

Magazines

Crisis

Crusader

Liberator

Messenger

Pullman Porters' Review

Southern Workman

Special Collections

Baltimore, Md. Morgan State College. Arthur J. Smith Collection of Negro History.

———. Morgan State College. Emmett J. Scott Collection (cited as Scott Papers).

Nashville, Tenn. Amistad Research Center, Fisk University. W. E. B. DuBois Papers (cited as Fisk Manuscripts).

New York City. National Council of Churches of Christ. Archives of the Federal Council of Churches.

———. New York Public Library (135th Street branch). Schomburg Collection of Negro Literature and History.

Washington, D.C. Association for the Study of Negro Life and History.

———. Fort McNair. Army War College Library.

———. Library of Congress, Manuscript Division. Newton D. Baker Papers.

———. National Archives (cited as *NA*).

Miscellaneous

Barbeau, Arthur E. "The Black American Soldier in World War I," Ph.D. dissertation, University of Pittsburgh, 1970.

Blount, Samuel E. "Reminiscences of Samuel E. Blount." Typescript. Schomburg Collection.

New York City, Writers Project. "History of the Negro in New York." Edited by Roi Ottley. Schomburg Collection.

Index